Shall
We Dance?

Titles by the same author include:

Like a Virgin: Madonna Revealed
Clint Eastwood: Sexual Cowboy
Michelle Pfeiffer: Age of Innocence
Hollywood People
Dudley Moore: On the Couch
Sharon Stone: The Biography
Fever: The Biography of John Travolta
Uncaged: The Biography of Nicolas Cage
Cilla Black: Bobby's Girl
Leonardo DiCaprio
Matt Damon: The Biography
Behind The Smile (with Paul Nicholas)
The Truth at Last (with Christine Keeler)
The Beatles Shadow: Stuart Sutcliffe (with Pauline Sutcliffe)
Leo on the Beach
The Hustlers
How to Rob Banks and Influence People
(with Victor Dark; John Blake Publishing)
Frank Lampard: The Biography (John Blake Publishing)
Lord of the Dance (with Michael Flatley)
Clint: Billion Dollar Man (John Blake Publishing)
Madonna: Queen of the World (John Blake Publishing)
On Her Majesty's Service (with Ron Evans; John Blake Publishing)
The First Lady (with April Ashley; John Blake Publishing)
Shadowland
Madonna vs Guy (John Blake Publishing)
Mafia Princess (with Marisa Merico)
Super Frank: Portrait of a Hero (John Blake Publishing)
The Dark Heart of Hollywood
Mafialand
Secrets and Lies (with Christine Keeler; John Blake Publishing)
Inside the Muslim Brotherhood (John Blake Publishing)
Stephen Ward: Scapegoat (John Blake Publishing)
Cilla: Queen of the Swinging Sixties (John Blake Publishing)

Shall We Dance?

The True Story of the Couple Who Taught the World to Dance

Douglas Thompson

WITH A FOREWORD BY CRAIG REVEL HORWOOD

metro

First published by Metro Publishing,
an imprint of
John Blake Publishing Limited
3 Bramber Court, 2 Bramber Road
London W14 9PB

www.johnblakepublishing.co.uk

www.facebook.com/johnblakebooks 🅕
twitter.com/jblakebooks 🅣

First published in hardback in 2014

ISBN: 978-1-78418-014-0

British Library Cataloguing-in-Publication Data:

A catalogue record for this book is available from the British Library.

Design by www.envydesign.co.uk

Printed in Great Britain by CPI Group (UK) Ltd

1 3 5 7 9 10 8 6 4 2

© Text copyright Douglas Thompson 2014
© Foreword Craig Revel Horwood 2014

The right of D[...]hompson [...] work has been
asserted by hi[...]ents Act 1988.

Papers used by J[...] made from wood
grown in [...]rm to the

Every attempt ha[...]s, but some were
unobtainabl[...]d contact us.

For Dandy

'Love is the sweetest thing.'
Al Bowlly, 1932

A pensioner has distributed 10,000 leaflets in the search for an old flame so that he can leave her all his money when he dies.

Herbert Riley, eighty-three, has not spoken to his former dancing partner, Reeni, for fifty-five years.

Unfortunately he never knew her surname.

He fell in love with Reeni when she was just twenty and he was twenty-four. The pair met at a Stockport dance hall in 1955.

They danced together four times a week and visited the Stockport Town Hall ballroom once a week. Mr Riley lived in Davenport, while Reeni was from Brinksway.

But after a four-year relationship, Reeni suddenly married another man she had known for only six weeks.

The former engineer married Margaret but she died from leukaemia in 1963. Mr Riley, of Longsight, saw Reeni fleetingly working in Hobson's Choice bakery in Reddish in the late 1980s. But the pair didn't speak. He now longs to see her again.

News item, front page, *Daily Telegraph*, 1 April 2014

Contents

Contents

Foreword

Craig Revel Horwood

Shall We Dance? is a fab-u-lous and informative look at one of the most iconic dance couples that have ever graced the dance floor. Leaders in their field and a couple that really did teach the world to dance. You know you're in safe hands when you follow the Castles' amazing 'don't' list for correct dancing:

Do not wriggle the shoulders.
Do not shake the hips.
Do not twist the body.
Do not flounce the elbows.
Do not pump the arms.
Do not hop – glide instead.
Avoid low, fantastic, and acrobatic dips.
Stand far enough away from each other to allow free movement of the body in order to dance gracefully and comfortably...
The gentleman's left hand and forearm should be held up in the air parallel with his body, with the hand extended,

holding the lady's hand lightly on his palm. The arm should never be straightened out.

Remember you are at a social gathering, and not in a gymnasium.

This excerpt has to be one of many of my favourite parts in this fascinating insight into the lives and times of Vernon and Irene Castle, and anyone would have to have a heart of stone to read the end of Part III without weeping. It's truly wonderful finally to have a book that explores, in depth, the love they had for one another through reading their personal letters while they were separated during the First World War.

The Castles were America's premier dance partners and were real trendsetters, encouraging the world to embrace new forms of social dancing, and they also helped to remove the stigma of vulgarity from close dancing. They made dance respectable, classy, and their enthusiasm was infectious. They often performed dances to jazz and ragtime rhythms, popularising African-American music among well-heeled whites. They appeared in a newsreel called *Social and Theatrical Dancing* in 1914 and wrote a bestselling instructional book, *Modern Dancing*, later that year. The pair also starred in a feature film called *The Whirl of Life* (1915), which was well received by critics and public alike.

When I first set to work to write *Teach Yourself Ballroom Dancing* I was captivated by their story and now, as you have purchased this book, I hope you will be too.

Douglas Thompson, thank you for writing this marvellous, detailed and most enjoyable book so everyone can share what an incredible couple the Castles were. You deserve a medal, darling – in fact, I can go one better, and say 'That's a ten!'

CRAIG REVEL HORWOOD

Preface

Chic to Sheikh

*'Ten cents a dance
That's what they pay me ...
... All that you need is a ticket
Come on, big boy, ten cents a dance.'*
Richard Rodgers and Lorenz Hart, 'Ten Cents A Dance', 1930

The decor was raving Nebuchadnezzar, a gorgeously vulgar rainbow of abandon, and, winking for attention with the fledgling and blinking electricity, was the most razzmatazz attraction in New York City. Between 43rd and 44th Streets on Broadway, close to a patch of properties which wasn't yet called Times Square, this latest palace of amusement was all about the desperate haste to be *new*. Rector's had its grand opening in New York on 23 September 1899. It was what was called a 'lobster palace', a venue for providing extravagant *everything* but principally eating and drinking pleasure.

Charles Rector had enjoyed success easing the frontier from Chicago with his restaurant, the Café Marine. He aimed to please, and for sophistication. It wasn't always understood. On an official visit to the World's Fair held in the city in 1893, Princess María Eulalia, the youngest daughter of Queen Isabella II of Spain, had been an honoured guest. On hearing the Café Marine served American whiskey to ladies in porcelain cups, she naughtily ordered her whiskey in soup bowls and lubricated her way through the fourteen-course menu of the day. She provided the stagger *du jour*.

Now, as the twentieth century also tippled forward, Charles Rector was opening the faux, if imposing, Greco doors to his emporium of excess. He had spent close to one quarter of a million dollars on dimension-daring, mirrored interiors of gold and a deep green; the walls cornered the 175 tables, which were dressed in sharply ironed Irish linen and personalised, hand-stencilled silver cutlery. The chief chef was Emil Lederer, whose *terrapin à la Maryland* had amused Queen Victoria. So much so, she wrote him a note of appreciation he so treasured he kept it snapped in his hat like a newspaperman. It was most appropriate: his glutton-friendly food was devoured in scoops.

As the Spanish princess had discovered, this New World was, indeed, the land of milk and honey – if only a breakfast appetiser. On the opening evening the menu was international: English pheasant, Egyptian quail, mounds of African peaches and Italian strawberries, towers of French pastries. Along the aromatic way were hors d'oeuvres comprising palmettes, mousselines, croustades, bouchées, and timbales; Lynnhaven oysters, lobster, terrapin, frogs, shrimps, crabs, canvasback ducks, chicken, beef, pork and lamb: whatever could be cooked had been; minced, chopped, sliced and carved, it had been poached and steamed, sautéed and grilled, broiled, braised, boiled and blanched, roasted and simmered and fried, dressed and anointed with the work of the renowned saucier Charles Parrandin, who himself was delicately poached from rivals Delmonico's for the first night. All about were more delights: from the figs and nectarines under glass to the champagne bottles lined up like a surrounding army on the sideboards.

Yet the celebrity crowd, led by recent world heavyweight boxing champion James J. 'Gentleman Jim' Corbett, almost didn't get to start on the clear turtle soup.

The evening's hurdle was Charles Rector's lust for the *new*: for opening night he had installed a revolving door at the entrance, the first such contraption in New York. The guests didn't want to get out. They whirled around and around, giddy with the fun of it and the sensation, a carnival ride of, seemingly, ever-revolving joy. It was only when 'Gentleman Jim' was spun out, as if to the canvas, with his wife in his arms that the cavalcade got on and festivities began.

Charles Rector beamed brighter than his lighting. What more could even the most demanding customer want?

There was the Yacht Club table for America's richest family, the Vanderbilts, and their wet-set cronies and the four *private* dining rooms, which kept the gossip columns and Fifth Avenue parlours in licentious speculation.

Yet, soon enough, a dance floor installed at Rector's was deemed *the* necessity. It was swiftly a talk of the town, a basic but powerful pull for the crowds of new devotees greedily seeking fun. By the time Rector's had moved to Broadway at 48th, next door to Times Square, and the twentieth century became a teenager, its legend had stretched to the heel of Italy.

So much so that immigrant Rodolfo Guglielmi went there on Christmas Eve 1913, just twenty-four hours after arriving in America from Taranto, Puglia. In his dark suit and white shirt, perked by the neatly folded white handkerchief in his breast pocket, the young Italian cast a striking figure. As he did on the dance floor – these dance floors which were now all over New

York and in the more suave suburbs, in restaurants and hotels, in the front of theatres, placed atop skating rinks... anywhere and everywhere so the daring could engage in this new craze, this dancing. Guglielmi found the way forward was to become a taxi dancer — a paid partner — for the thousands of women seeking afternoon and evening excitement with public dancing and music, especially the jaunty syncopation of ragtime. Yet, cabaret and stage work paid more than the dollars and cents a dance engagement. Forget Rector's and the rest, he was quickly advised by the well-connected Frenchman George Ragni: 'See the Castles in cabaret...'

He did and watched in awe, as they all did, the swells and the chorus girls, the dishwashers and the tycoons, those who had and had not, as the Castles manifested at midnight and danced.

Vernon and Irene Castle captivated every evening. Vernon Castle, the tall, lean Englishman in his chic, tailless evening coat, leading his all-American girlish wife, comfortably free of corset and social restraint, lightly and with unbuttoned elegance, flowing about him like a silk scarf.

They offered a shimmering simplicity of love, of romantic marriage, of unthreatening excitement, of passion without sin, yet they were dancing all over the social architecture of their time. They were a tempting combination but provocative, as much so as the evolving era in which they taught the world to dance.

It was the night that Rodolfo Guglielmi, who after a remarkable metamorphosis became Rudolph Valentino, cinema's first matinée idol, the screen sheikh and master of the menacing tango, said he first believed in the magic of performance. He never forgot Vernon and Irene Castle, who became the most famous couple in the world by having a good time. The Castles presented something he'd never witnessed before but somehow, mystically, had the quality of a memory. For Rodolfo, as for so many, their dancing illuminated a mythical past and cast a glow on a time yet to come. Vernon and Irene Castle were extraordinary at enjoying themselves. Their joy was contagious.

Prologue

Dancing in the Sky

'It is never right to play ragtime fast.'
Scott Joplin, 1899

—

Vernon Castle flew as gracefully as he danced. Conditions might alter his tactics but not his style, which favoured panache over panic.

He had confidence, maybe not completely in himself, but in the mission, in the purpose of bouncing around at 10,000 feet in the air above Belgium in a Nieuport 17, a V-strut biplane that squeezed its pilot, guns, fuel tank and engine into a fretfully small space.

By this particular afternoon of 11 March 1917, the French makers of the deftly manoeuvrable 20-foot-long single-seater aircraft hadn't yet quite figured out a way to synchronise shooting at the enemy without riddling the spinning blades of the flier's own propeller. The compromise was to have a Lewis machine gun wedged on to the larger top wing.

Vernon Castle wasn't too scientific about it either: he pointed his plane at enemy fighters and blasted away. Stalling or overstretching the capabilities of his aeroplane and 'spinning' never overly concerned him; he knew the real danger would come from the sky around him.

So, that day he did raise a neatly shaped eyebrow when he saw four Albatros DIII biplane fighters – the particularly deadly favourite of the flying aces like Manfred von Richthofen, the 'Red Baron', of the *Deutsche Luftstreitkräfte*, the German Imperial Army Air Service – swift-moving below him, for all the world like an unpleasant diamond-shaped insect.

He stamped one out. He dived down on the tail of the fighter at the rear of the tiny swarm and took it out with rattling clacks of machine-gun fire, soaring off and climbing out of visibility before the surviving trio of German pilots could turn on him.

The next day he was, as always, in the air and flying over the German lines on the Western Front. His primary objective was to take surveillance photographs. It wasn't easy to compose clear images through the deafening bang-bang bursts of anti-aircraft fire zipping through their own black puffs of smoke. You had to concentrate, pay photographic attention, while inside what was little more than a narrow wooden box with extra bits and a propeller. The trick was not to be intimidated by the acute possibility of instant death. Vernon Castle had flown 150 of these reconnaissance missions, a legend commended by the French Government who awarded him the Croix de Guerre, the highest gallantry medal afforded those not sainted to be born in France.

Yet, luck, inherent talent, skill, courage and a genetic parcel of optimism which comprised Vernon Castle's attitude, could only be pushed so far; and he was a man with a naughty, ring-a-ding smile who enjoyed pushing his luck. Still, he had a feline streak. The enemy's anti-aircraft guns, which the fliers called 'Hun Archie' – British pilots referred to being 'archied' – got a little revenge that day for all the sensitive material Lieutenant Castle had gathered.

He was not more than a thousand feet up in the spotless sunlight when his engine, as close as any co-pilot, took a direct hit. More than half of the machinery was ripped off – which didn't leave him much linen and plywood to fly. The engine's control cables dangled with nothing to connect to. The noise was remarkable: he could hear the bones in his ears crackle, and the air rushing at him was like punches in the chest. He flew by dead reckoning. He brought the debris down with a deep breath and a giant bump behind his own second-line trenches. What was left of the Nieuport 17 snagged in the defensive barbed wire and flipped over. Vernon Castle was left dangling from the wreck. He suffered bruising to his arms, legs and dignity.

The show, as he knew so well, had to go on. By 'Bloody April' 1917, when Germany was dominant in the skies of Europe, he'd flown mission upon mission. That month his latest Nieuport 17 betrayed him and inexplicably fell out of the sky over Abeele, a hamlet in west Flanders. As it swooned towards the ground he managed to bring the flimsy frame into a glide and smacked into a confusion of barbed wire; happily protecting France, not Germany. This time he suffered a nasty knock to his left leg which hobbled him a little. The injury didn't harden him; if anything he became more and more sensitive to the misery affecting all involved in conflict. While on the ground recuperating at the Royal Flying Corps hospital, he proved a life-safer, in a literal sense, helping the morale of enlisted men and officers to combat not just their physical pain but suicidal depression; he was a most famous entertainer but he was also one of them. He was a hero. He was admired and he was listened to. He was also a hell of a pilot.

The War Office recognised this talent but also his propaganda value and, anxious to boost recruiting in Canada and America, put Vernon Castle on a ship to New York from where he would be assigned duty as a flying instructor.

Crossing the Atlantic, close to the second anniversary of the German U-boat torpedo sinking of Cunard's liner the *Lusitania* – the outrage over the death of 128 US passengers among the 1,198 who perished in the Celtic Sea on the afternoon of 7 May 1915 had hastened America into the First World War – Vernon Castle marvelled at his charmed life since he had first sailed from Liverpool to New York in 1906. So much had happened, and so fast; too fast, for there had rarely been time to think about it. There certainly hadn't been time to follow Joplin's instructions, to take it slow.

For the moment, he was ordered to the training fields of Camp Deseronto – the cadets called it 'Camp Deserted', and indeed it was far from the fast lane : in Ontario, Canada, Fraser's Ice Cream Parlour was as chilled out as it got.

He drove into town in his sunshine-yellow Stutz Bearcat. With him, like an escort, were two German shepherd police dogs. On his shoulder was sand-coloured Jeffrey, his rhesus monkey.

Everyone had their eyes towards Vernon Castle.

Which was just the way he liked it.

Vernon Castle enjoyed making an entrance.

Book I
Showtime

'Do it big, do it right, do it with style.'
Fred Astaire, 1924

Chapter One

Great Expectations

'Looking on the bright side of life.'
Al Bowlly, 1932

Vernon Castle found fame by falling flat on his face.

The boy from the East of England did everything, even a pratfall, with élan. Which much impressed the American entertainment maestro Lew Fields, who'd seen most, if not all, before.

With the look of a Dickensian caricature, Lew Fields had a face to launch a thousand seaside postcards, but his kindness made him endearingly attractive. His antecedents accounted for his compassion. He'd witnessed and experienced much misery growing up around the whisky-and-flophouse culture of the Bowery in New York. Punctuating his life, in and out of the decaying dwellings, were the indigent gangs, the girls with lots of panstick and no pants, the extortionists and political bullyboys and, throughout his boyhood, the freed black slaves and newly arrived Eastern European Jewish families like his own, the Schoenfelds, who docked in 1872.

His days could be as freakish as a P. T. Barnum show. Lew Fields, side-stepping the sweatshops and the gangland culture, wanted to put on a very different sort of show. Amused as he was by the dime museums with their 'Chinese Giants' and 'Turtle Boy' exhibitions, their displays of Custer's last strand of hair and other detritus from the Little Big Horn, his ambitions stretched towards legitimacy.

It was a social need he shared with many, this legitimacy; it equated with respectability, which itself meant majority acceptance, and that was the vital accolade. Audiences had to accept and like you if they were to pay to see you perform. Lew Fields was popular for half a century.

He was helped in that by Joe Webber, another Jewish-comic survivor from Manhattan's Lower East Side, the origin of so much popular culture. They became a touring vaudeville double act, masters of malapropisms, presenting a much-loved and slapstick mixture of sentiment and silliness. In 1896, these Bowery graduates opened the Weber and Fields Music Hall, producing Victorian burlesque sell-out shows (not bump and grind but rather a clever comic pastiche of operas and the classics). For eight years, they showcased the early comic and musical talents of the coming century. Then, instinct-driven, Lew Fields moved on alone and more towards formal theatre, albeit often upmarket vaudeville. The distinguished actress Helen Hayes, who in an eighty-year career remains one of only a dozen performers to win a full house of entertainment awards: Emmy, Grammy, Oscar and Tony, was 'discovered' by Fields in 1906 when she was six years old. She said that next to Charlie Chaplin, her mentor had 'the most perfect comic mask I have ever seen'.

He was also, as a producer and inventive showman, as significant if not as flamboyant as Florenz 'Flo' Ziegfeld, the creator of the

Follies, and *Yankee Doodle Dandy* patriot-producer George M. Cohan. He was the partner of the entrepreneurial Shubert Brothers, who established Broadway as America's pre-eminent theatrical district, and he set the stage for Broadway boomers like Al Jolson and Fanny Brice and Eddie Cantor, for a future of entertainments. He put on a show.

Which is why, one August evening in 1906 he adored it when he first saw Vernon Castle comically collapse on stage.

'Style!' he cried. 'That boy has style!'

Lew Fields, the former Moses Schoenfeld, creator of the first theatrical 'pop' stars, a man who was sought out by the double cream of theatre and literature, George Bernard Shaw, Oscar Wilde and the young lyricist P. G. Wodehouse, was cognisant of what it was like to arrive young in a new world. He'd faced off life in the Bowery aged five years old. Vernon Castle, who had sailed in from Liverpool aboard the SS *Teutonic* four weeks earlier, on 19 July 1906, was nineteen years old; older maybe, but also a dreamer. It wasn't only precocious pratfalls which gave them an affinity.

In that sense, Fields 'adopted' Vernon and regarded himself as a mentor to the teenager who, like him, was tall; Vernon's lean frame ran up to just short of six feet, most of it a jangle of legs; Lew Fields couldn't do enough for this 'English string bean'. As with all such arrangements, there is no arithmetic to them: it was simply timing, happy happenstance.

The actor-producer had established the Lew Fields Herald Square Theatre on New York's West Thirty-Fifth Street with Lee and Sam Shubert, the business end of this showbiz entanglement, in early May 1906. He'd signed the contracts with the Shuberts in the stalls bar of the theatre over two bottles of champagne: one was smashed on the bar rail and they drank the *cuvée de prestige* in a toast to a musical entertainment enterprise 'of the highest order'. Fields had also agreed to pay a share of $20,000 worth of red satin and other, arguably in themselves burlesque, renovations; he required a success.

He then sailed off to review the shows playing in London; the constant source for American producers of musical scripts. The play he'd been told about he didn't like so he acquired the rights to another, *The Orchid*, but that too quickly wilted on him. He spent three days in London, extravagantly buying the rights to the play *The Girl Behind the Counter* and the services of the whole company, despite knowing it would take months to produce in America.

In immediate post-Victorian theatre, the producers, the stars, the writers and the musical style setters were interchangeable back and forth across the Atlantic; as well known in New York as they were in London. Nothing was shared more than a success and, from time to time, a little decadence. Nothing succeeds like excess. So, it made sense to buy the rights to the package, the play and the players, as insurance for a repeat of the box-office magic. For the actors, an ocean voyage was but a lark set against the prospect of fame and, with lottery luck, fortune.

While Fields was on the high seas, Vernon's sister Coralie was high on London theatre wish lists. She'd enjoyed a run of success through diligence and appeal. One uncredited interviewer was much taken with her in *Mr Popple of Ippleton* at the Apollo Theatre in London and it showed in the 1905 interview with her for the monthly show people magazine *Play Pictorial*: "'I have never been late for a cue," said Miss Coralie Blythe, as she arranged the masses of beautiful fair hair that she "lets down" so effectively during her dance in *Mr Popple*, "I have never had any adventures, I have never forgotten my part, and things have always gone just as they should;

so you see there really is nothing for me to talk about," and Miss Blythe gazed meditatively into her own blue eyes as they gazed back at her in the mirror.

"'Things usually happen to most people, and if I had a fine imagination I would tell you that I had fallen from a flying machine and been caught on one of the arms of the golden cross of St Paul's Cathedral, and had then been rescued by an adventurous youth who crawled over the dome and carried me down in his arms. It would make a good story, but people wouldn't believe it, and would say rude things about my imagination. One day I will try and manufacture some real good anecdotes – oh, I mean quite nice ones – and then I will get them printed, and everybody will say, 'Dear me, what an interesting life she must lead!'"'

With a shine in her eyes, she was delightfully deprecating about her achievements. Her family had previously only provided one element of entertainment – booze. Now, she was a headliner of Edwardian musical comedy and married to Lawrence Grossmith, a star of the genre. They were also leading lights in the London production of *The Girl Behind the Counter* at Wyndham's Theatre.

The former Caroline Maud Blyth (for 'Coralie Blythe' was but a dramatic stage name) proved a threatening combination for the times: a beauty and an independent career woman. She could turn on an intimidating look – but that was appealingly dismantled by her smiling, bright eyes. A 'modern', born on 28 January 1881, she was part of the *fin de siècle* resistance against what had been and what 'should' be. Puritans said she and those like her, such decadent youth, were flirting with damnation. There was a growing constituency which comprised the moral middle class that held views so sharp andbrittle you could scar yourself on them. Yet she was never blooded.

Taking the stage name Coralie Blythe and becoming an Edwardian theatrical was in itself a huge rebellion: against convention and family. She knew her own mind: she was only fifteen years old when she became engaged in 1896 to the then nineteen-year-old Lawrence Grossmith yet, although always a couple, they did not formally marry until 1904.

Caroline had three younger sisters: Gladys, Stephanie and the family's last born, Marjorie. Before Marjorie, William Vernon Blyth arrived on 2 May 1887. He was named after his father but always called 'Vernie' at home. The family patriarch William Thomas Blyth married Jane Finley in north London in 1879. They moved to Mill Hill Road, Norwich, Norfolk, shortly after Caroline was born, a true Cockney, in Bow, East London, within easy sound of the bells. Vernon's grandfather, another William, ran the Great Eastern Hotel in Norwich. Hospitality, a lively version of it, was the family business. The Great Eastern (in 2014 the blander Norwich Nelson Premier Hotel Inn on Prince of Wales Road) specialised in its own brand of theatre. The drink was always good and strong, much like the conversation, if not all the customers.

The Blyth family were in the Victorian tradition of early Dickens, archetypical like the Cratchits, like a wedding vow: they stuck together through rich and poor, upset and tragedy. Vernon was just four years old when his mother Jane died, aged twenty-eight, from being weary, after five children, and so devoured by a maverick infection. For a decade Vernon had run free with his sisters, their lives choreographed by necessity. When the twentieth century became a reality, in 1900, his father remarried: his bride Lucy Johnson, aged twenty-five, who was thankfully kind and not wicked, or Vernon's early days would have been ridiculously Dickensian, a rich feast of appropriate metaphors.

At school, the new generation Vernon learned all about 1066, and in the 'all that' one local point fascinated: how William the Conqueror had established Norwich Castle in 1067 to keep the peoples of East Anglia in their place. It began, in an extraordinary oblique way, an enthusiasm for all things French. Needs must, of course: on holidays from Norwich Grammar School, Vernon set aside consideration of the Norman invasion of England and learned to entertain the clientele at the Great Eastern. He was at ease with this; all his life he and his sisters had created their own entertainment, from playing chase to charades.

He also 'performed' at a pub called the Albert Arms near Paddington Station in London, on which his father held the licence for three years. There he picked up snug-room card tricks, his long fingers deftly dealing magic, confounding 'find the lady' enthusiasts. He took these talents still further on the perimeter of 'The Magic Circle' in London, through the work of the Victorian genius of illusion and stage tricks, John Nevil Maskelyne. Maskelyne, like America's fantastical escape artist Harry Houdini, disdained ideas of the occult and supernatural power and formed 'The Occult Committee' to expose spiritual fraudsters. He conjured his fame simply by magic. Which is rather how it happened for Vernon Castle, too.

The teenaged Vernon concentrated – as much as he ever could – on card tricks. How did they do that? He spent energetic hours at St George's Hall, in Langham Place, Regent Street, which Maskelyne refurbished in 1905 as 'England's New Home of Mystery'. Vernon learned quickly, and once he had mastered card tricks he moved on to investigate conjuring and illusions and the mystery of levitation – the creation of which, despite other claims, is rightly credited to Maskelyne. (Anyone who has ever 'spent a penny' is in debt to him, one way or another. He invented the door lock for Victorian London toilets which required a penny to operate. Vernon was more fascinated by a royal flush at cards.)

As Vernon Blyth, he took his first professional engagement (fifteen shillings, no tip) mystifying the guests at a London dinner party. Vernon didn't bore; people listened to him, believed him. He was so good he could sell you your own horse and cart. He was a natural. He received his first, and always treasured, fan letter. He also got experience. He glimpsed those who lived the life of gin and music halls; the corners of London which were an abandon of smoke, beer and poverty.

In May 1906, the family's eldest daughter Caroline, a.k.a. Coralie Blythe, a.k.a. Mrs Lawrence Grossmith, was causing friction. She and her husband wanted to take Vernon to New York where Lew Fields was paying them to go with *The Girl Behind the Counter*. Her father was not keen for his only son to leave England for any time. All the arguments were presented to William Thomas Blyth; the most convincing being the opportunities which would be available for his teenaged son. Vernon had been studying structural engineering, but was clearly happier performing magic tricks and picking up pocket money with comic routines at private parties than building bridges or pouring pints. His father said he could go – but he had to travel with him. Also with them went George Grossmith's friend, and contributor to West End shows, Jerome Kern, who would compose 'Ol' Man River', 'Smoke Gets In Your Eyes' and scores of memorable show tunes.

It was a frolic for Vernon but serious business for his sister and especially his brother-in-law: Lawrence Grossmith was a transatlantic regular since a 1900 tour with the actress–producer Lillie Langtry, a truly intimate Edwardian performer. Grossmith was a thoroughbred theatrical; he had the full pedigree and the paperwork to prove it. His father George Grossmith was a Gilbert and Sullivan contemporary performer and a friend of Charles Dickens, whose work he presented on stage. His brother, George Jr., tall with a floppy frame, was a big star of the Edwardian stage, an actor, writer and stage manager, but, as Lew Fields found out, somewhat silly. But, like Vernon, he adored him. As did P. G. Wodehouse, who used him when he created his foil for Jeeves. George Jr. was the model for Bertie Wooster. Inspiration was derived from moments like an audition involving an early George Gershwin collaboration, *Primrose.* Wodehouse recalls the moment in the 1953 memoir *Bring on the Girls.* George Grossmith was interviewing the multiple prototype 'model–dancer–actress' Sylvia Hawkes (married five times, Douglas Fairbanks Senior and Clark Gable were among her husbands) for a lead role. The somewhat precious English actress, a victim of that draining artistic paranoia, was asked by her producer to show what she could do:

'Must I sing, Mr Grossmith?'

'Yes, Sylvia, you must. The Gershwin score demands it.'

'Oh very well… ' she sighed.

She presented her music to the pianist and his fingers skipped across the keys:

'God save out gracious King, long live our noble King, God save the King… '

Grossmith immediately stood to attention. As did all his hangers-on. Where the National Anthem usually ended, the patriotic pack, led by George Grossmith, began to sit down. But Sylvia had other plans. There were, like her talents, many stanzas and even with the pianist silent she sang them all. No one dared call a halt. Sylvia got the job.

Like Bertie Wooster, the gregarious George Grossmith had many well-placed and connected friends to placate. He was admired for his success. He may have fumbled and fussed about details but it was the attention to them, application and rehearsal, that constantly produced his success. He was also a kindly man and was there to welcome his brother and the Blyths when they arrived in New York. William Blyth, seeing his son so comfortably placed, returned almost immediately to England, sailing on a ticket provided by Lew Fields. George Grossmith had made enquiries about work for his brother and in-laws but Lew Fields trumped him. While *The Girl Behind the Counter* was in pre-pre-production, he cast Lawrence Grossmith and Coralie Blythe in *About Town*, which was a scattergun of theatrical tricks, comedy and music vaguely connected to *The Orchid*. It also marked the début of Vernon Castle – the man and the name.

Vernon was still Vernon Blyth when Lew Fields placed him and, most importantly, personally coached him in a small but attention-getting 'silly ass' role. Vernon thought of home, of Norwich, of Norfolk, of the Normans, and Norwich Castle. 'Vernon Castle' was born on 30 August 1906, on the first night of *About Town* at the Herald Square Theatre. He was very good at falling gracefully on his face and that landed him on his feet with the *New York Times* and several others who reviewed the show. Soon he was taking other roles, including standing in for Lawrence Grossmith, which was an accolade in itself. *About Town* went on the road; another commercial success for Lew Fields as it scrambled across America and sent his teenaged discovery further up the casting beanstalk.

Vernon appeared in a run of productions, usually as the comic feed for Lew Fields: Vernon, in a tight, bright green suit and hat, as daft as an eight-day week, leaps into a shop and requests an order of rat poison. Shopkeeper Fields: 'Will I wrap it up or will you eat it here?'

Vernon was bemused by the speed of his success, but not by his good fortune – for he never realised what it was like not to be wanted. He'd taken a stage name because his sister had, not to avoid charges of nepotism. He never thought of favouritism and, surprisingly, his luck did not foster envy in too many of the Broadway crowd. He made friends in his own and other theatrical companies as he saw America through the bedsit-and-landlady repertory-style experience. But Lew Fields was *his* benefactor. The roles planned for his sister and brother-in-law got lost in the rewrites of *The Girl Behind the Counter* as, with Fields as the star, it became more about his madcap character. Yet, there was plenty of room for Vernon – he had three roles.

His best scenes involved him as one of five waiters – the other four were outlandish-looking non-actors from the Bowery, a four-foot-tall shoeshine boy, an enormously fat masseur from the Murray Hills Baths, a street tough, and a miser with the look and manners of a bloodhound – who in Edgar Smith's freewheeling adaptation of the London production took instructions from Fields: 'Always remember, the first duty of a waiter is to look insulting. Never go near a customer until ten minutes after he has come in. If he goes like that [a snap of the fingers], don't pay any attention to him. If he gets excited and jingles on the glass with his knife, go out in the kitchen where you won't hear him. In about ten minutes, come round and brush the crumbs into his lap. Then, if he asks for a programme [menu], look at him as if you pitied him, give him a glass of ice water and walk away. When you come back, he has found his programme and knows what he wants. Then, you take out your pad and write it down – and then go into the kitchen and order something else.'

It was brash entertainment, and as played by Fields – who was an authentic comic and dramatic talent – and Vernon – who had no reason to harbour any inhibitions and pushed his role to the eccentric limit – it worked. The accompanying line-up of grotesques enhanced the amusement.

The New York critics hailed it as the best scene and Fields was saluted as 'never funnier'. After a sell-out three-week out-of-town run, this was heartily welcomed material on Broadway. Vernon was elevated by the general cavalcade of acclaim. He was in a huge hit, one making $15,000 a week – for thirty-seven weeks from October 1907. Essentially, he showed that he moved well on stage, hit his marks, and could improvise. He spun on, whizzing around the roulette of showtime in an increasing variety of guises. With fickle audiences and economics, some shows never opened, or closed quickly – but Lew Fields's players enjoyed absolute success. He seemed immune.

In 1910, the producer had seven musicals on Broadway, including *Old Dutch*, which had a dozen child performers; the standout was the nine-year-old Helen Hayes, who shared crucial scenes with Fields. When they were completed, his co-star Vernon would hoist her into his arms and carry the girl they called 'the baby' to her dressing room. The actress said of Fields in a 1937 newspaper interview: 'He loved me like a daughter; and Vernon Castle he loved like a son.' It was true in so many ways for the producer–actor; through theatrical pressures, he spent more time with them than with his own two sons and daughter. Helen Hayes elaborated much more in her 1968 autobiography *On Reflection* about her own crush on Vernon:

In *Old Dutch*, I found my Prince Charming and fell in love for the first time. He was tall and he was skinny and he wore a green suit. He looked just like a string bean. His name was Vernon Castle, and he became the centre of my life. He took me to his tender heart. The iron stairs backstage were too

14

steep for me to climb quickly enough and at each performance, after my scenes with Mr Fields, he would sweep me up and carry me to his dressing room. I would wait breathlessly for the moment.

He became my reason for being, and his funny little mash-notes and jokes and gifts were like draughts of life-giving oxygen. I ate, drank and talked nothing but Vernon Castle. Poor Mother. I drove her mad with my adoration of him. Vernon was a delight. He knew how to enter into a child's world and, better still, how to make a child feel grown-up. His games were enchanting, our mock romance fraught with drama. He would have his dresser hand me a note as I walked offstage and I would rush to the privacy of my dressing room to read it. The note would speak of his extreme wretchedness due to some fabricated attention I had paid to old Mr Fields or the porcine John Bunny. He would sometimes, in the conceit, play my husband or sometimes an ardent suitor. The notes would be answered by me as quickly as I could think up a clever reply. Vernon was playing a game. I was not. I was the string-bean's adoring dream-wife.

And Vernon Castle discovered he wasn't playing; he was a professional. Aged twenty-three, he discovered he no longer had a job; he had a career he had neither planned or imagined but was beginning to enjoy.

Lew Fields had worked his success with the Shuberts and produced his own shows, including *The Midnight Sons*, which had a lush role for Vernon. He played the stage drunk, which enjoyed the talents of his lanky body; cleverly acrobatic he could bend this way and that with all but a whisper stopping him from collapsing in a heap. To heighten the theatre of his agility, Vernon had the help of the influential choreographer Edward 'Ned' Wayburn, who followed the French teacher François Delsarte 'method', linking inner emotion to an actor or dancer's movement. It led to exaggerated gestures, perfect for his early minstrel productions – and for Vernon's stage work. Wayburn had dazzling parameters and they encompassed Vernon's quick and quickly bored mind: Wayburn's showtime ethos relied on acrobatic work, musical comedy, tap and step dancing, toe specialties (not quite a Nijinsky *en pointe*) and, remarkably, a concept close to exhibition ballroom dancing.

As the star of the opening scene of the theatrically adventurous *The Midnight Sons*, Vernon employed much of Wayburn's thinking into the antics of Souseberry Lushmore and it delighted from the first night. Wayburn was creating a musical extravaganza (as he did in his collaboration creating the *Ziegfeld Follies*) with the largest chorus Broadway had ever seen. And with Vernon too: a speciality act as slush sentimental Lushmore, he bleatingly sang 'Call Me Bill' ('never mind my real name now...') and with a One-Step or Hesitation Walk presented his drunk dance to an applauding audience as he tripped, dipped and swayed his way from one chorus girl to the next, something he was most adept at doing sober and offstage. But there was nothing suggestive in the shows, or any offensive language; Lew Fields made money by not being objectionable in content, by being family-friendly. One reviewer emphasised that:

Vernon Castle as Souseberry Lushmore typifies the show as it is in general character. He is the young man who enjoys himself hugely at the banquet and thereafter is wandering about aimlessly, not getting home but seeing a good many things on the way. His part typifies the spirit of the show. While he may get soused, he is nevertheless always a gentleman. For his humour he may descend to climbing upon chairs or ladders and falling down on the floor, but he does not call in the risqué to get his laughs.

Vernon learned that being different, a novelty, attracted attention. He found he rather liked the adulation. For the first time, he began to feel the buzz of show business, that he belonged; he told the cast that he got more enjoyment out of playing Lushmore than anything else he had experienced. Everything was now officially *fun*. And there were now even fewer restraints on him having as much fun as he wanted. His sister had returned to London with Lawrence Grossmith, where he took over the running of the Savoy Theatre and she remained a busy actress but with, always, a watch on the family in Norwich. As such, Vernon Castle found his only responsibility was to the theatre.

He relished swimming and horse riding and walking, the comics, the cartoon 'funnies' in the American newspapers, gossiping and drinking and the ladies… and had the vitality to pursue his multiple interests. Sleeping bored him. There was so much to do. He didn't want to miss a thing. He loved life. As such, he enjoyed getting out of the city and found he was spending more time in New Rochelle a renowned (through the 1906 George M. Cohan song) forty-five-minute journey from Broadway aboard one of the five shiny and varnished, deep green carriages drawn by a giant 4-4-0 Baldwin locomotive. The residents were higher income and convinced that money elevated the tone of the place, but it was mostly their aspirations which were high. The New York suburb was their heaven-on-earth: white picket fences and neat, rolling lawns seeded by the American Dream, bankrolled by those on the city streets driven by avarice and, increasingly, by Henry Ford's 1906 production line of success, the Model T motor car.

Vernon, with his tireless energy, found New Rochelle was the template for twentieth-century America, 'bigger and better' and not coy about reaching out for advancement. Possibly, he saw the deeper picture and understood then the nation's domineering trait, of wanting the enormous to do the work of the excellent. It's as likely New Rochelle simply offered more comfort than apartment life in the city; on Echo Bay, a sheltered inlet on Long Island Sound, there was a yacht club and a rowing club, while in town there were plenty of theatres and accommodation available; Vernon took a small, two-connecting-rooms arrangement. He commuted back to Broadway where he was being paid $75 a week in alternating Lew Fields's productions, including *The Midnight Sons*, and deftly handling the agile attentions of a dancer-actress, a Southern belle from the foothills of the Blue Ridge Mountains.

Life, and the weather, were very good that summer of 1910. Yet he was feeling weary putting the same show on night after night after night. There was no room for improvisation and he knew – he'd witnessed it – that the discipline of movement insisted on by Lew Fields worked. But it could be tiresome for a young man with a head packed with inventive ideas. He needed a quest, a challenge to keep him on his toes.

Be careful what you wish for. He met a manipulative minx named Irene Foote.

Chapter Two

A Mutual Friend

'Without promotion something terrible happens... Nothing!'
P. T. Barnum, 1850

It was with a splash and a giggle that Irene Foote, just seventeen years old, a precocious, privileged pain in the neck – caught the comet which changed her life and the amusements of the future. In the moment she couldn't have been luckier. She controlled it like a circus ringmaster – as she should have. Her links extended to one of the greatest showmen of them all, the truly remarkable P. T. Barnum, who really could make a monster out of a molehill. Her grandfather was Barnum's spin doctor, David Stevens Thomas, a highly charged haphazard of promotion who declared in headlines and could match the great P. T. for over-selling, over-stretching, over-pitching any of the attractions he offered his adoring public. Barnum would invent the impossible, his *spinmeister* would endorse it. Yet, the story the teenaged Irene told Vernon Castle the first day they met was even more remarkable for it was true (sanctified by Harvard University archives). It also underpinned her adventurous attitude, wanting to be first at everything, to be free of the stifling nineteenth-century restraints of simply being a woman. Her mother Annie had paid no attention to convention and her indulged daughter wasn't going to either.

Annie Elroy Thomas was fourteen years old in August 1875, when she proudly became the first female to rise into the skies over America in a hot-air balloon. Her publicist father was a ballooning enthusiast and himself delighted with air travel, with a freedom subservient only to the weather. And the whims of traditionalists like Sitting Bull and Geronimo, who were still sending nothing but smoke signals into the sky, and actively resisting the encroaching, if euphemistically phrased, pioneer spirit.

Warpath smoke talk didn't intimidate P. T. Barnum – little did – or his Great Roman Hippodrome, a 500-strong touring family of trapeze artists, Wild West shows, ladder-balancing acts, Mexican horse-riding displays, Roman riders and a vast tent as large as an ordinary circus, containing twelve cages of animals including four elephants, five camels and what are announced in that year's yellowing route map programme as 'a number of curiosities': P. T. Barnum liked novelties. His attraction and fortune was built on them, for decades much of it on the tiny shoulders of Charles Sherwood Stratton, who was twenty-five inches tall and weighed fifteen pounds when he was five years old. As he grew (finally to three feet, four inches tall), Barnum taught 'General Tom Thumb' to sing and dance; he wasn't more than a toddler when he was impersonating Napoleon and attracting huge audiences. P. T. Barnum never kept his feet on the ground; there always one more grand plan: the one involving Irene Castle's mother was a balloon flight from New York to Boston. Her father, in charge of the public relations, was booked on the flight with a group of newspapermen. No one bothered to check the wind velocity. It was believed the balloon would head in the 'general direction' of Boston (out into the Atlantic was the disregarded option) and they did consider the overall weight. Mr Thomas was replaced by his much lighter daughter. The perils of the flight were not an issue, but it was insisted that if it grew dark before the balloon arrived in Boston, the teenaged girl would be 'grounded' and the trip continue. It was not deemed proper that a young girl should remain in the basket of the hydrogen balloon overnight.

'Mother wanted the balloon to go higher and higher, to go faster,' Irene told Vernon Castle, insisting: 'She said she could hear herself living. She wasn't frightened for a moment.' And Irene found a way to reject fear too. Oh, yes, she was apprehensive and concerned and stressed and worried and all the rest of the emotional A to Z but not, not ever, *frightened*. Halfway, in a straight line, from New York to Boston, Irene's mother was 'landed' at New Haven, the home town of the balloon's pilot, Captain 'Darling Donald' MacDonald. He took position over a field and swung the anchor overboard. He picked up a megaphone and requested someone below to attach the weight to something stable. The farmers ploughing the fields below looked up, screamed and ran from this voice of Satan from the sky. The horses were left. The anchor swung about drunkenly – it was all over the place, in the tops of trees, a church steeple – and then grasped and lodged in a brick wall stiff with mortar. More ropes went over the side and the basket was brought down safely, and with it the exiting passenger, Annie Thomas. Irene Castle held the image of her mother curtseying to Captain MacDonald and then taking herself off, quite calmly, to arrange a horse and buggy home. It had been quite a day.

Irene beamed as she gushed out the story to Vernon, who quite suddenly had become the centre of her own over-inflated world. Five minutes earlier, she had branded him as 'not my cup of tea'. For one thing, he was far too thin. She had plunged off the Rowing Club's high diving board and pulled herself on to a float platform to dry off. By chance, Vernon climbed on to the other end of the float from the waters of Echo Bay and briefly glanced at the girl with the boyish haircut. They sat in the sun ignoring each other and gazing out at the blue haze. Irene believed your life is decreed before you are born and an unexpected encounter gave her argument a boost for a matchmaker arrived in the most unlikely of guises. The theatrical manager Gladwyn MacDougal, aged forty-five, was a hunk of a man, Canadian, with the affability of a cuddly bear but not one to be angered. He'd served with the 2nd Battalion of the Black Watch, forming part of the Highland Regiment, which during the Boer War saw some of the bloodiest fighting in South Africa. A Rowing Club regular and a friend of Irene's parents, he strolled over to the float.

'Irene, have you met Vernon Castle? Vernon, this is Irene Foote.'

There was a set of noncommittal nods. Gladwyn MacDougal was not a man to retreat: 'Vernon is one of our promising young comedians. He's been doing awfully well on Broadway with Lew Fields...'

Broadway and Lew Fields were the magic words. Unashamedly, Irene launched an offensive: 'I turned loose every ounce of charm I could muster to hold his attention. My mind immediately began to make plans and weave schemes.'

Vernon was polite but he had other business that afternoon. The damp giggle of a teenager, all enthusiasm and eyelashes, was somewhat overwhelming on a hot day. He said, truthfully, that he had a guest waiting for him. He looked towards the veranda of the clubhouse, at the guests in white linen carefully positioned on the wicker chairs and loungers. He *had* to go.

That might be, but Irene, already convinced there was a conspiracy to conceal how remarkable she was, had decided: 'I felt sure if Lew Fields could be persuaded to take one look at my dancing, my career would be on its way...'

It was Vernon who was on his way. Irene chased after and walked with him as far as the ladies' dressing room, where she swiftly changed and then 'oozed out on to the veranda to try to persuade him to get me an audition with Lew Fields'. The most immediate and spectacular obstacle was Vernon's 'guest', the gorgeous Southern girl Kathleen Clifford, a dancer and a veteran of Broadway's most elaborate and popular shows. The sight of the dancer took the gusto out of Irene's indefatigability: 'She was so resplendent in diamonds, I forgot everything else.'

Vernon's close friend was best friends with diamonds. They dressed a lavender wool outfit set off by an arrangement of violets in her hair. She clasped a mesh bag with her initials picked out in diamonds. About Kathleen Clifford were comfort in her own presence and more diamonds, placed every couple of inches along a gold chain which teased across the bust of her jacket and down through her belt to goodness knows where. Irene had never seen anything like it. She was impressed with the display of sparklers but Kathleen Clifford wasn't with her. She gave Irene a brief once-over and introductory 'How do you do?'

Irene's thoughts stumbled, ever so briefly: 'I was quite certain that my budding friendship with Vernon Castle had begun and ended within fifteen minutes.' But not if she could help it. The confidence is quite breathtaking in how it extinguished that flare of pessimism. The 'budding friendship' had involved her berating Vernon with requests to audition for Lew Fields. He, in turn, had been as polite as he felt socially acceptable and ducked out of the conversation. Irene never gave up. She recruited Gladwyn MacDougal as her go-between. MacDougal, as a 'theatrical', had often been treated to Irene's auditions, including the comic song 'The Yama Yama Man', which was a Broadway success performed by her idol Bessie McCoy in the show *The Three Twins*. Bessie McCoy, forever dubbed 'The Yama Yama Girl', was twenty years old and Irene's neighbour in New Rochelle: where Bessie could go, Irene could follow. She'd been brought up to believe she could achieve whatever she wanted.

Irene's father was a trained homeopath (a health discipline increasingly popular towards the end of the nineteenth century) and a qualified doctor working with his father out of a practice on Lexington Avenue in New York, when Annie Thomas became his bride on 29 May 1884. They moved to New Rochelle, where their first daughter, Elroy Bertha, was born on 17 September 1886, and it was a suburban life, chestnut trees surrounding matching homes and values. The couple made careful family plans and it was on 17 April 1893 that Irene arrived on schedule. The idea was that Elroy, with the intended age gap, would bond more closely and care for her sister; instead, she regarded Irene as a burden and the animosity ran on into their teenaged years.

Dr Foote was a progressive like his wife: in 1904 he patented – under reference number US 766106A – an intimate female cleansing device, the Foote Vaginal Syringe, and pursued medical research constantly. Which was a little irritating for his daughters, who were always being quizzed about their bowel movements. Dr Foote was a man concerned with the digestive system. He also had his own health to treat. He had tuberculosis, which chipped away at his energy, and each winter he sought comfort with the more caring climate in Mexico. His wife also got him involved in the new exercise of bicycling. Dr Foote cycled to the local tavern; a couple of drinks brought comfort too.

Irene's parents had a strong and loving marriage, a comfortable financial and social life. Her family worked for her like a trampoline, she could fall on it and bounce back higher. Where her father had his health preoccupations, her adored mother would indulge with her in talk of fashion and make-up, of hairstyles and romance. She also taught her daughter a no-nonsense approach to life. Annie, known in the family as 'Nell', was physically fearless and, just as she'd soared in the flyaway hot-air balloon, did so daily over high jumps on Vesta, a thoroughbred mare. When a German gardener, dismissed for pilfering, returned and shouted abuse at Mrs Foote, she took a rifle down from the gun rack as the former help fled down the driveway. She shot him in the left leg. When Dr Foote said he believed her actions rather rash, his wife complained: 'I only meant to wing him.' Dr Foote replied: 'Now, Nell, don't excite yourself.' Irene said that her mother had long learned that anything she did was always going to be fine by her husband: 'My father never allowed himself to be shocked by anything my mother did. He regarded her as a creature more precious than gold.' Her father was as vigilant about his wife's temperament as he was about her and his daughters' disgestive system. Irene said Dr Foote was convinced emotional upheaval was as bad for health as 'poor elimination'.

Irene felt herself entitled to similar carte blanche to shock but she ran at life a little too fast for her parents, who slammed on the brake: they enrolled her as a mid-teen in a private girls' boarding school, the National Park Seminary in Forest Glen, Maryland; an educational establishment which attracted money not brains. Irene was, as always, forthright, arguing that growing girls were shoved off to finishing schools like National Park to ease parental life at home during the 'difficult stages'.

Irene found it difficult adrift in hormone hell. She was pining for the athletic Cameron Whiting, a regular swimming partner at Echo Bay; she was convinced, aged fifteen, she would marry Whiting, almost as much as her parents were convinced she wouldn't. She was miserable.

The one enjoyment was being recruited for the boarding school's swimming team; the snag having to practice during breaks from lessons. It was also compromised by the elaborate boarding school hairstyle: the girls were supplied with 'puffs' of fake hair which were, after much time-consuming preparation, fastened with a multitude of pins to the top of the head. To train for half an hour in the school swimming pool meant removing the 'puffs' and then drying off and replacing them. It wasn't possible. Irene took a pair of scissors to her traditional pile of curls and snipped and snipped much of it off, creating a blunt bob. This was radical hairdressing – sausage curls were more of a norm – and the precocity raised attention and the blood pressure of the school administrators. They could cope with Irene's new 1909 look, but not the complaints of aghast parents when her classmates began chopping their hair into short bobs too. Irene attempted to run off to escape the furore but was returned to school – before finally being asked to leave for plotting an elopement with Cameron Whiting. In tandem time, her sister Elroy's early marriage failed. Her parents were getting sun in Cuba, and they sent for their children.

It was a mess and the girls were apprehensive about seeing their parents. Irene was especially nervous because her father had paid for Whiting to be exiled, or as he called it, 'apprenticed', as a Canadian lumberjack, and she planned to see him before he went.

The sisters waited uncertainly at the home of family friends in Cuba for the arrival of their father. Dr Foote was breathless and red-faced: 'Now, I don't want anybody to get upset. It's bad for the nervous system to get upset.' His girls collapsed into his arms.

Something Irene mirrored a few days later when she wrapped herself around Whiting at Grand Central Station before he left New York for British Columbia. They kissed. They promised to write every day. She wanted to die when the train had gone. Her legs wouldn't move. She sat on one of the hard station benches for two hours before she could walk home. The pain was not permanent, as Irene explained: 'Fortunately it is impossible for a person with robust good health to pine very long or very hard.' They wrote to each other, but after a few weeks there were no letters sent either way.

Irene was much more interested in her prospects in the theatre. And, so, in Vernon Castle too. She had put on 'shows' which were really imitative turns of Bessie McCoy doing 'The Yama Yama Man' at garden parties and charity events. Her mother indulged her with costumes and encouragement; Dr Foote told her she was 'a good little dancer'; and Bessie McCoy's mother saw her perform and told her she was 'very good'. She was also an excellent schemer. Gladwyn MacDougal did his duty and Vernon was invited for Sunday lunch at Irene's family home. Her parents liked him: Vernon was easy to like, softly spoken and pleasant with warm family manners. Dr Foote and his wife had brought up two difficult daughters (Irene insisted: 'I was not a wilful girl, not really') and to have a charming man about the house was an enjoyable contrast. He became a Sunday lunch regular, his place at table always set. Vernon listened to Dr Foote's medical theories and the topics local to New Rochelle. It was so very different from his conversations with Lew Fields, who enlivened him with stories from the streets of the Bowery. Here, in New Rochelle, almost everything on display was white: the suits, dresses, tennis gear and the people; even the refinement was aerated. In a way, Vernon didn't really exist for, in the local imagination, there was no immigration, only Americans. There most certainly were no 'Negroes'. Which put Walter Ash, the son of a plantation slave, in a spot. He was the Foote family's manservant. In much of this society he didn't exist either – which is possibly why he and Vernon got along so well.

Walter Ash had joined the Foote family a few months before Irene was born and she had grown up with him around the house. He was not a black retainer, he was a servant, but he was Walter, and part of the family. It was a paternalistic, patronising attitude: Irene said he was used to serving people because his mother had been a slave. Her words reflected her time and place, concreted notions Harry Houdini would find tricky to escape. It was not so long since the nation had fought the Civil War on the supremely divisive question of skin colour, an ever-present factor on the streets of New York and the backstairs of New Rochelle. But not at the dinner table or skipping over the waters of Long Island Sound.

Vernon was given Dr Foote's full approval when he was invited out on the doctor's boat, a 30-foot motor launch called the *Hully G*. They'd take Irene and Mrs Foote's chicken sandwiches and a sense of adventure with them. They were soothing, comforting days for them all. On land the atmosphere was more lively. At home Irene would badger Vernon about an audition with Lew Fields. Dr Foote and his wife treated Vernon like a son, a brother for Irene, much as she did in the early days of this friendship. He *was* too thin, she thought. His nose had a comic character all its own. Yet, he was composed and nice and understanding. Except about Lew Fields.

Irene snuggled up to Vernon but only for advancement; there was no instant romantic attraction and most certainly none of the teenaged red-faced *longing* that had signalled her love-at-first-sight crushes. Yet, she snuggled on for, she told herself, her greater good. She was cute at it and one Sunday evening at the Foote family home, with Gladwyn MacDougal as witness, Vernon, stung by a WASP, finally promised to set up an audition for Irene with Lew Fields. It took much effort, even for Fields's favourite son of the theatre.

Yet Vernon didn't succeed alone. At first, he did it for Irene and then they pursued *their* dream, for their lives were now captured by kismet. Lew Fields didn't love any of this. Anxious working actor that he was, he still rejected the role of Cupid: he wanted Irene out of his – and Vernon's – life. And very far away.

Irene remained close to Vernon and Broadway. She and her sister Elroy, who was studying catering, were sharing rooms high up in a Columbus Avenue apartment block in New York; standing on tiptoe, neck stretched like a swan in full flight, she could glimpse a slim corner of Central Park. Elroy did the housework and the cooking, chores which Irene insisted were good practice for her sister's studies. Irene floated around the theatres, watched endless performances by Vernon, couldn't bother with Ethel Barrymore 'emoting' or Douglas Fairbanks 'being energetic' and made herself a scenic walkabout. Her persistence paid off and after many, many weeks of being badgered by Vernon to give this 'sweet young girl' a chance, the parental Lew Fields agreed. He had spent five years fondly turning Vernon into a profitable, comic headliner, and felt Irene was 'stealing' his boy, luring him away from comedy to dance, which he considered a grave career misdirection.

He had much on his mind. Fields was enduring misunderstandings with the Shubert Brothers over what shows to grandstand and where to place them. He wasn't in the best of health at that moment, almost crippled by exhaustion. He was grumpy; he was also reluctant to disappoint Vernon, who just by jauntily walking into a room made him feel less weary and much, much better. Yet, harried and tired, he remained grumpy one warm Saturday afternoon in September 1910, at the Riveria Theatre on 96th and Broadway, where, after fourteen weeks in Atlantic City, his new success *The Summer Widowers* was playing. On stage was a standard stage lamp with one naked bulb. Whispers echoed like gunshots in the vast theatre, all but empty between the matinée and evening performances. Except for the few onlookers (Helen Hayes and her mother were at the back of the stalls) and that pushy socialite, that spoiled swell, who was tempting Lew Fields's star turn from him. Irene, after many postponements, had her audition. She was on show.

The musician she'd engaged to play the piano, who'd arrived from New Rochelle before time on the Baldwin 4-4-0 with spoked engine truck wheels, was idly seated, her fingers running over the keys with this and that melody. Vernon stood close by.

'So – go ahead!'

Lew Fields, steaming a little like the Baldwin, was feeling his way down the aisle of the theatre in the darkness. He shook hands with Irene, glanced at Vernon, and then turned back into the stalls, Vernon at his heels, to take a seat and watch the show with him.

'Can't we get some light?' asked Vernon.

'Go ahead, I'm waiting.'

'You won't be able to see what's been worked out.'

'I came – I'm seeing.'

Manifestly, he was not making it easy for anyone. Irene looked out, trying to see Vernon. She tugged at imagined creases in her costume, looked around, and Vernon slipped off backstage. A few overhead lights and a couple of footlights sparked alive, but you couldn't say Irene was in the spotlight. She indicated to the piano player to go for it and a resounding capriccio brought Irene bounding on to the stage doing a saucy can-can kicking routine, then she switched to another lively number using castanets. Irene was rarely a self-analysing teenager but at this moment: 'There is nothing more exciting than castanets in the hands of an expert who can coax unearthly music out of them. In my hands castanets sounded like the hoofs of a very tired horse crossing a wooden bridge.'

As it transpired, across a romantic Rubicon: 'I was terribly aware of the two people sitting out there in the darkness but, strangely enough, it was Vernon I wanted to please.'

He was. He coaxed Lew Fields into offering Irene a job – to dance in the fourth road company of *The Midnight Sons*, which was touring in Colorado and all points west. That delighted Fields. And Irene. She, as Vernon knew she had to, turned the opportunity down. Honour was satisfied and Irene's self-awareness flew away as the Baldwin locomotive on its way back to New Rochelle built up steam: 'I was thrilled beyond words. I was bursting to tell everybody that Lew Fields had offered me a part in one of his great successes and I had turned it down!'

The young Helen Hayes was less enthusiastic about Irene's audition: 'I saw a nervous, skinny non-professional who had never appeared on stage before. She followed Vernon around like a puppy, unsure of herself, tripping over ropes, bumping into props, under everyone's feet.

'It was doubly painful to me.

'It was an absolute betrayal!

'My Vernon had fallen in love with an amateur.'

Indeed, he had. Fallen in love, that is. Irene's 'amateur' status became debatable very quickly. In November 1910, *The Summer Widowers* (three husbands go on the town until their wives return early from holiday) had moved to the Majestic Theatre in Brooklyn and the actress Billie Coupier had moved on too. Vernon had been lobbying to get Irene a role in the show and with only a couple of weeks left of the run, she got the job, which involved three lines and not much stage time. She also had to share a dressing room, with Helen Hayes, who had the much greater role of Psyche Finnigan. Both ladies remembered it vividly. Irene recalled: 'My first night at the theatre was the most thrilling night of my young life. I came in at the stage door with Vernon and he led me up the winding iron stair to the dressing room I was to share with the other two wives and the little girl who played the part of Psyche Finnigan. The little girl had long curls and a much bigger part than mine.

'Helen Hayes had a crush on Vernon, a violent, unrelenting crush, and when I arrived to share her dressing room it was like the snake entering the Garden of Eden.'

That was accurate. Helen Hayes: 'My world was rocked when I heard that Billie Coupier was leaving the show for some glamorous, amorous reason. It was shattered when I heard it was a sweetheart of Vernon's who would replace her and share my dressing room. Sweetheart! The drums of doom began to beat in my heart. I hid in the shadows the day Vernon proudly strolled in and introduced the slim, beautiful girl to everybody. "Where's Helen?" Vernon asked, as I retreated further into the dark corner. I wished a trap door would open under her.

'*She's a bean pole*, I decided viciously – conveniently ignoring the fact that they were obviously made for each other. These two string beans were beautiful. It was so unfair. Everything about Irene was chic. Vernon certainly knew what he was doing when he chose her. His eyes were keener than Mr Fields' and less jaundiced than mine.

'I couldn't have been meaner. When Irene walked into the dressing room for the first time and asked what she should do about make-up, I quickly answered: "Ask Willis B. Sweatman what he uses." Mr Sweatman was a famous black-face comedian in the show. She bought a box of minstrel's make-up. I don't know what I expected to happen; but I was foiled. Vernon found her naiveté touching, and I just made him love her more with my mischief.'

On Christmas Day 1910, Vernon Castle asked Irene to marry him. She said yes. Any doubt on her part was about her father's reaction when he returned with her mother in March from wintering in Mexico. Mrs Foote would have to be warmed to the nuptials first. Dr Foote, his pain nagging him that he was slowly dying from TB, wanted a solid future for his daughters. Elroy was training to earn her own living. Irene was incapable of cooking or housekeeping and wanted a career on the stage.

Now, her plan was to marry a man earning $75 a week – when he was working. It was not a practical match in Dr Foote's consideration, no matter how much he liked and admired Vernon as a good man with a suitable age demographic, he being a reliable six years older than his intended bride. He didn't object to the vines of his daughter's deepest emotions being trained around Vernon. His concern was if Vernon had the roots for them to flourish. He agreed to a family conference and leaned a little more comfortably back into his leather armchair and waited for the ambush. He varied his objection by saying weakly that marriage was difficult enough without an 'international marriage'. Vernon was a British subject and that meant their backgrounds were 'diverse'. His wife eyed him through her lorgnettes, firing an effective warning across the swell of her bosom: yes, well, he'd think about such a marital union. His wife suggested that their younger daughter's future was not a matter of American foreign policy. They too had been young and aspiring. This was a matter of the heart, of love. Didn't they still love each other? Didn't Vernon love Irene and vice versa?

Dr Foote despaired: 'Now, Nell, don't upset yourself. It's bad for the nervous system to get upset...'

The girls, this time mother and daughter, collapsed into his arms. His future son-in-law shook his hand, and the formal announcement of the engagement was made the next day. The wedding date was an easy pick, Sunday, 28 May 1911, the twenty-seventh wedding anniversary of the warmly benevolent Dr and Mrs Foote.

It was also the day Vernon Castle got lost up the creek, up the Swanee, even with a paddle.

Chapter Three

A Foreign Country

'One day you really must try Tom's Negro ragtime. I know you'd love it.'
Vivienne Eliot, T. S. Eliot's first wife, writing in
December 1917 to London society hostess Mary Hutchinson

Vernon Castle lived for ragtime and these, as Scott Fitzgerald said, were the great days to be dancing to it. Irene Castle was born in the same year the syncopated sound made its formal début. While the thirsty Princess María Eulalia of Spain celebrated the World's (Fair) Columbian Exposition of 1893 in Chicago in her particular fashion, the background music being readied for the twentieth century was receiving its first popular ovations. It was lively and it was most certainly democratic.

The first Eisteddfod choral competition staged outside of Wales was held in Chicago at that grand celebration for the 400th anniversary of Columbus's discovery of the New World. There was much more *new* to toast, including the first Hawaiian hula and Indonesian music performances in the US; a 250-voice Mormon Tabernacle Choir competing in the Eisteddfod; Joseph Douglass becoming the first black performer to tour as a concert violinist after his appearance; and soprano Sissieretta Jones ('The Black Patti', after the Italian opera singer Adelina Patti) enhancing her already glorious reputation. She sang for four Presidents and the British Royal Family, and her supreme salute to the wealthy diversity of life was to perform in concert 'Swanee River' and selections from *La Traviata*.

Scott Joplin played piano and, even with all the *new* around, that in itself was shamelessly daring. It telegraphed a style of music which stimulated change not just in the trivial pursuits of a good time but in how people dealt with and respected each other. Not everyone liked it – or the thought of any siege around the status quo. The Ku Klux Klan bonfired some crosses and whistled Dixie. Nevertheless, Joplin hit the right time and the right notes and became the vivid champion for ragtime, what he called 'Negro music'. He invited an audience rapport that became indispensable to his success. Once the sound sticks in your head, it tends to book in for the weekend and stay the week. Even then, it never totally completes checkout.

Ragtime, the music of black America, first offered competition to the classical music of Europe in Chicago in 1893. The 'freedom' of slaves in the tattered aftermath of the Civil War and the future of themselves and their culture as 'American' was still constantly debated. Black and white segregation in public places was an ongoing fact of daily life, 'free but not equal' went the complaint. At the World Fair an incomer, the Czech composer Antonín Dvořák, said that by living in the United States he had become convinced of one thing: 'The future music of this country must be founded on what are called the Negro melodies. These beautiful and varied themes are the product of the soil. They are American.'

Dvořák, so celebrated and versatile, who was the composer in

1893 of the 'American' String Quartet at the invitation of the New York Philharmonic Orchestra, was acutely prescient. As the 1890s ended, Scott Joplin's 'Maple Leaf Rag' was a true success story. As was its composer, a slave's son born in 1868 – the year the proclaimed, but discerningly ratified, Fourteenth Amendment, which promised legal equality for black Americans, was introduced. Joplin, whom many built up as a crusader when he was essentially a pioneer, popularised the music, but he didn't invent it. Ragtime, with unlikely happenstance, began at the Castle Club in St Louis, a decade before Scott Joplin first lived there. The prissy teenaged Irene Castle would have freaked at the chance of that name: this Castle Club was one of the most imaginative brothels in America, run by the flamboyant madam, Sarah 'Babe' Connors. The Pulitzer Prize-winning and obsessively inquisitive cultural historian, the late Professor Russel Nye, pinpointed the infamous cat house, which offered piano-playing entertainment for those requiring further amusement, as the birthplace of ragtime in *The Unembarrassed Muse: The Popular Arts in America*. Ragtime or variations of it was the music of Babe Connors's establishment. She was born into slavery in 1857 and opened the Castle Club in 1890 when, having quite miraculously survived that far, she was as hard as the diamonds she draped herself in. She had gold inlaid in her upper teeth but it was diamonds she liked most, around her person, parasol and feather boa. It cost an American 'double eagle' ($20 in gold, no currency) to step through the front door of the Castle Club and see the sparkle.

Sensual and driving unexpected rhythms featured around the black cellar clubs, the dives and the doorways and cabarets of St Louis, but the bordello was customised for wealthy white men and they too equated that beat with a good time; Babe delivered fine wining and dining and a revolving selection each evening of at least ten Creole girls guaranteed to be authentic Louisianan. Her 'parlour' in the double-fronted house on Chestnut Street also offered singers and musicians and the more rustic enjoyment: the 'parlour' floor was mirrored, allowing Babe's ladies, minus underwear, to dance in demure, long skirts but still keep the clients as perky as the music which many were hearing for the first time. It became acceptable and then accepted, a cultural and inventive transition for so many.

By 1904, Joplin had published 'The Entertainer' and a concert of other work, and that year, along with a crowd of other ragtime piano players, he was in St Louis for the city's Louisiana Purchase Exposition. His music was popular across the nation but he and his fellow musicians were banished to a segregated area. It was unofficial but it was done. It couldn't quieten the sound, the piano playing that echoed around the St Louis days and evenings and into the small hours in the clubs and cafes, a soothing, soft tempo. Ragtime, believed Joplin, required some dignity, some class; he always, always insisted: 'It's never right to play ragtime fast.'

It soon provided Vernon and Irene Castle with a musical platform on which to dance. The banshees of good taste said they were dancing on the edge of doom but the rhythm, the joyous give and take of it, begged for dance invention, for spontaneity, for creating individual magic. With ragtime and their collaborators, the couple became pivotal in the world's acceptance of the revolution in music and social dancing.

Like so many marvellous things, it wasn't remotely planned. As Irene Castle happily admitted, 'We became professional dancers by necessity.'

Because Vernon Castle wasn't too well organised. He adored the big picture; details were for people in the back office, not the true creatives. A chaotic volley of this was on his wedding day. He forgot about it. More precisely, the time: he was so enjoying himself out rowing on Echo Bay, where he might have recalled this whole wedding business had first begun... But, no, Vernon was AWOL from the Foote family home in New Rochelle where family guests (tuxedos and finery) and bridesmaids (in the yellow chiffon) and Irene in her wedding gown (a long flow of crêpe de Chine with weights in the train to make it hang properly, and wax orange blossoms in her hair) were nervously tugging at their finery. The Reverend Benjamin T. Marshall was piously patient in the downstairs reception room but anxious to begin the ceremony. Irene's parents gave her a last-minute inspection and full approval. She asked: 'Where's Vernon?'

No one knew. The bridegroom had vanished. Dr Foote, already gaunt from his illness, told the pianist to keep the music going. His wife called the Rowing Club. 'He's done what? He's gone canoeing?' Mrs Foote's questioning squeals down the telephone could be heard around the house. Irene looked distraught and then she heard Vernon's voice; he'd 'lost track of time'. He did a quick change, entered from stage left into the second reception room, and the Wedding March began. They could hear the bride arriving down the polished oak stairs; the weights in her train hit every other step, bang, quiet, bang, quiet, bang, up a beat, down a beat: it was a syncopated start to the marriage of Vernon and Irene Castle.

Any concerns about Vernon's lackadaisical approach to marriage were drowned in several cases of champagne and the sight of the newlyweds taking to the floor for the first dance. Vernon could dance; he was exceptional. Irene's huge talent was to follow him, never to get in the way of Vernon or the music. Shall we dance? Absolutely, but first there were thespian pursuits.

When he married, Vernon had a couple of weeks to complete

in the summer run of Lew Fields's spectacular new success, *The Hen-Pecks*. He and Irene could see the show's name in lights from their honeymoon suite at the Knickerbocker Hotel in Times Square. The show's box office had refreshed Vernon's Broadway status. It had also given his theatrical career an immense boost, but not helped his fading relationship with Lew Fields, who saw the Englishman as his successor. The *New York Times* did too, endorsing his performance in *The Hen-Pecks* as 'genuinely amusing and clever'. Still, Vernon, so easily bored, was finding Fields and the show heavy going, despite the acclaim. The story was simple, and silly, enough: Vernon in a red fright wig was the zany Zowie, a magician called the Monarch of Mystery, who was intent in the seduction of farmer's daughter Henolia Peck, much to the displeasure of her father Henry, the lead role taken by Lew Fields. It gave Vernon and Lew Fields a huge amount of conflict onstage, an extravaganza of slapstick between the musical numbers. What most delighted the packed-in vaudeville audiences was a scene where Fields, disguised as an Italian barber, takes revenge on Vernon's Zowie. They would be unaware of the sadistic undertones; what that new visitor to America, Sigmund Freud, might make of it. The knockabout sequence involved clever timing and the antics were risky. Vernon carefully annotated the uniquely vaudeville routine and it is filed with his other scrapbook materials in the New York Public Library at the Lincoln Center:

1   Barber hacks tie. Barber grabs tie and ties it to the back of the chair.
2   Barber rips collar off victim. Victim jumps up. Barber pulls him down, twice.
3   Barber tilts chair back, takes victim's face, and bumps head down four times. Punch line: 'Now don't you move!'

4   Barber strops razor on tie, hits victim on head with razor; he starts to get up when barber winds tie around neck, pulls him down, and continues stropping.

5   Victim twists legs around. Barber tries to untwist victim's legs, jabs knee with razor edge, knocks feet off stand.

6   Barber gets shaving cup, bangs victim's head into correct position and dabs brush first in left eye, then in right eye, and then nose, etc., etc., etc.

7   Barber lathers mouth and then tries to insert brush between lips. Punch line: 'Say something.'

8   Barber jabs brush in mouth. Victim bites it. Barber tries to get it out again.

9   Barber starts to shave victim. Wipes razor on victim's trousers twice and then on lapel once.

10 Barber pulls nose back over chair to shave upper lip. Wipes razor on neck.

11 Barber pushes victim's stomach down.

12 Barber grabs hot towel, puts it on victim's face. It's too hot etc., etc., etc.

13 Barber gets second hot towel, places it on victim's face with tongs.

14 Barber straightens chair, sets fire to victim's wig, pulls his shirt out, gets fire hose and shoots chair, exit chasing victim with fire extinguisher.

Vernon survives, as he must, for he spends most of the show on stage fooling around, doing magic tricks and dancing. He was also fascinated, as were the whole theatre company and the audiences, by Blossom Seeley, the former Minnie Guyer of San Francisco and 'Queen of Syncopation', whom Lew Fields imported east for

The Hen-Pecks. She was an original 'coon shouter' like Sophie Tucker, whose success 'Some of These Days' she had introduced. Blossom Seeley ('Way Down Yonder in New Orleans', 'Yes, Sir, That's My Baby') belted songs out through the rafters and that provided a noisy fanfare for ragtime as it flowed into the mainstream. Vernon and Irene Castle were staggered by the reception she achieved. Lew Fields milked it. For her big number he placed the sleek, long-legged singer from the Barbary Coast on a table centre stage and she performed what she established as her signature song, 'Toddling the Todalo'. With it, to the delight of the Castles who noted the rave reaction, she previewed a roaring dance routine called 'The Texas Tommy'.

Along with Sophie Tucker and several other 'coon shouters', Blossom Seeley merged black and white into more colourful entertainments, at a time when racial and gender acceptances were raw and delicate, the boundaries as disputed as Balkan national frontiers. They, and oceans, were crossed. The British music halls and Paris revues became stages for 'coon imitators' and tinkles of ragtime; variety bills in America included such performers close to the top of the bill. It was an intriguing mix, often a collision in culture. Sophie Tucker recounted in her autobiography her role in this hangover from the nineteenth-century minstrel shows, when in 1906 she was reluctantly persuaded to black up by a Harlem theatrical manager who didn't believe she could deliver a sexy song and ordered: 'This one's so big and ugly the crowd out front will razz her. Better get some cork and black her up.'

On stage, the singer wowed the audience and then removed her gloves and waved her clearly white and fleshy hands; it was something of a royal wave, the crowd all but curtsied. They loved her. For next half dozen years Tucker was billed on the vaudeville circuit as the 'world-renowned Coon Shouter'. Songs being sung around the piano were shamelessly titled 'If The Man In The Moon Were A Coon', 'My Little Zulu Babe' and 'Pickaninny Nig'. With Blossom Seeley's breakthrough star turn in *The Hen-Pecks*, the sound and the music went to a more breathless altitude.

It also became automated, everything from sheet music to pianos were being factory produced, affordable and in turn respectable for the aspirational home: the family photographs were often displayed across the piano, and children were encouraged to take up the 'pianny', the close black and white keys sending a subliminal message of enlightenment, of unity of purpose. Possibly too subliminal for some. Self-appointed white tastemakers branded ragtime as the anthem of dangerously out-of-control black sexuality.

There were nasty remarks. Edward Berlin, a renowned scholar and author of a cultural history of ragtime, quotes in his many works an unnamed director of the American Institute of Musical Arts: 'Ragtime tunes are like pimples. They come and go. They are impurities in the musical system which must be got rid of before it can be considered clean.' Berlin adds another viewpoint of the time: 'The counters of the music stores are loaded with this virulent poison which, in the form of a malarious epidemic, is finding its way into the homes and brains of the youth to such an extent as to arouse one's suspicions of their sanity.' music magazine offered: 'The American "ragtime" is symbolic of the primitive morality and perceptible moral limitations of the Negro type; with the latter, sexual restraint is almost unknown.' Berlin quotes the interestingly named Karl Muck, the German conductor of the Boston Symphony Orchestra, as giving his classical opinion: 'I think what you call here your ragtime, is poison. It poisons the very source of your musical growth, for it poisons the taste of the young. You cannot poison the spring of art and hope for a fresh clear stream to flow out and enrich life.'

T. S. Eliot was enriched by ragtime. He was there at the birth. He was born, in 1888, at 2635 Locust Street in St Louis, west (a long way) from the red-light district and Crawford's Theatre where Joplin's 'lost' work, *A Guest of Honor,* débuted in August 1903. This was Joplin's 'ragtime opera', his pursuit of 'serious' music but damned by purists as a shameful oxymoron. Eliot insisted he never escaped the influence, the pulse, of his upbringing near the Mississippi, crediting it with his early 'nigger drawl' and the river, 'the brown God' he creates in 'The Four Quartets', published so much later in 1945, with everlasting inspiration.

T. S. Eliot, like millions of others, tapped his toes to the ragged melodies and danced 'Negro ragtime'. Joplin strove to write more serious material but there was constant commercial pressure from the white music publishers for 'pop'.

Some never gave a thought to that or the incongruity of race relations. Others pondered how so much joy, so much joviality of hope was most extraordinarily created out of the misery of poverty and slavery. Irene Castle's manservant, the pragmatic Walter Ash, was succinct: 'It's about surviving.' Which Irene Castle believed she never would in England. Her upbringing was obviously many miles from the banks of the Mississippi. England? The flighty teenager thought she'd die in East Anglia. It was, without any doubt, horrid.

A few days after *The Hen-Pecks* went on hiatus for the summer, Irene and Vernon sailed from New York on 11 June 1911 on the SS *Minnehaha* for Tilbury in east London. All was well for them on their honeymoon voyage aboard the Harland-and-Wolff-built ocean liner. They were young and fun and in love; they were waited on. It was the life Irene was accustomed to, her needs, her everything, being cared for, arranged for her comfort and benefit. She and Vernon left for Britain as the preparations were building for an even more cosseted couple. The Coronation of King George V and Queen Mary was held on 22 June 1911 at Westminster Abbey. George V had been King since his father King Edward VII's death on 6 May 1910, and began his rule when a technology-changing world was learning to live and die in altogether different ways.

It was still the days of the British Empire. George V was the only monarch present at his own Delhi Durbar, the Indian assembly to salute a British monarch's Coronation; he founded the House of Windsor, pushing the House of Saxe-Coburg and Gotha into the pages of reference books, all to quieten animosity towards his family's German ancestry. He was a standard bearer for the emerging middle classes, more puritanical than indulgent and, if possible, more Victorian than his grandmother.

This was the world Irene Castle read about in America – but not in the new formatted newspapers, the tabloids, when she arrived in Britain. Even so, London was so remote to New Rochelle; for Irene, New York and the bright lights of Broadway weren't worth comparing. She was to be shocked by the lifestyle of Vernon's family. Goodness knows what she'd have made of that summer of the libidinous cyclone whirling through London society. Depending on your pride or peccadilloes it truly was the best of times or the worst of times, for the daughters and fated sons of Empire. The teasingly great beauty, Lady Diana Manners, who became Lady Diana Cooper, Viscountess Norwich, and calmed her nerves with needles of morphine, recalled in her memoirs the extreme hedonism around her; her life a reflective A to Z, from Asquith to Zanzibar. Cocaine, opium and heroin were available over the counter at the High Street chemist. Postprandial cocaine was served in salt cellars. Although the new tabloids, particularly the *Daily Sketch*, condemned the 'snow snifters', the nightclub crowd involving Diana Manners called itself 'The Corrupt Coterie'. She announced they were proudly bohemian: 'There was among us a reverberation of the *Yellow Book* (a monthly magazine for those keen, by definition, on immoderation), Aubrey Beardsley, Ernest Dowson, Baudelaire and Max Beerbohm. Swinburne often got recited. Our pride was to be unafraid of words, unshocked by drink and unashamed by "decadence" and gambling – Unlike-Other-People, I'm afraid.'

'The Corrupt Coterie', this Algernon Charles Swinburne poetry-spouting set, were enthused by narcotics, vision-endangering absinthe and the new booze, vodka, which, like the drinkers, appeared to mix with anything at all. Especially at house parties, those grand bohemian rhapsodies. The aesthete Osbert Sitwell wrote that, for these gatherings, 'One band in a house was no longer enough, there must be two, three even.' The chilling of the drinks became such an obsession that great blocks of ice were formed and placed to be cooled by electric fans. It was very modern but decor and good taste demanded the electric function be disguised: the chilling paraphernalia was hidden behind banks of hydrangeas.

Irene would have adored ice in her ginger ale when she got to Vernon's family home in Norwich. Metropolitan London had found no favour with her, what hope the wilds of Norfolk? Travelling through London for the train to Norwich had provoked the first shudder of horror. The men looked well dressed and prosperous, but she was aghast at the appearance of the women. Through Irene's nineteen-year-old flapping eyelids they were dreary and dowdy and so, so inconspicuous. Norfolk, she felt, must be better – yet it didn't seem so when she first arrived at Norwich Victoria Station. Vernon's family were there. Young, nervous and possibly wary of what she'd landed herself in, jealous of the affection showered on the prodigal son (Vernon hadn't written to his family in three years), she began badly.

Irene was not enamoured by Vernon's family home. The upset was it wasn't Dickensian; it was new with the one bathroom in the basement, the bedrooms two floors up. Her father-in-law was nice but normal; his chief advantage, for Irene, was he could have stepped out of Dickens's pages, a short man in a dark suit, bowler hat, and an impressive watch chain dangling from his waistcoat. Still, he was void of Vernon's flair – where did her husband get his style from? It was not from Norwich where she said he felt like a circus act, a curiosity for the locals in her stylish New York coat with its black satin hood. It was the 'little things' which made her visit difficult: 'I shuddered every evening when Mrs Blyth headed for the pantry and the bottles of warm ginger ale.'

It was bananas on which she truly slipped up. They had spots. Vernon's stepmother offered them with pride, bought for a favour and price that day, but Irene felt her stomach turn as the brown speckled bananas were presented to her

Irene, not very politely, turned the offer down. Later, in their bedroom, she was laughing about it and Vernon asked: 'Private joke?' She explained her thoughts about the brown-spotted bananas. As he took off his tie her husband told her: 'They're the same bananas you eat in New Rochelle.'

'*Those* bananas. *Those* bananas!'

'They're identical, very same ones.'

So began a lively domestic.

'Impossible! '

'I think it was rude of you to pass up on the bananas. She was very proud of them.'

'She can have them. And you can have them. But *I'm* not going to have them.'

This banana business was silly but it emerged as important – for it made Irene take a close look at herself. At first, she couldn't explain what had gone on; neither could a bemused Vernon. What *was* the problem? It wasn't until they were sailing back to New York that she took her husband out for a walk on the upper deck and said:

'I'm sorry. I was a spoiled brat.'

After dinner that evening, they went for another turn around the deck before retiring. They leaned over the rail looking out into the black and wavy Atlantic, and Irene recalled thinking to herself: 'That was the day I began to grow up.'

It was a start. Smooching with an eager and alternative fan in Paris was an altogether different lesson in life. Which she could have blamed on Vernon. Instead, Jacques took the rap for that one.

Vernon and Irene were waylaid by the French theatrical producer Jacques Charles weeks after their return to America. Lew Fields had given Irene a small role in *The Hen-Pecks* on $25 a week for saying three lines (Vernon was getting top dollar: $100 a week) to keep his theatrical 'family' happy. It didn't ease the tension between him and Vernon, who was still brooding about the tardy arrangements for his wife's audition.

They went on tour, Pittsburgh and Philadelphia and, as the ice started forming on the lakes, Chicago. Irene was ambitious for Vernon who was – and, of course, she couldn't put it quite this way – playing second banana to Lew Fields. They had many discussions about their future when Jacques Charles visited them as the show opened in Kansas City. He wanted Vernon to appear in a Paris revue reprising the barbershop scene: he'd bought the rights from Lew Fields and would cast a French comic actor in the Fields role; he wanted Vernon to play the hapless and absurd victim in the barber's chair. Yes, scenes would be created for Mrs Castle.

They had some savings – $500 of which Vernon promptly spent on a diamond ring, a 1911 Christmas gift for his wife – and a romantic notion of Paris. It would end the regular paydays; there would be no cash released during rehearsals, only when the revue began. It was a terrible proposition... which they immediately accepted. Vernon said they would worry about the details when they got to France. Wasn't it exciting?

Irene squeezed her outfits into steamer trunks; only a green linen suit – 'not Paris' – remained in her wardrobe at the family home in New Rochelle. They travelled with the English bulldog they'd been given by Dr Foote when they married. He was one of the doctor's much-loved seven show dogs and had a red flash on his back left paw; they called him Zowie as a salute to Vernon's raspberry-coloured fright wig in *The Hen-Pecks*. Vernon was passionate about animals and from then on he and Irene indulged themselves and were surrounded by them; they adored Zowie, he was their 'baby'. They liked Walter Ash too. He would travel with them for no pay but, as Irene pointed out, 'glad of the opportunity to see Paris'. She remembered the voyage many years later and her memory remained that of the Daddy's girl from New Rochelle: 'We all regarded Walter as a member of the family. He came along as cook, valet, and general utility.'

The Castles sailed first class for Europe aboard the SS *Zealand*. The stoic Walter Ash was in steerage. Irene, in 1958, gleefully recalled: 'Every day we stood at the first class deck railing and tossed goodies down to him on the deck below. He was beaming with excitement.'

Vernon, typically, had given little thought to this first marital enterprise, trusting that all would 'happen' much as it always had before. He and Irene had written themselves into Hans Christian Andersen; they were engaged in such an infatuated love, such an engrossing and tactile confection of self-indulgence, that they were floating above reality. Irene, with reflection, saw how foolhardy it was – a spectacular tilt at chance. If Lew Fields had but made a tiny, reasonable offer to them she believed they would have stayed in America. But Fields, with the choreographer Ned Wayburn whispering like Iago in his ear about Vernon's fidelity to him, did not. Europe awaited. Irene was supported by Vernon's enthusiasm, his joy of a new adventure, and she saw how much he enjoyed people and they him. Still, she knew 'he could get most delightfully bored; things had to keep up a lively tempo to hold his interest and even those he loved bored him at times.' He loved the Continent and it never bored him. Or Walter Ash. Or Zowie. It flustered Irene a little.

The Castles docked in Antwerp and, with no racial segregation in Europe, Walter Ash went everywhere with them. Even stalking milk carts through the narrow streets of the city: Irene and Vernon were fixated by the unwavering concentration of the dogs trained to draw the carts, of milk and hay and people. They had money, a still bulging 'roll of francs', and moved on to Brussels en route to Paris. The shops were more fun than those in London and Irene liked the Belgian lace and bought five Dutch caps in the material, neat little numbers which flatteringly framed her face. She knew she looked good in them and they became part of her style.

The two of them were in a very big sweet shop. They were dedicated tourists in Brussels and saw all there was to see: monuments, cathedrals and three theatrical shows at which they did not understand one spoken word (their interpreter charged them more than their week-long hotel stay). With their 'roll' diminishing, they boarded the train for Paris and another elegant hotel, a small, discreet establishment expensively reserved by their French management, the producers of *Enfin... Une Revue*. Which was highly romantic.

French Customs were not. They had their particular rules for travellers. Irene's 500 cigarettes would be confiscated. As would Vernon's matches and his five decks of playing cards and no amount of argument, even regarding his professional magician status, could stop that. Protests were met with Gallic shrugs. The officials wouldn't even speak American. Or English. It was, as the customs officer might have said, a débâcle. It was also a hefty fine: 600 francs (at 25 cents to the franc) and a lump out of their Paris cash fund. Yet, the show was about to open and they were in the city of romance. Of course, Vernon offered: 'Isn't it exciting?'

It took him a couple of days to ask how much their hotel was costing. That was so exciting it turned him pale. Irene was 'horror-struck, our guarded pile of francs was evaporating'. They moved to an attic apartment above a white-shuttered antique shop and grander apartments with cramped balconies on rue Saint-Georges in Montmartre. It was an unlikely garret. There were two bedrooms which took care of the Castles and Walter Ash. Zowie had a bed on the kitchen floor, the better to catch scraps, but shared the Castles' bed too. There was also a bathroom with running water and a toilet. The ceiling slanted down from the roof and Vernon had to duck his head moving from one room to another.

True to form, he made it into a comic turn and never saw their situation as a predicament but a pause in their good fortune. He even turned the bad news that there would be a delay in the opening of the Paris show into a 200-franc advance from Jacques Charles, which turned their daily drinks into champagne again.

And sent them on a ten-franc ride on a *voiture à bras*. Vernon said it was better to spend, to get some air on a handcart ride: anyway, he hated coins in his pockets as they spoiled the line of his trousers, which he carefully pressed himself every day; he could never imagine being seen out without having shaved and dressed with precision.

He and Irene were preparing (it took an hour or so) for an afternoon walk when a tiny bottle of Guerlain eau de cologne with a stubborn stopper spilled from Irene's hands and the perfume splashed into Zowie's eyes. The dog yelped with the burn of the pain. Irene screamed with guilt. Much of their reserve cash went on paying a vet to treat Zowie; a supply of special eyewash saved the bulldog's eyesight but postponed the champagne supply. They were down to their last few francs. They began to spend their stash of copper penny coins – the ones too big for Vernon's pockets – and soon they were gone. When rehearsals began, they received another advance of 200 francs.

That went quickly, what with a bottle of wine with dinner each night and 20 francs a day in cab fares to and from rehearsals. It was an all or nothing life. When flush it was champagne and steak dinner for themselves, Walter – and Zowie – or, the funds low, snacks and evenings playing cards, 'Seven Up', which Walter Ash had taught them; or strolls through Montmartre sneaking looks inside the nightclubs. Walter Ash, the French speaker in the family, became the scavenger with local shopkeepers and brought home treats.

It was wonderfully cavalier, so *c'est la vie*. The artistic temperament and sentiment can be applauded but the arithmetic of reality finally added up to a future of potatoes and cheese and then nothing, no food, no rent money and, probably, no champagne. But not quite yet. They discovered a gold watch which Irene had inherited from a great aunt: Walter pawned it.

He got 15 francs and Irene revelled in how they spent it: 'We were so hungry we spent all 15 francs on a big meal at a little outside café on the boulevard, washing it down with five-franc champagne.'

This pioneering spirit continued and they juggled life and an increasingly hectic rehearsal schedule for Vernon. Walter cushioned the enterprise as they were running out of time and fried eggs, their survival diet.

Walter, short, dapper and burly with a neatly trimmed moustache and attitude, presumably now a specific rather than simply a general utility, came to the rescue. He was not strait-jacketed by illusions, in love with love, and was keen to continue living well. He was also almost as tricky with a pack of cards and the roll of the dice as Vernon. Walter had befriended the staff working in other apartments along rue Saint-Georges and on their downtime had arranged gambling parties. He taught his new friends the American game of 'craps' with dice shooting across the table (an apartment floor and a couple of satin cushions as 'the block' were the stand-in arrangement) and as a veteran player had a big edge. So, not quite magically, he produced the francs which bought the American trio chicken and steak dinners, and champagne and flowers for the apartment, where on frugal evenings in the attic of 44 rue Saint-Georges they sipped house white, a rich Sauternes, after dinner and played the more innocent 'Seven Up'. Walter usually won and there were no complaints. Vernon and Irene Castle were not so innocent that they starved in Paris. Their 'breadline' French life made more for amusing anecdotes than suffering. That was provided by Vernon's 'art'. Or, in the eyes of the Castles, the sad lack of it.

The Olympia Theatre in Paris was aged and the plumbing facilities had the whiff of the Bastille. The Lew Fields–Vernon slapstick had been rewritten and was, of course, to be played in

French; it was Walter who had learned some of the language, not the star. Yet, the immediate problem was Vernon's costume – he looked ridiculous. He was, for some theatrical reason, called Duncan, a Greek poet, and dressed in sandals, a short skirt-tunic and a long wig. Even at his zaniest on Broadway he'd never felt so silly. This time around it wasn't even funny: for the Castles or the silent French audiences. Appeals for artistic renovation were overturned and they had little argument; they were the architects of their own denouement, in hock to the producers for 1,000 francs of advance payment. The show went on. Vernon and Irene endured those first two weeks of March, 1912. The show didn't work, the comedy routines didn't translate, the audience didn't laugh. Vernon's act was a flop: Why was he setting fire to his hair? Of course, if you have to ask…

In life as in art there is, we must trust, a reason for everything. No one cared if the Englishman immolated himself. But they were enraptured when he danced with his wife.

The show craved a big finish to send the audience away smiling and celebrating their evening. Irene's mother, pining for her daughter and the son-in-law she loved for bringing joy to Irene, had sent newspaper cuttings of the latest entertainment news in America to her absent family, including reports of the fashionable dances like 'The Grizzly Bear'. Vernon easily added up that if they hadn't seen 'The Grizzly Bear', the French audience hadn't either. *Hot diggity*, Mr and Mrs Vernon Castle would present a version, an 'exclusive' to excite them.

The Castles won Paris by thinking of Broadway, of Blossom Seeley and 'Toddling the Todalo', and improvising 'The Texas Tommy'. They launched their great professional dancing partnership and the public adoration of their enduring love story to 'Alexander's Ragtime Band'.

They sang, and not very well but that didn't matter; the music worked the wonder: you must simply conjure it in your consciousness:

Come on along,
Up to the man,
Who's the leader of the band,
Come on and hear,
Alexander's Ragtime Band.

Imagine it at eardrum-rattling blast, emotions akimbo. It was rough and tough and Irene said she spent more time flying in the air around Vernon than with her feet on the ground. Vernon let it all go and Irene, never ever afraid with his arms around her, flew with it.

'Bravo, bravo!' cried the crowd, jumping to their feet and clapping along to Irving Berlin's song. Several couples joined them on the dance floor. The noise, reports a faded – possibly *Le Figaro* – newspaper clipping, was deafening.

The Castles went on dancing, which was the way it was always meant to be. Whenever there was a hint of a pause in the action, in the insistent rhythm of the song Berlin stole from Scott Joplin, the cry went up for more, more, more.

The Castles danced on.

Chapter Four

Dangerous Liaisons

'My father warned me about men and booze, but he never
mentioned a word about women and cocaine.'
Tallulah Bankhead, *My Autobiography*, 1952

The lady in black with raspberry-coloured lips, her face flushed
by crème de cassis and an overwhelming fancy, gave Irene
increasingly frequent glances which swiftly became gazes. Much
as she tried not to, Irene kept catching her eye across the tables of
the Café de Paris. The woman, her tall, full figure plunged into a
velvet dress with a huge V in the back, and howling for attention
with an oversized velvet dinner hat adorned by a curling plume
of bird of paradise, smiled at Irene. She returned the smile and
then to Vernon. A waiter appeared by their side. The woman
would like to speak with her. Vernon and Irene's dancing was now
known in Paris. She thought the lady in black was a fan. She asked
the waiter if the woman spoke English. She didn't, but Vernon
urged: 'Go on – your French needs polishing!'

Irene left that bad joke at the table and went over to greet her
admirer. The woman gushed away, as the bemused Irene kept

smiling and repeating '*merci*'. She hadn't a clue what was being said. She did pick up when the lady asked her for tea. Irene said she would be delighted, as would her husband, who was English and the English loved their tea. Tea? More pertinently: 'Do you love him?' When she said she did, the lady in velvet pulled back from the conversation but gazed on at Irene, who was glorious to see: tall, slim and radiant. She was the antithesis of the fashionable Edwardian woman; young women and girls did everything possible at that time, including elaborate hairstyles, heavily corseted figures and ornamental, frilled gowns, to look as alluringly mature as they could. They invited the dowager look some years before it would present itself free of charge; you couldn't retrieve time from a safe deposit box. Irene, who simply wanted freedom of movement, accessorised her unusual style with her youth which, like a diamond necklace, requires no public relations.

Bemused by her encounter, Irene, with her boyish, short hair, squeezed her trim body past the packed tables and back to Vernon, who had arranged for them to join friends and go dancing on the Left Bank at l'Abbaye Thelesme and on to Maxim's for breakfast. It was chilly outside and they grabbed coats and wraps and were off; a long table for them had been reserved at l'Abbaye and Irene found herself at the end of it. The nightspot was busy but the waiters zipped around the tables and soon they had drinks – and Irene the attention of the lady in black velvet, who was sitting next to her and smiling ever so much. Irene was puzzled by why, but she felt so fidgety, so uncomfortable.

An English friend drifted over and asked her to dance. She accepted instantly. It was moments and a couple of turns around the floor before Raspberry Lips took action. The dance partner suddenly vanished, inelegantly removed by the apparition in black velvet who, pressed in body-to-body with Irene, began what Irene called a 'hootchy-kootchy' dance. This was too sensual, a little too much French for the girl from New Rochelle who could not comprehend her state of discomfort. Her friends were amused but Irene was so distressed Vernon rescued her. With some effort. Raspberry Lips hissed at Vernon but kept her claws sheathed as he danced Irene around the room as if nothing untoward had happened. Later, at home, he explained the desires of Irene's ardent admirer. She said she wasn't shocked but surprised. Her mother had never told her about it, so it must be a French exclusive, like some of the fashions.

Irene's naiveté and Vernon's theatrical illusions were being tempered in Paris. With their dancing success at the Olympia Theatre they'd paid off their advance, saved (well, those nasty, big copper pennies) and, with a stoicism appropriately inspired by short-skirted Duncan the Greek, resigned from the show; life was again dependent on Walter's knack with the dice. It wasn't arrogance, more devil-may-care in an uneasy world. Irene glowingly reported how they wandered the boulevards hand in hand, the chestnut trees in blossom; how they giggled together as they window-shopped and, in the evenings, laughingly peered between the legs of the heavily uniformed doormen of the nightclubs. Their days were rushing on; there was no time to take anything too terribly seriously. Irene: 'We were still children, of course, and we were in love, and nothing else mattered.'

Children of their unsteady time, however. When an exuberant headwind of garlic swept up the stairs of number 44 rue Saint-Georges, dancing became most important again. The theatrical agent Lucien Marc, a more rotund version of the French politician and future President, Raymond Poincaré, brought a proposition along with the piquant aroma. He was as diplomatic as his lookalike but also as pragmatic. He had seen the Castles do 'the greeezly bahr' to 'Alexander's Ragtime Band' at the Olympia. He wanted to hire them to dance at the Café de Paris but with a caveat: if they did not please, it would be strictly a one-off. They would be paid 50 francs for their evening of dancing: it was like discovering hidden treasure.

Yet, they couldn't quite comprehend the offer. The Café de Paris was *the* society spot in Paris, the watering place for all aristocratic species and those with the cash, if not the pedigree, to be entitled to a good table. The proprietor Louis Barraya ran his establishment like an embassy; there was protocol for every eventuality, but he remained his own man. He defied the perception he created with his huge physique and short, razor-cut hair: he was as intrigued to talk of Gobelins tapestries and Sèvres porcelain as the new American dances. He too had seen the Castles appear at the Olympia and had been enchanted. He was not as confident, however, that those who paid his exorbitant prices would be as won over as he was; his clientele saw themselves as the entertainment, the headline cast, their presence a joy for all others. They were a rarefied caste, a jaded bunch, confused about their faith and identity, lost in the partisan politics of Europe, protectively blinkered to what might come. Louis Barraya saw in the young Castles an affirmation of life, of a good life. Which was, indeed, his business to provide. Every evening.

With the serendipity of the opportunity, Vernon and Irene had little time to prepare. Vernon made notes and he and Irene stepped out their bespoke 'Grizzly Bear' in their attic rooms. There was one emotional crisis – she didn't have anything to wear.

There was a rush. Louis Barraya had suggested they grace the Café de Paris twenty-four hours earlier than planned, to have a table by the dance floor and dinner, on him, at 'ringside' as it were.

Irene wore her lightweight crêpe de Chine wedding dress, her only accessory a gold bar pin Vernon had given her on the first night of their honeymoon. Vernon was elegant enough for Paracelsus, so light in his dancing shoes he was sylphid, his minute waist accentuating the form of his New York-cut mohair suit.

They looked so elegant, even if the butterflies were swarming inside them, as Louis Barraya led them to the centre of the prized ten tables reserved for VIP patrons. Irene felt dowdy, surrounded as she was by so much pretension, finery and jewellery. You could hear the trust funds stretch as the crowds turned to inspect her and Vernon, who'd added an encouraging smile to his wardrobe. It was Irene's shoes tied with satin ribbon and one of the lace Dutch caps from Brussels, which highlighted the symmetry of her features, which elevated her from the other women around the tiny dance floor. She quickly realised that less was longevity.

At nineteen, Irene, in a way, had the world looking at her that spring of 1912, for the Café was buzzing with international aristocracy: Russian grand dukes and duchesses, French nobility, Austrian and German royals, London lords and ladies, Argentine and American millionaires. Many American women, aristocrats by marriage, were involved in this revolving group, from London society to the Tsar's court in Russia and the palaces of the Austro-Hungarian Empire. This American-born new class – they had their own magazine published in 1912 in New York, *Titled Americans* – comprised 42 American princesses, 17 duchesses, 19 viscountesses, 33 marchionesses, 46 ladies, 64 baronesses and 136 countesses. The denominator figure – the average age of the women was thirty-five – told something more of this aspect of international affairs. Now, another young American was on display, being guided around the Café de Paris dance floor by her husband: the Castles had been caught on the hop.

At a few minutes after midnight, when the diners' cognac was beginning to taste less expensive, Louis Barraya had begged their indulgence. One of his best and favourite customers, a Russian aristocrat, had seen them in revue and would like to see them dance that evening. It was a shock. Irene, especially, was reluctant but Louis convinced her and she pinned up the train of her dress with the gold bar. For both Irene and Vernon, life and work was not about the individual, it was about *them*, Mr and Mrs Vernon Castle, professional dancers.

They stood up from their centre table and moved to the dance floor. Irene felt Vernon give a squeeze of her hand. The butterflies flew away and never returned. Paris, the leader of the small orchestra, had been alerted, and his baton and the Castles went into action. Irene moved in a haze: 'All I recall of the dancing was Vernon's supreme confidence. Vernon was ingenious and sure-footed and I followed his lead.'

The proprietor and their patron, Louis Barraya, was pleased for them and for himself; his gamble had paid off. It also did for the dancers when he presented them with 300 francs from his Russian friend who had pleaded for an encore. They danced once more and went home richer and happier. Their dancing had been requested, applauded and rewarded, as was Walter Ash who was woken by 300 francs being waved in his face. Their confidence was high, helped by success and the wine, and the next evening their 'audition' was a pleasure not a terror. Previously, cabaret entertainers had been kept away from the guests, sequestered behind the piano or by the kitchen door, but when they arrived at the Café de Paris the next night Louis Barraya gave them 'their' VIP table.

From then on Louis Barraya was always 'Papa Louis' to Vernon and Irene. This was the man who had helped, and calmed all fears.

Now Vernon and Irene Castle had made a magical entrance, their first steps on to the world stage. Vernon had been more diligent at writing home to Norwich and had promised that he and Irene would visit, but the profitable demands on their dancing became all-consuming. Irene believed their success was helped by their no-frills elegance at the Café de Paris: 'We were young, clean, married, and well-mannered. My clothes were simplicity itself, and I had no jewellery; the youthful enthusiasm we showed for our work and the real joy we derived from dancing demanded attention.'

Vernon and Irene were smarter than their years or experience. When they were offered a six-month contract at the Café de Paris they delayed waiting to see how popular they became – and so were able to ask top dollar in negotiations.

Yet, now money was no longer a problem. Their fee was 100 francs an evening – but that was champagne money given the tips, usually huge amounts in a variety of currencies, which they received every evening. Both of them were regularly slipped 1,000 francs 'in appreciation'. Walter Ash instantly went on salary, plus 30 per cent of the tips; supper every evening was on the Café de Paris and for their engagement they retained *their* table. It was a lucky omen: they became the most sought-after couple in Paris and their reputation travelled with their international fans. Soon they were invited to appear at soirées and do exhibition dances: they often performed three an evening (at 300 francs a time) before getting up from their Café de Paris table at midnight to dance again. They became careful in their choices of 'freelance' venues; if Vernon was wary, he asked for 1,000 or 3,000 francs for an hour's dancing – and to his great astonishment such a contract would be agreed and paid.

His wife became a fashion leader. *She* was smart enough to

know it was her youth which gave her the edge; and, subconsciously, that American East Coast restraint, which when matched with a flare of fun, promotes clever, innovative looks. Irene Castle was *different*. She became a pin-up for the 'New Woman', the 'Modern Woman', the 'Twentieth-century Woman'. When money became hugely available in Paris, she was tempted to have elaborate dance costumes made, fine and fancy affairs which would rival those of the nobility, but that, she knew, would be tilting at bejeweled dowagers bankrolled by nations. It would have been pointless. She stuck to the satin ribbons in her shoes for effect, her one luxury her adored black-and-white striped petticoat. She asked a local rue Saint-Georges dressmaker to sew up demure dancing gowns of crêpe de Chine in simple cream.

Her slender frame, that titillating androgynous puzzle, together enhanced the clothes and the demographic of her appeal. Something similar could be said of Vernon. As a team, they had all bases covered. They were the look, the new perspective of the future, they were about *change*. They were also going to rearrange a world of attitudes and vice versa. Irene Castle sparked the twentieth-century fashion industry; she helped make how you dressed part of public life. It began undetected, like a sly virus, and then took on the bedlam of evangelism: you *can't* go out in *that*. Irene, of course, went out as she pleased; she was showing the way, and the trends evolved from her. You dress and groom like those you admire or trust – and Irene looked good and safe. An incredible paradox given the sexual awareness of the 'New Woman'.

The Castles were the sensations of Paris. Fashion archivists enthused about Irene Castle, with one uncredited historian writing of the time:

Vernon's and Irene's impact on social dancing was nothing compared with Irene's effect on the Paris fashion world. Irene's young, slim, athletic form symbolised all that was new and exciting. She defined the brave new woman. She was more like her husband's equal and sexually ambivalent friend than a passive, child-bearing dependent female. Her *raison d'être* was still to be desirable, but desire was no longer defined by dynastic power, pomp and prestige. Independence, individual initiative and innovation was the new ideal. Irene was sending the message of youth, equality and freedom as she flew around that dance floor at the Café de Paris.

Fame attracts. It wasn't only Irene who was making waves, creating new standards and aspirations for women and style. Elsie de Wolfe was her own energetic standard bearer and had a huge influence on the lives and careers of Irene and Vernon. The biographical books tell so much about Elsie de Wolfe by simply stating: 'She was born in New York and died in Versailles.' There are many pages in between, but that's a good insight about the woman, known as Lady Mendl through marriage (platonically to British diplomat Sir Charles Mendl), who invented interior design as a profession and breaching convention as her life. Elsie de Wolfe was comfortable with herself and everywhere she went, as long as she didn't encounter anyone or anything that snapped her back to her Victorian childhood. Her mother, with exaggeration, had called her ugly – but she called herself a rebel in an ugly world. She used colour and light in her life and her work to vanish dark Victorian days and design. Irene Castle was doing that by being alive.

Elsie de Wolfe, later named in Paris as one of the world's best-dressed women, was amused that Irene had knocked her off the fashion pedestal that summer of 1912. She was a customer of Mrs Josefa Osborn of New York who confidently advertised in newspapers across America: 'Mrs Osborn is the most renowned individual authority on matters of dress in America, and the creator of the most exquisite costumes produced for the stage and women of society.' Elsie de Wolfe had commissioned a 'walking skirt' from Mrs Osborn which hung six inches off the ground and was a design repeated by four Paris fashion houses. It got lost in the scramble for all things Irene. Author Jane Smith, in her book *Elise de Wolfe: A Life in the High Style*, notes: 'The fame of Elsie's invention was soon eclipsed that summer by the rush to copy every gown, hairstyle, step, and gesture of a younger and considerably more beautiful arrival from the United States, the dancer Irene Castle.'

The French fashion archives record a wider impact: 'Everything the American teenager chose to wear became de rigueur for the fashionable.' Shoe manufacturers copied Irene's satin-ribboned evening shoes and called them Tango slippers. Women demanded simpler hairdos like Irene's and shed the rats and appliances that they had previously used to create their elaborate coiffures. The enormous Edwardian picture hats were dropped for little hats more in keeping with Irene's petite lace cap. Diamond dog collars, elaborate jewellery and massive tiaras started to go out of fashion because Irene wore no jewellery. Ornamentation and frills also started to disappear as Irene preferred youthful, unadorned lines.

Many of the elements of change that had come together that night in 1912 at the Café de Paris had not originated with Irene. They were the result of six years of social revolt. Isadora Duncan, Ida Rubinstein, and Ruth St. Denis had startled in 1906 with their interpretive dances wearing transparent chiffon chitons, oriental veils and bangles. To see an uncorseted female body move in public was something that had not been seen for almost 500 years.

The following year, Lady 'Lucile' Duff Gordon, of fashion house Lucile, caused a sensation when she designed a soft, flowing, lightly corseted empire gown and marvelous hat for Lily Elsie, who was starring in *The Merry Widow*. That same year Lady Duff Gordon's sister, the novelist Elinor Glyn, created the first real sex novel of the twentieth century, *Three Weeks*. It was about an Eastern European queen who so dreads perpetuating her husband's barbaric nature that she seduces a young English aristocrat to produce a proper heir. She lies, uncorseted, upon a tiger skin wearing a soft chiffon gown to excite her lover.

Whether literature, Elinor Glyn did a great deal for the aphrodisiac reputation of tiger skin. Which was emphasised in verse:

Would you like to sin
With Elinor Glyn
On a tiger skin?
Or would you prefer
To err
With her
On some other fur?

Lady Duff Gordon and the French couturier Paul Poriet now replaced the corset with a lightweight elastic girdle and the provocative-sounding *soutien-gorge*, a.k.a. the brassiere. The orphaned seamstress Coco Chanel was making hats from her apartment at 31 rue Cambon, across the street from the Ritz,

which set off the sleek Lucile designs. It was the sort of arrangement a good public relations company would invent, but all was
not good PR. Pope Pius X frowned on behalf of the Vatican.
Women were arrested for wearing too little; their indiscretion
apparently an invitation to natural disaster, floods and locusts and
the like. The fire-and-brimstone men in the pulpits announced
doom: these flimsy fashions were, so to speak, the Devil's design
and it was eternal damnation all round.

Until Irene Castle took them on parade. She was exempt from
damnation. She made it all smart and sensible and wholesome.
She was elegant and she was young and she was married. This
teenager made change safe; we are told the young are the motive
power of history and Vernon and Irene Castle were historic
landmarks. She validated the free, modern woman, who must be
more engaged with society and men and life than her mother's
generation. It was only the beginning.

Irene and Vernon took what were previously feared as satanic
and 'dangerous impulses', accompanied as they were by ragtime
music, and on the dance floor made it fun and aloof from sexual
metaphors. They looked like a couple of kids having a good time.
That Vernon and Irene were married, and happily so in such a
public romance, excited a psychological appeal: you too could be
slim and healthy and in love – if you danced. Vernon's years on
Broadway and their months in Paris had earned them 'overnight'
fame. By then Vernon was a veteran of attention and able to deal
cleverly with the attendant tricks, traps and trifles which rode in
tandem with success – but not the money; he liked to spend. Irene
simply swept celebrity around her like a piece of silk and wore it
just as well. Of course, she'd always believed she was someone.

The Castles were also most acceptable in polite society. Elsie de
Wolfe and her longtime companion, the intuitive Elisabeth

Marbury, who had lived intimately together since 1892, introduced them to an international audience. It was the Castles' relationship with the two women which was important in their success, for the power of prescience and the connections that these two formidable women possessed were quite remarkable. The world was expanding in the twentieth century but in some areas it remained small. Vernon and Irene, beautiful and charming, even together as slim as a whisper, danced at parties organised by Elsie de Wolfe for her friends, and for many others including Charles de Noailles, the Vicomte de Noailles, a rich aristocrat as young as the dancers but rather more wanton in his general interests. From that appearance, one soirée followed another.

An extravagant supper party at the Ritz Hotel in London in July 1912 bestowed greater 'star' power on the young dancers. Colonel Anthony J. Drexel, Jr., a banker-businessman (Drexel & Company of Philadelphia was a foundation stone of the J. P. Morgan colossus), enjoyed important friends: the late King Edward VII and the very much alive-and-kicking Kaiser Wilhelm II. Drexel wanted the entertainment for his guests, who included a Russian grand duke, to reflect his status. A star of the evening was the Italian tenor Giovanni Martinelli, who had made his début a year earlier singing for Toscanini at the Teatro Dal Verme theatre in Milan. The fragile and brilliant dancer Nijinsky, from Sergei Diaghilev's Ballets Russes, also performed, as did Diaghilev's ravishing and mesmerising prima ballerina, Tamara Karsavina. Mr and Mrs Vernon Castle completed that extraordinary line-up. 'People were marvellous to us,' said Irene, and they were, for the couple retained a freshness, a 'golly gee' attitude to the people they were meeting and the money they were earning. It was as if they remained adolescents being rewarded, kids being allowed to stay up late with the grown-ups.

From their attic at 44 rue Saint-Georges they visited grand houses and chateaux, but they always returned to the Café de Paris and to Louis Barraya, who completed their circle. The Café de Paris proprietor was also close to the American-born dancer Maurice Mouvet, who had been brought up in Paris. Maurice was an innovative ballroom dancer and in 1911 had married Florence Walton from Delaware (whose 1907 stage début was in the chorus of Lew Fields's *The Girl Behind the Counter*) following the death of his first wife and dance partner, Leona Hughes. She had died from pneumonia, brought on by overexuberant performances with her husband of the Apache dance, which Maurice had co-created.

Irene didn't like the Apache routine and its violent choreography casting the woman as the victim: 'The male dancer tries to demolish the female dancer, spectacularly, and usually succeeds.' There may have been some jealousy in her animosity as Maurice and Florence were, in 1912, the only true dance rivals the Castles had. Now, they were sharing the bill with them at the Café de Paris. The kindly Louis Barraya had promised Maurice, following his wife's death, that if he returned to Paris he could work for him. The promise had been kept and Vernon Castle had welcomed the kindness; he recognised it as the gesture of a friend.

Maurice wasn't quite as much the gentleman. The Castles retained their table by the orchestra but Maurice and Florence, internationally renowned as they were, had to appear from behind a screen which was, not too discreetly, concealing the kitchen door. Also they were the newcomers and didn't receive the adulation the 'resident' Castles had created. It made the evenings somewhat tense. Maurice, born in New York's Bowery, was used to sharp elbows. After his dance, he would wander over to Vernon and Irene's table, glower at Vernon and murmur: 'It must be nice to be a star.' Vernon shrugged it off but one night Maurice hadn't corked the bottle soon enough and invited Vernon to step outside where he would rearrange his face. To escape the embarrassment, the Castles told Louis Barraya they would leave until Maurice and Florence had completed their engagements. Which is the way it went; the run-in with Maurice had tainted the Café de Paris a little even if Vernon wrote it off as more wine than Maurice.

The Maurice *contretemps* deflated Irene. She was already a little low; she missed her parents and was concerned for her father. Her mother had written daily to her in Paris giving full reports on Dr Foote and his losing battle with TB. It was taking a vicious toll on his body. Nothing, it seemed, could ease the pain of the tuberculosis. The winters in Mexico had helped, but only a little, and Dr Foote had insisted in returning to New Rochelle in late February, 1912; if he was going to die, he'd do it at home. The pain was unforgivable.

The inevitable telegraph cable arrived for Irene in May that year. Dr Foote, beaten by the pain, had refused to eat and drink, and finally succumbed. Irene and Vernon were a little lost by this. Understandably, Vernon felt he should visit his own father; death plays the conscience like that. Irene would take Zowie, the best-fed dog in France, and go home.

She sailed four weeks after the sinking of the RMS *Titanic* – the biggest, safest liner in the world, on 14–15 April 1912; a disaster from which the survivors included Irene's friend and designer Lucile, Lady Duff Gordon. Sailing from Southampton and out into the Atlantic, Irene took to the top deck and sat with Zowie wrapped up in a steamer blanket in her arms. When a night fog swept over the ship, haunting it with gloom and menace, Irene made a plan with herself should they too be hit by an iceberg. She would rush with Zowie in her blanket as though she was taking a baby into a lifeboat. Otherwise the dog might be banned.

They made it to New York, where her mother waited on the dock. Irene waved and waved from the upper deck and then stopped. She was outraged. Her sister Elroy was there, and wearing the green linen suit, the only outfit Irene had left behind. Irene said she raged at the 'perfidy' of her sister. It was forgotten moments later, dismissed as the trifle it was, as mother and her two daughters were reunited for the first time with the family patriarch gone. The girls tried to comfort their mother but it was she, who had endured Dr Foote's final months, who kept consoling them, holding them ever so tight and sincerely telling them it was 'for the best, what he wanted at the end'.

Irene explained that Vernon was on the next sailing. He'd look after them. For Irene, her husband, despite his casual approach to the business of living, his joking and 'don't-cha-know' chatter, still had the authority of the decision-maker. Times were changing but too much time had gone before. She was Mrs Vernon Castle.

Vernon arrived in New York with good news from Norwich – his family were all well and prospering – and a letter of introduction from Louis Barraya of the Café de Paris, Paris, to Louis Martin of the Café Louis Martin, New York: the former Café de l'Opera on Broadway between Forty-First and Forty-Second Streets, a spectacular 'lobster palace'. This post-theatre cafe and nightclub had been created from the gutted structure of the eight floors of the Saranac Hotel by an investment group, who apparently decorated with pots of gold; the refurbishment looked like Dali had painted a weekend in Babylon. The *New York Times* reckoned the Café de l'Opera had cost upwards of $4 million. The *New York Tribune* said the 18,000 electric lights turned 'night

into day, and balustrades and pergolas of black marble in the glare
of brilliant lights, statues and sculptures, winged bulls and other
fantastic and artistic conceits contribute to the general scheme.
The Café is nearly barbaric in its lavishness.' Ouch, that was a
sting in the lobster tail. The newspaper described the main floor
as: 'in Assyrian style, heavy gold and black marble being
predominant. A marble palace of music is featured from the time
of Alexander the Great. It rises 50 feet and is entirely constructed
of black marble. The pedestal is formed of one large solid block
of marble, on which reclines an immense Assyrian lion. Bronze
figures ornament the steps, and from the temple run pergolas to
the balconies, which are supported by Assyrian columns of black
marble, the capitals being double griffins taken from casts of
originals.'

Good, barbaric stuff which included a 22-foot-wide walkway,
modelled after the great staircase of Persepolis, leading to the
second floor. Along the staircase was a series of bronze Assyrian
lions, each one supporting a flickering flame. From the balcony of
the second floor eight life-sized bronze statues glared down on
the diners. From the third balcony hung what they said, and
hoped, was the largest silk rug in existence, hand-embroidered in
Assyria. Hot food was a problem. By the time it got to the table,
the steam had long gone out of the dishes. Staff could move
quickly through the building because newfangled escalators had
been installed between the eight floors – but that was no help to
the food trolleys. Miles of pneumatic tubes connected all sections
of the restaurant. Electric buttons at each table allowed the guests
to call their steward or chef. This was revolutionary. The
restaurant's dining rooms occupied four floors, with its main
kitchen located above them. Manager Henri Pruger, hired on
$50,000 a year from the Savoy in London, had a staff of 750. It

was all too much and New York's most expensive manager went back to London richer if not wiser in July 1910, when the venture went bust. Louis Martin took over and hired Vernon and Irene Castle as insurance.

Martin was a hospitality business professional; he'd successfully run the Café Martin at Broadway and 26th with his brother Jean, and with the renamed location he was intent on lifting the tone and lowering the overheads. He moved the kitchen to the basement to solve the problem of food arriving cold at the tables. He installed a bar on the first floor and revoked the unpopular formal dress requirement. He wanted all to be low-key. Yet, like George Rector and all entertainment and hospitality pioneers, Louis Martin felt pursued by the *new*, the need to be modern. Why else have a dining room lighted by a dozen perched owls with electrified eyes the size of silver dollars? (Vernon would wink at the owls as he danced. 'Look 'em in the eye, don't-cha know.')

Vernon and Irene negotiated a favourable arrangement with Louis Martin whose English, despite the years in New York, was poor. But he knew his arithmetic. When he'd enquired about salaries, Irene had jumped in with $300 a week. Louis Martin said for that money he would dance himself. He would ponder on it. Vernon and Irene went off to her mother in New Rochelle. They had been making good money but immediately spending it and they had not lost their taste for champagne. They were energy rich but cash poor. That didn't last long: Louis Martin did his sums and the Castles added up.

His financial projections with them attracting many new late-night customers were strong enough to prompt him to meet their $300-a-week demand and to give them accommodation in the Café Louis Martin's building, a fourth-floor suite with more space than Paris but not the charm. They had a staircase which led down to a balcony overlooking the supper club where they danced. Each evening they'd go down to the balcony, light cigarettes, and watch the crowd. No longer would they be on show all evening. They would make a proper entrance. There were cards neatly printed on all the supper-club tables: 'Mr and Mrs Vernon Castle will appear at twelve o'clock.'

A few moments before the gifted moment, they'd slip quietly to their table, the drums would roll, the guests would clear the dance floor, a spotlight on the balcony would pick them up and they were on, gliding gracefully for many miles around the floor to the delight of the room. The astonishment was that they made it up as they went along. Or, rather, Vernon did. He was like a composer who can't read music. He could imagine the movement, the steps of the dance, and once performed it would be logged in his memory. He had an uncanny ability of recall. He'd copy down steps on the back of menus, lose his notes, and start again. He and Irene had rarely spent a night apart since they married and they were tuned to each other. It helped in the dance, as Irene explained: 'By keeping my eyes firmly fixed on the stud button of his dress shirt, I could anticipate every move he was going to make and we made it together, floating around the floor like two persons sharing the same mind.'

They'd taken Paris and, now, Manhattan was rushing to anoint their feet. Elsie de Wolfe's partner, Elisabeth 'Bessy' Marbury, was their official agent (15 per cent). Gladwyn MacDougal, the unlikely Cupid, became their manager (good faith, good cigar). The group – they could never be a *team* – had a gusto about them, a social ideology founded on the need for freedom and sophistication…and making a buck. Bessy Marbury was transparent about the financial potential: 'I saw the fat years ahead.'

They met to celebrate at the Marbury–de Wolfe showroom of

a home, on Irving Place in New York, which was decorated with chinoiserie furnishings and a satirical hint of naughtiness: dark Victorian furniture enamelled white; colour picked out by striped wallpaper. They drank Mumm champagne and – to make the toasts extra special – added a touch of crème de cassis. It brought the warm and exciting glow of expectation, of new adventures, of a grand new stage to dance on.

Book II
Dance Time

'The afternoon was already planned; they were going dancing – for those were the great days: Maurice was tangoing in Over the River, *the Castles were doing a swift stiff-legged walk in the third act of* The Sunshine Girl *– a walk that gave the modern dance a social position and brought the nice girl into the café, thus beginning a profound revolution in American life. The great rich empire was feeling its oats and was out for some not too plebeian, yet not too artistic fun.'*

F. Scott Fitzgerald, 'The Perfect Life', one of the *Basil and Josephine* stories, first published in the *Saturday Evening Post*, 5 January 1929

Chapter Five

Russian Roulette

'When you hear that Lady Mendl standing up
Now turns a handspring landing up
On her toes,
Anything goes!'
Cole Porter, 'Anything Goes', 1934

Irene Castle said that Elisabeth Marbury looked like Queen Victoria 'with the plumpers in'. True, Bessy Marbury didn't require cosmetic cheek fillers to get the look. She did like to be amused. She enjoyed the gaiety in Elsie de Wolfe's eyes and her penchant for doing acrobatic body flips at parties. That followed cocktails, usually the Pink Lady (one-third gin, one-third grapefruit juice, one-third Cointreau), which Elsie had created, believing grapefruit was good for the dietary system; a system which Irene knew only too well from life with Dr Foote. It was a remarkable ménage, wild *and* dedicated; miraculously, they were enlightened fogies.

Yet, for all the eccentricity, both Bessy Marbury and Elsie de Wolfe got on with business. Their lives might look like a frolic but they were social reformers, philanthropists, and enchanted by

Vernon and Irene. They were believers in marketing and promotion. There was also self-belief – and that confidence over-whelmed the eager Castles.

There arrives a time for all performers of all disciplines when they are told they can walk on water. Also, a moment when they believe it. Each evening at Louis Martin's increasingly popular nightspot, the applause for Vernon and Irene and cries for encores endorsed their worth. Jack Reagan, the manager across the street at the Knickerbocker Hotel, installed a dance floor and offered to double their money if they'd appear for him. It was a temptation, but only that – until Louis Martin's good drinking buddy Maurice Mouvet appeared. Maurice and Florence Walton had returned to New York and were booked at the Café Louis Martin as an added attraction. Not for Vernon, and especially Irene, who found Florence beyond irritation, especially when Irene believed she copied her dancing dresses 'to the last button'. It was one thing Maurice offering to punch Vernon's lights out in Paris but this, said Irene, was 'ridiculous'.

They confronted Louis Martin with this problem and mentioned the Knickerbocker Hotel offer. He doubled their money and Maurice and Florence abruptly left. Vernon and Irene had the fabulous showcase of the Café Louis Martin all for themselves. It was like an ongoing worldwide audition for their talents. They got better by the night, Irene so comfortable with Vernon, rarely missing a step, never missing a beat. Vernon, of course, couldn't put a foot wrong: he was creating the dances. But all who saw them mention 'the fun' which the Castles presented on the dance floor.

Other performers – like the vaudeville dancing child stars Fred and Adele Astaire, who began their careers half a dozen years earlier, when he was five and his sister eight years old – were influenced and inspired by them. The Astaires talked about the Castles in 1926 when they, themselves, were dancing stars. Fred Astaire said he and his sister 'idolised' Vernon and Irene, and Adele revealed: 'They were our ideals. We tried to ape them a lot. We thought they were wonderful. She had beautiful clothes. Naturally, I tried to copy everything she had even at my tender age. They were both so tall and thin and lithe. Fred and I just went goo-goo over them. When they were really tops in New York, society flocked around them like bees to honey.'

Society could sometimes be more predatory, like wasps to rotten apples. Invitations to 'exclusively' appear at the homes of the rich and famous were as constant as the applause. Before Bessy Marbury took strict control of these engagements, the dancers made their own arrangements and the detail could be wanting. Neither of them was good with train timetables: they thought the locomotives went one way and then steamed back again; schedules?

It was an adventure to get out to Long Island, to perform for a famous and wealthy family whom Irene, to avoid embarrassment when she told the story, called the Chatfield-Smiths, and still be back in New York City for midnight at the Café Louis Martin. They made it – but wished they hadn't. Even many years later when she repeated the 'Long Island affair', people swore they could see steam coming out of Irene's ears. She was, they said, *so mad*. The couple were accustomed to Continental sycophancy but that was most absent: they were walked directly into a huge home of wall-to-wall entitlement and self-regard. By the butler who was, at best, charitable. They had taken the train and then a car through the snow; Irene had fussed to stop her flesh-coloured dancing tights being snagged, her knife-pleated skirt rumpled. They were led down a long hallway by the butler who opened a door at the end for Irene, who intoned like Lady Bracknell: 'It was a clothes closet, a large one to be sure, but definitely and unmistakably a clothes closet. There were coats hanging on racks on either side.' She then offered full-volume Augusta Bracknell: '*A clothes closet!*'

Vernon was not as upset. They were being paid $100 and expenses for a couple of hours. The butler returned with two straight-backed chairs. Vernon said they could, at least, sit down. Irene gave him a withering once-over. 'I was as mad as a snake.' He said he could have worked that out by the hand signals. An incensed Irene kicked the door of this prison cell open and the butler attempted appeasement with a tray of coffee. A silver bowl of sugar lumps caught their eyes... as did the portrait of a family ancestor with a very large nose. They took bets on who could hit the nose most with the sugar lumps. Vernon was winning 3-2 when the time came to take to the floor. They laughed now, giggled maybe about dancing the Sugar Lump Fairy, and Vernon followed his charming routine and first asked the hostess to dance. This landed Irene to dance with the gentlemen. The dancing talent was indifferent to gender.

One dancer, each slower and frailer, followed another. This was hard work. The Castles put their price up to $300 an engagement and found they were invited even more. They were also careful to remember the tactic of the Russian dancer Anna Pavlova. The story had been in the *New York Tribune*. When she was invited to perform for a famous couple, she gave her fee as $1,500. She was told: 'Of course, my dear, you won't be required to meet the guests.' The prima ballerina responded: 'My price will only be $1,000.' Irene was miffed at being disdained: if she didn't like it from Lew Fields, she abhorred it from these self-centred swells and the ones who forgot consideration to musicians, especially black musicians with whom the Castles established an everlasting empathy.

Vernon enjoyed spending the money they were making but was eager to resume a stage career, to combine his dance and comic talents with more dramatic roles. He had good vaudeville instincts and he didn't want to play Hamlet, but he had aspirations. He wanted to be taken seriously as a man and as a performer. Many of his theatrical friends had Bowery antecedents and they were not above snide comments about the tall, thin Englishman with a twee voice who was a ballroom dancer. The more famous he became, the more insidious the inferences and published comments. The circumstantial evidence was strong but his life delivered straight testimony. His marriage to Irene grew stronger; they'd finish each other's sentences, order the same dinner, take in two puppies rather than argue over which one to give a home to – and every evening revoke the stigma from close dancing. They were the perfect argument against the perceived vulgarity of couples dancing together and magically made a man and woman entangled around each other no threat to decency: they invented chaste romanticism. The most they could be accused of was consensual elegance. If they, the wholesome Castles, could dance with propriety, then everyone could.

Their attraction was extensive and not exclusive. Suburban housewives and debutantes wanted to look like Irene and were a little in love with Vernon, youngsters like the Astaires aped them, political and social leaders were equally bewitched by the Castles and this new phenomenon of dance. Some feared and hated them, their eyes shuttered to what they regarded as seditious and sordid. Others, like William Earl Dodge – the patriarch of a post-Civil War family of Wall Street 'merchant princes', abolitionists, champions of Native American rights and the temperance movement – hired them. Earl Dodge Junior's sister Mary was fascinated by the tango which she'd read about in the newspaper. She was paralysed from the waist down following a riding accident and not able to see it performed in public. Her brother asked the Castles to accommodate her and arranged a private room with a ballroom floor at Delmonico's. Mary Dodge lay out on a chaise longue with a velvet robe wrapped around her legs. Vernon and Irene stepped out and did the tango and the delight was so evident in Mary Dodge's eyes that they did it again, as well as the madcap Grizzly Bear and Bunny Hug, the Argentine tango, the Brazilian tango – which was a swaying two-step called the Maxixe (pronounced Mah-SHEESH) – the Half-and Half, which was a hesitation waltz in 5/4 or 7/4 time, and the classic one-step, which was just that: one step in front of another.

Vernon and Irene found it a pleasure to please so much, the engagement another stamp on their passport to the swells of Fifth Avenue. It was still a society where money led and on the avaricious streets of New York some families still persisted in the past, their servants in satin breeches and powdered wigs, but the majority had leaped on to the machine age, and the speed of it. Vernon and Irene's dancing was important to the social and cultural renaissance. The great progressive Jesse Lasky, vaudeville player turned producer of Broadway musicals and the original Hollywood mogul, a founder of Paramount Pictures, talked of the velocity of change: 'In 1911 it was still scandalous to dance in a public place. A year later the prejudice was swept aside, and nightclubs blossomed like magic.'

There was some design with, of course, chance, as the world began to learn to dance. Charles Bancroft Dillingham played his part. He wore a bowler hat, a handlebar moustache and an easy air, which defied his wily negotiating talents and handling of ballerina Anna Pavlova. He was rated on Broadway as a talent like Flo Ziegfeld, but he was a more eclectic producer: he took Sapper's Bulldog Drummond to the stage as well as Peter Pan – for now, he had his sights fixed on Vernon and Irene. He intrigued Vernon into taking a role in *The Lady of the Slipper*, which was a musical comedy version of 'Cinderella', with Elsie Janis providing the glamour as the fairy-tale star and Fred Stone and David Montgomery, a renowned comic act, the laughter. Vernon had plenty of stage time in comic scenes and dancing. Charles Dillingham wrote Irene into the show, with one dance with Vernon in the second act, and moments, dressed as a harlequin, as a side-stage presenter.

Irene would rather not have been in Philadelphia where the show was to open. She contrived to escape without contract penalty. She quickly had a plan. Elsie Janis was a delight, but her mother was a horror, a stage mother who would keep Dracula home at night. Irene was aware of 'Ma' Janis's deep disgust at seeing a scintilla of flesh from the neck down. Which worked while her daughter was 'Little Elsie' on the vaudeville circuit – but not as she matured as a comedy star and singer ('Give Me The Moonlight, Give Me The Girl'). As protection for Elsie's dignity, Mrs Janis insisted on having a veto on all costumes in shows in which Elsie appeared. All went well at rehearsals until Irene perked on to the stage, picked her skirt up to her waist, and revealed 'very snug and very brief panties of the same material, which fitted like a wet bathing suit'. If that was not shock enough, her legs were bare. She did her dance with Vernon before allowing her specially designed skirt to fall and modesty return. Charles Dillingham told her how much he liked the costume but added: '"Ma" is shocked beyond words at your dress.' He attempted to mediate but Irene wriggled out of her contract as fast as she had her skirt. The dance number went and so did Irene. Vernon, with some encouragement from his wife, followed before *The Lady of the Slipper* moved on to Broadway and became a marvellous success for all involved.

Especially Elsie Janis who, despite her 'Ma', had become a good friend of the Castles. They adopted her, chaperoned her around her mother. 'Ma's' life was her jewels and furs and ostrich plumes, cases of chilled champagne and first-class suites in grand hotels and on ocean liners. All Elsie, who had been put on the stage as a two-year-old, wanted was to be loved. She had her share of blasé roués, she got flushed over the French entertainer Maurice Chevalier, dancers in musicals in New York and London, and all was intense but brief. Her dreams were of Scott Fitzgerald's 'heaven of romance' but they miserably ebbed away.

Elsie was delighted when Vernon, as there was no replacement for him, agreed to rejoin her show for a few weeks. She could team up with him and Irene again. After negotiations with Bessy Marbury, Vernon agreed to Charles Dillingham's request that he return, without his wife, briefly to *The Lady of the Slipper*. Following the show, Elsie would join Vernon and Irene at Louis Martin's most evenings.

Vernon's kindness in accommodating Dillingham's request was soon returned by the producer who, with Bessy Marbury urging him on, persuaded his close friend Charles Frohman to give Vernon a grand opportunity: a headline role in *The Sunshine Girl*. He had five song and dance numbers; Irene, billed as Mrs Vernon Castle, appeared in Act 3 for one song and dance ('It was my only bit in the show, nobody forgot I was in it') through the wiles of their manager. It was like taking a huge billboard high up in Times Square announcing their conquest.

Mr and Mrs Vernon Castle were on Broadway every evening.

Mr Castle, said the critics, was 'original', he was 'unique', he was 'delightful' and his 'fascinating dancing with the lovely Mrs Castle was the sensation of the night'. As the applause calmed, they'd be off to Café Louis Martin to perform again. Vernon and Irene were carefree on those glorious nights. *The Sunshine Girl* was fully booked through until the summer, Louis Martin met their every demand, financial and for more elaborated 'digs' on the premises; society was running Vernon off his feet asking for dance lessons. He was in such demand that he could name his price which Irene did for him.

Across America, in San Francisco, the *Sunday Call* newspaper found the demand for Vernon's talents so remarkable it was worthy of page-one news headlined: 'Teaching Dancing at $1 a Minute.' On 16 March 1913, the newspaper excitedly reported:

For every twenty-minute lesson he is paid $20. Of all the cabaret dancers who have appeared on the restaurant horizon, Vernon Castle is the most popular. Society has taken him up and it is no exaggeration to say that he is the most sought-after dancing teacher in America. He has dozens of private pupils whose names are to be found in the Social Register. He has weekly classes at the homes of Mrs George Gould, Mrs W. K. Vanderbilt, Sr., Mrs W. K. Vanderbilt, Jr., and Mrs Benjamin Guinness. It was the turkey trot that started this young Englishman on the road to fame and riches.

Twenty-four hours after this dance was invented or evolved – it is difficult to say which – Vernon Castle was trying the steps. When he wasn't dancing he was making love to Miss Irene Foote, daughter of a physician in New Rochelle, N.Y. One day when he wasn't stepping at all he persuaded her to leave New Rochelle and marry him. She bade goodbye to her parents and sailed for Paris with her husband. Paris didn't seem to be gay enough to suit their fancy and they decided to enliven it and incidentally enrich their family pocketbook by dancing. The Café de Paris was the scene of their first appearance. In the French capital and to the strains of 'Alexander's Ragtime Band' they turkey-trotted before the tables of the astonished diners. Their success was instantaneous. Mrs Castle had never before danced in public, but she knew the steps better than most professionals. Returning Americans brought wonderful accounts of the success of Vernon Castle and his pretty American wife. Restaurant men who six months before had never heard of him cabled enticing offers. But life in Paris was agreeable and not until last fall did the Castles think of returning. However, the call of the cabaret could not be resisted, and after Vernon Castle finished his work at the theatre he and his wife danced at Louis Martin's.

At the present time they are dancing in *The Sunshine Girl* at the Knickerbocker Theatre, New York. Mr Castle has one of the important roles in the piece, but Mrs Castle only dances. After the performance they hurry across Broadway to Louis Martin's to appear in the cabaret show.

There is no late sleeping for them, however. Mr Castle's first class begins at 10 a.m. and until dinnertime he is kept busy teaching wealthy men and women the mysteries of the nestep. In his classes at Mrs Gould's and Mrs Guinness's are a score of socially prominent people, and they regard his opinion as the last word *la dancing*.

Faraway San Francisco knew all about the Castles, but they owned New York, or at least the part with people spending as fast as they could dance. They bankrolled a grand twenty-fourth birthday party for Elsie in an upper ballroom of the Café Louis Martin. They hired an orchestra to play through the night. It was adrenalin that kept the Castles on their feet. Elsie squealed with excitement that evening in March 1913 as she watched her friends create their great dance sensation.

Elsie, the birthday girl, who had sharp features softened by her deep, often sad, brown eyes, was glowing: the party, the people, it was all such fun. Vernon and Irene were messing about on the dance floor, a busman's night out for them, and while they clowned and bounced around the floor they tried something different with the one-step. Instead of the normal, going *down* on the beat, they went up. It resulted in a step close to a skip, and they skipped and skipped. When they returned to Elsie she was laughing: 'What on earth were you doing? You looked ridiculous.' Irene admitted: 'It wasn't very graceful to be sure, but it did provide a variation and a great deal of amusement.' Elsie Janis looked over at 'Ma' and, after some persuasion, Vernon took her on to the floor for a birthday treat and again went *up* on the beat. Elsie and Vernon danced and danced the new steps. Other couples wanted to see how to do it too.

It was the birth of the 'Castle Walk', which led the cavalcade of modern dancing. Scott Fitzgerald said it was so simple it could be perfectly danced when sober. 'They look more like a pair of schoolchildren out for a frolic than a staid man and wife in dancing as a business,' was the verdict of the *Chicago Examiner*. In their book of instruction, *Modern Dance*, which became an inspiration as well as the manual for ballroom dancing, Irene admitted that the 'Castle Walk' looked silly and was silly: 'That is the explanation of its popularity.'

Millions knew the Castles before Henry Ford was in *Who's Who*. Ford's cars were now selling quite well. Vernon's 'Castle

Walk' instructions, which came from his scribbled notes, sold out:

The Castle Walk

There are very many different figures, but they are in this same strict tempo. It is simply one-step – hence its name. I am going to try to explain the different figures, more or less in the order in which they should be learned. This will make the dance comparatively simple even for those who have never tried it – if there are any.

First of all, walk as in the one-step. Now, raise yourself up slightly on your toes at each step, with the legs a trifle stiff, and breeze along happily and easily, and you know all there is to know about the Castle Walk.

To turn a corner you do not turn your partner round, but keep walking her backward in the same direction, leaning over slightly – just enough to make a graceful turn and keep the balance well – a little like a bicycle rounding a corner. If you like, instead of walking along in a straight line, after you have rounded your corner, you can continue in the same slanting position, which will naturally cause you to go round in a circle. Now continue, and get your circle smaller and smaller until you are walking around almost in one spot, and then straighten up and start off down the room again.

Even the clumsy-footed could make something joyful of it. The professionals loved it, it was easy and, most important, it was *new*. Adele Astaire said: 'Fred and I immediately began doing the Castle Walk.'

What Vernon and Irene weren't doing was having a love life. They were too busy dancing. Irene complained to Elsie Janis about the lack of romance due to their exhaustion after a day of dance lessons (given by Vernon), an evening of *The Sunshine Girl* and their midnight dancing for Louis Martin. 'When our heads hit the pillows, that's it,' she reported. Soon, she knew, when the show went on hiatus, they were off to France and the familiar haunts and romance of Paris, and that relaxed her.

The summer of 1913 was warmer than average and the hot weather made for slower days in gay Paris – but the evenings and nights were still frantic for Vernon and Irene. At the now even more prestigious Café de Paris they were on display and this time, if not quite their best friends, the richest of the names in the audience were now acquaintances: the Vanderbilts and the Astors and a mix of royalty, with and without kingdoms. All, it seemed, wanted to be able to boast that they, personally, had seen Vernon and Irene Castle dance.

That summer's engagements included two weeks at the new and stately Casino de Deauville across the rue de la Mer from the Normandy beaches. Vernon and Irene's spins had to compete with those of the roulette wheels but, with generous tips and fees, without risk they added to their fortunes. More cash came from private parties, one of which was organised by the free-spending Mrs Bertha Potter Palmer, who had taken an impressive Deauville estate for the season. It was in these surreal surroundings, created especially by the Kentucky-born multi-millionairess (by marriage, Mr Potter Palmer of Chicago), that Vernon and Irene met Grand Duke Dmitry Pavlovich, the cousin of Tsar Nicholas II. Irene was especially taken by the handsome young man: 'He looked like an Englishman, blond, smooth-shaven, tall, slight and possessed of a definite Oxford accent.'

Dmitry Pavlovich was the son of Pavel Alexandrovich, who was a son of Tsar Alexander II. He was with his father and his aunt, the Grand Duchess Anastasia, in Deauville. Irene told Vernon the gossip that Anastasia had her lovers beheaded when she tired of them. Vernon said Anastasia was a little too old for him. Dmitry wasn't too old for Irene and she took a fancy to him, one in which she daydreamed of being the Tsarina of Russia.

The Russian saw the Castles as a social helping hand. Aunt Anastasia was a bit of a big lump and heavy on her feet. Vernon was called in and through his good nature and patience taught Anastasia how to do the one-step and the tango. Irene said the Grand Duchess wore dance shoes the size of canoes so Vernon's educational abilities were clearly special.

Vernon was also amused at their Russian friend's passion for Irene. He laughingly told his family in Norwich: 'He's a Russian bear but he won't get my honey.' Vernon saw it as a lark of life, even when they returned to Paris and found they had a new besotted fan. The Grand Duke turned up to watch them dance every night at the Café de Paris. Afterwards, they went dancing at l'Abbaye and between dances Vernon and Irene would write out the lyrics of ragtime songs for Grand Duke Dmitry. He said his father enjoyed it when he returned to the Ritz Hotel and awakened him with 'Waiting For The Robert E. Lee' or Cecil Macklin's '*Très Moutarde*' ('Too Much Mustard'). That's not quite the eyebrow-raising assertion it seems; Russian aristocrats did enjoy ragtime. As intended, it impressed Irene – but not nearly as much as the cartons of Russian Sobranie cigarettes and the onyx-and-diamond buttons from Cartier. Orchids and pledges of adoration followed but Irene could not be persuaded to turn her fancy into anything more: 'If I was on the throne of Russia, what would I do with Vernon, whom I dearly loved?'

Vernon went to Norwich to visit his family, Irene joined him and they sailed from Liverpool back to New York. Dmitry

Pavlovich went off to help in plans for the assassination of Grigory Efimovich Rasputin, the 'Mad Monk' whom the aristocrats of Russia feared had too much influence over Russian Tsarina Alexandra. Irene's friend was briefly banished to the Persian Front after Rasputin was finally murdered on 16 December 1916, while 'Yankee Doodle Dandy' was playing on an upstairs gramophone. (St Petersburg society adored ragtime and especially the tango; young aristocrats had replaced their dance orchestras with gramophones so that they could dance to American ragtime bands. 'Yankee Doodle Dandy' was playing to convince Rasputin a dance was in progress and it was fun and games that were about, not murder plots.)

Her friendship with the Grand Duke in the summer of 1913 had been a fine distraction for Irene. In America, she was again the centre of fawning attention; she became a national obsession receiving pliable coverage from the press. Bessy Marbury knew Irene was a gift in front of the camera and her image, with controlled interviews, began appearing in newspapers and, increasingly, in fashion and general interest magazines. The public wanted to know everything about Irene, including her favourite sandwich (bacon, lettuce and tomato). With Elsie de Wolfe's fashion and style connections and Bessy Marbury's remarkable marketing instincts, the two women created a confection of Irene which was more and less of the real thing. They could not conceal the adventure and fun in her and did not want to try. They did chip away at some of the sharp edges of her manner, mainly her big mouth, for she spoke as she thought. Bessy Marbury was an idol for the entrepreneurs: the strivers and successes around her came from poverty or riches, rarely anyone from the middle, a slowly bulging amount of people who panicked at the parody of a hymn ('Nearer My God To Thee' becomes 'Nero, My Dog, Has

Fleas') or the hint of a petticoat, and were becoming less silent than their shrewish instincts dictated.

Bessy Marbury and Elsie de Wolfe had a vast company of contacts and most of their associates were champions of the machine age, of modernity. These protégés were decisive characters, themselves youthful or working with the young, the girls over-rouged, the boys – for they were only that – keen to make a difference. Vernon and Irene were models ripe to be cast. It was a generation bursting to get on with living, thriving on inventions and innovations; there was a whole new world out there. Bessy Marbury used that to install her own definition of the era.

Irene was twenty. Her friend Charlie Chaplin, the Londoner hailed as the 'emblem of popular culture' (he made thirty-six films in 1914), was twenty-four; Vernon only twenty-six. Everybody was so young. Bessy Marbury enjoyed the youth and the energy. She said it kept her lively. She also recognised popular taste, talent and was rare in her instinct for genius. She'd taken *Little Lord Fauntleroy* to Broadway as the agent of writer Frances Hodgson Burnett. She also represented Oscar Wilde and George Bernard Shaw and, along the way, Edith Wharton, Eugene O'Neill and Somerset Maugham; and she forwarded the careers of P. G. Wodehouse and – her discovery – Cole Porter. The songwriter witnessed one of the social wonders of the age, Elsie de Wolfe in several 'Pink Lady' acrobatics, before including her in 'Anything Goes', when she became Lady Mendl.

With the Castle Walk a sensation, Vernon was teaching for upwards of six hours a day at the newly formed Castle School of Dance. The Castles were also wanted for society parties, for which their agent received 'fabulous prices'. Bessy boasted: 'They earned $2,500 in Washington with one function in the afternoon and an evening engagement.' She didn't manipulate Vernon and Irene, they were too headstrong and confident for that, but she did influence them in their choices of engagements and of fashion. Groups, of both sexes, are vague, sometimes nervy, about what looks right, what is old-fashioned, what is too new, too trendy or daring. Vernon, deemed rakish for wearing a wristwatch, with dapper manner and suits, had the style and sharpness but not the self-regard of a true aesthete; he was comfortable in himself.

Irene, meanwhile, had the services of Lucile, Lady Duff Gordon, through the graces of Elsie de Wolfe, who saw no limit to style. Was there such a thing? James Whistler, the painter, had dyed his butter blue to match his clothes. Elsie and Lucile contained themselves with necklines which bordered on the indelicate and skirts which had a slit at the side and were tight across the bottom, with a sting in the tail like Whistler's butterflies. Bessy Marbury, who had an interest in the female form, described Irene: 'She had a body lithe and graceful, her swanlike neck suggested the highest distinction, her features and colouring beautiful. Her limbs, ankles, and feet were perfect.'

The enterprise which the marketing of the Castles had become was a generosity for Lucile, who provided between three to half a dozen gowns every week for Irene to wear or model; they were never fussy or with dangles of material which would interfere with the dance. The arrangement was a kindness to Lucile in tense times. The year before, Lady Duff Gordon and her husband, Sir Cosmo Duff Gordon, had taken first-class passage on the *Titanic* with her secretary, Laura Mabel Francatelli, whom they called Franks. They sailed as Mr and Mrs Morgan to avoid publicity. Of which, in turn, they received a great deal. When the *Titanic* began to sink, Lucile and her husband and secretary found safety in Lifeboat One. It was lowered with only those three and nine others, seven of them crewmen, despite the lifeboat being capable of holding forty people. When they were taken, with other survivors, aboard the RMS *Carpathia*, the crewmen on Lifeboat One were given cheques by Sir Cosmo drawn on Coutts Bank in London. Later, by gossip, the newspapers and at the British Board of Trade Inquiry, he was accused of bribing the crewmen not to rescue other passengers and crew for fear of their lifeboat being overturned and sunk itself. When Lucile and her husband gave evidence at the Board of Trade inquiry in May 1912, they attracted the largest crowds of the hearings. Sir Cosmo Duff Gordon was cleared, officially, but the shame was indelible.

A year later, Lucile was thankful for the support of her friends, who included one of the first newspaper and magazine tycoons, William Randolph Hearst. She wrote a weekly syndicated fashion column for Hearst Newspapers and a monthly version for *Harper's Bazaar* and *Good Housekeeping*. Lucile benefitted in superb publicity from Irene's custom but it worked the other way just as grandly. Lucile was 'franchised' out: she designed the interiors of the new motor cars, she licensed her names to scents and shoes and brassieres; any products that required some marketing refinement.

Irene was her own endorsement. She had the refinement; Vernon had the talent as a dancer – and Bessy Marbury had the flair. Irene had bobbed her hair long before Bernice and her 'look' – the 'Castle Bob' – was a gift to the press. Irene helped them with different stories of her 'bob': one for the New York papers (with longer hair she'd have to use hairpins and in the swirl of the dance they'd fly off and hit customers), another for the worshipping Hollywood scribblers out on the Coast (she had to stay in hospital overnight and didn't want the nurses messing with her hair). The Hearst-owned *San Francisco Examiner* decided her hair was 'a cross between an ancient Greek runner and a child's bob'. When she wore a pearl necklace as an improvised headband, it became the 'Castle Band' and versions were in department stores within a week. Her influence was monumental on millions and, for the frostily frugal, totally unfathomable. Irene's youthful and literal clean-cut image was leased, selling hats and shoes and beauty creams, the bigger contracts with cigarette and car companies racing Henry Ford. Her image decorated publications worldwide, her presence at an event guaranteed the right people, and plenty of them.

The deliciously precious Cecil Beaton witnessed that at an early age and much later, in his writings in 1954, pronounced what must have reflected one of his first moments – a pash, really, on Irene. It was a complimentary flurry: 'When Mrs Vernon Castle suddenly appeared she was greeted by the shock of recognition that people always reserve for those who *create the taste for which they are to be appreciated.*' He'd borrowed that from Wordsworth but went on: 'It is no coincidence that Stravinsky's early music and Picasso's cubist period coincided with the success of a woman who has to be one of the most remarkable fashion figures the world has ever known. Mrs Castle was as important an embodiment of the "modern" in the social and fashion sense as these artists were in the world of art.'

The style and the look and the fashion were vital but all was dependent on the dancing, which had become a mania, spread across America, into Britain and the rest of Europe. Classical or artistic reference was applied to the Castles as their career soared, but, in a little time, the answer to the puzzle of their enormous popularity returned to the dance. To Vernon Castle. Gilbert Seldes, a man who influenced cultural America and educated all who read him, was certain of their place in the history of the art of entertainment. It's breathless simply to read his words; how must he have felt in 1924 when he wrote them? They arrive in a rush:

That these two determined the course dancing should take is incontestable. They were decisive characters, like Boileau [Nicolas Boileau-Despréaux] in French poetry, Berlin [Irving] in ragtime; for they understood, absorbed, and transformed everything known of dancing up to that time and out of it made something beautiful and new.

Vernon Castle, if it is possible, was the better dancer of the two; in addition to the beauty of his dancing he had inventiveness, he anticipated things with his rigid body and his evolutions on his heel. But if he were the greater, his finest creation was Irene. No one else has ever given exactly that sense of being freely perfect, of moving without effort and without will, in more than accord, in absolutely identity with the music. There was always something unimpassioned, cool not cold, in her abandon; it was certainly the least sensual dancing in the world; the whole appeal was visual. It was as if the eye following her graceful motion across a stage was gratified by its own orbit, and found a sensuous pleasure in the ease of her line, in the disembodied lightness of her footfall, in the careless slope of her lovely shoulders. It was not – it seemed not to be – intelligent dancing; however trained, it was still intuitive. She danced from the shoulders down, the straight scapular supports of her head at the same time the balances on which her exquisitely poised body depended. There were no steps, no tricks, no stunts. There was only dancing, and it was all that one ever dreamed of flight, with wings poised, and swooping gently down to rest.

Vernon *and* Irene were leading the dance, and their society connections by now were impeccable. Elsie de Wolfe talked to London and Paris and Rome; she and Bessy Marbury constantly travelled with their friend Anne Tracy Morgan, the youngest daughter of moneybags and financier John Pierpont 'J. P.' Morgan. The three of them had bought Petit Trianon next to Versailles in 1903 and in the summer they entertained there. They were known as 'The Versailles Triumvirate' and society wanted invitations to their salon. With another golden name, Ann Vanderbilt, the second wife of William K. Vanderbilt, they were founders of the Colony Club, the first women's social club in New York City. They used their status – and the dynastic wealth – to pursue suffrage and the human rights of women, especially those of lower-class immigrant workers. They were mocked for their efforts by union activists and headline writers as 'the mink brigade'. It wasn't slander but it was slanderous. They created the Vacations Association, which offered charitably rated boarding house accommodation in rooms designed by Elsie de Wolfe, as well as weekly dance classes and exhibitions of the Castle Walk. Vernon and Irene appeared for free; at fundraisers they donated their fees to the charities supported by 'the mink brigade'. Which put dancing on the curriculum of respectable life. Bessy Marbury, naturally, saw the potential of merging her belief in social reform with her business acumen by creating a genteel environment for teaching dancing, and doin' it.

Everybody was. Hotel ballrooms, cabarets and cafes which previously only staged exhibition dances now had their own dance floors. It was a unique craze – there really had been nothing like it – which provoked much discussion and newspaper investigation. *Current Opinion* magazine in October 1913 went to town on 'New Reflections of the Dancing Mania' and concluded: 'People who have not danced before in twenty years have been dancing, this past summer, afternoons as well as evenings. Up-to-date restaurants provide a dancing floor so that patrons may lose no time while the waiter is changing plates. Cabaret artists are disappearing except as interludes while people recover their breaths for the following number.' The new venues replaced fun fair dives and seaside resorts as public dancing locations. Dancing was the entertainment for everyone. Vernon explained why crowds no longer simply watched dancers but had become them: 'When a good orchestra plays a "rag" one has simply got to move.'

For many, ragtime defined debauchery. There was furious contemporary discussion: pulpit versus progress, human rights against moral right. The twenty-first-century academic view offered by Christopher Martin, a scholar of American Dance in Florida, is this:

> The Castles' work lies in the mediation of African-American dance forms for European American consumption. During the first decades of the twentieth century there was fierce debate regarding the performance by European Americans of the ragtime dances which originated in African-American culture. Vernon and Irene Castle were at the leading edge of a cultural trend that aimed to encapsulate and incorporate certain elements of an African-American aesthetic even as they neutralised and eliminated others. The aesthetic which emerged from the Castles' work on behalf of Elisabeth Marbury and her coterie of social reformers became the template by which European American artists would safely transcribe subaltern dance practices – valued and forbidden for their differences from similar European American

practices – into forms that satisfied European American notions of propriety throughout the twentieth century.

Ultimately, the Castles' work led to the erasure of even the memory of African-Americans from the inception of modern ballroom dancing, instead framing the battle over aesthetics as a part of the struggle to move from Victorian to Modern sensibilities. The Castles presented a desexualised, elegant and refined version of ragtime dances such as the Turkey Trot, Grizzly Bear, and Bunny Hug, refashioned as variations on a single dance they called the 'One-Step'. They retained the popular ragtime music while eliminating the specific body movements that were problematic for white performance.

The Chicago Tribune gave the contemporary editorial view rather more easily and bluntly in 1913:

Cabarets and dance halls have brought people of all classes together in what were sometimes disreputable settings, and exposed more Americans to new styles of music and dance. Unlike the genteel salon music that had typified the Victorian period, ragtime music has its roots planted firmly on the other side of the tracks. Previously, evenings in the ballroom meant a few waltzes and polkas and endless variations of the German [the cotillion]. Women had to coax their husbands on to dance floors. The simplicity of the two-step and the jaunty syncopations of ragtime music have made dancing accessible and enjoyable to every class and to both sexes. This breakdown in the strict Victorian code of behaviour worries many people. Dance halls and public dancing are being condemned as 'paths to hell' that will lead a young girl to ruin. Traditional-minded moralists and clergy bewail the unchaperoned mixing of the sexes, the ubiquitous presence of alcohol and the shocking vulgarity of the new dances that are appearing across the country. Not all their fears are groundless.

The dance floor is turning into a barnyard. Rowdy new dances like the Turkey Trot, Grizzly Bear, Bunny Hug, and Chicken Scratch and the Monkey Glide are invading dance halls. Like ragtime music itself, early ragtime dance steps and movements were born in the black community. Elegant European salon dances had always emphasised a quiet, erect carriage and dignified bearing. These dances, with their shoulder shaking, slouching and tight embrace are stomping and wiggling their way from rowdy west coast honky-tonks, bordellos and lower class dance halls to every ballroom across the nation.

The popularity outran the perceived vulgarity. It wasn't only dancing which had changed direction. Attitudes had too. When the twentieth century began it remained rare for white dancers to follow black dance steps. Sometimes what was known as the Negro cakewalk, a two-step dance begun by slaves on plantations, would be performed to make a change from the waltz. William K. Vanderbilt found it a 'unique diversion' for a 1906 family ball and with that it became social. Four years earlier in 'The Ragtime Dance', Scott Joplin had given mention:

Let me see you do the ragtime dance,
Turn left and do the cakewalk prance,
Turn the other way and do the slow drag,
Now take your lady to the World's Fair
And do the ragtime dance.

The dances which followed, the various farmyard trots, the black bottom, the Charleston, all had their roots in black communities and culture. The Texas Tommy – Blossom Seeley's version of which had so magically inspired Vernon and Irene in Paris – was, like Blossom herself, from the Barbary Coast, and had first been seen in black cabaret in San Francisco. Before that, it was a turn-on with red-light districts, a racy favourite on the mirrored floors of Babe Connors's Castle Club in St Louis.

The century was still to get properly into second gear and the Vanderbilts, one of the world's richest families, had accepted what they, and a majority of others, had previously decried as disreputable. A huge percentage of people continued to believe that public dancing was apocalyptic with the mass degeneration of all morals, public and private. The End was truly nigh. Instead, it was the beginning of a new order of behaviour, of life between the sexes. The gentility of past dancing, in controlled and private affairs, at grand houses, in government buildings and outposts, had been achieved by figure formations, a sort of hands-off dancing. It was all about a nod to a partner, never, never a wink, and then on down the line; there was rarely time to say 'hello', never mind become truly acquainted; even the waltz was performed at (a formal six inches apart) short arms' length. Propriety, directed almost exclusively at women, pronounced that if you danced at all it was within restrictive rules; you even had to swoon gracefully. Such rules vanished, of course, with dances with names like the 'Bunny Hug'. In Britain and America it was couples like the Castles who set the rules of the dance. Arthur Marwick reminds us in *The Deluge: British Society and the First World War* that the control of the dance card was gone; the convention that you never danced with the same person twice in succession vanished with it.

Couples had the time, and the desire, to do as Vernon Castle did: have fun and, if you must, make it up as you go along. Grand ladies fainted at the tango with its requirement for legs to meet and pelvic areas to touch. While couples stretched for excitement, others did so for the smelling salts. The traditional role of men and women was being readjusted; the Castles were showing that a good time, dancing, wasn't just for adolescents. The married, the parents, could dance too: doing the Turkey Trot was not quite the Devil's work. Soon, Bessy Marbury had convinced a good section of the world that the Castle Walk was God's work.

Vernon and Irene certainly had a vast congregation. They also knew the need to reinvent their dancing continually and to keep a fresh look. Irene, with her shorter, slim-cut skirt and hair and dancing legs was the prototype flapper. She looked wonderful. With Vernon, *they* were wonderful.

They were also making themselves very famous and very rich. If only there was more time in the day. Yes, there was, announced Bessy Marbury. Vernon and Irene were free in the afternoons. What better to do between 4 p.m. and 6.30 p.m. each evening than dance? There would be tea dances, sophisticated *thé dansants*. A dozen of the wealthiest women in New York agreed and, over lunch with Bessy Marbury just in time for oysters to be back on menus, the foundations of 'The Castle House' were laid. Or, hatched. It was a chicken and the egg conundrum.

Chapter Six

Tea Dancing

'I find it harder and harder every day to live up to my blue china.'
Oscar Wilde, 1877

Vernon was like a toddler with a train set. The kindly executive from the car company, Minerva of Belgium, had recognised the strength of his wallet and explained how the engine, with double sleeve valves, drove almost silently. He was a fine salesman. He flattered Vernon that in his home country, in England, the Minerva cars were becoming popular; a Mr Charles S. Rolls was their official dealer there. In New York, they were presenting the latest models with the Charles Yale Knight engines. Modern? The cars were so sought-after that the kings of Norway, Sweden and, of course, Belgium had one. Henry Ford had bought two only that week.

Vernon was engrossed by the technical details, enamoured by the sleek and glamorous look of this luxury car, which had won first place that afternoon at the Grand Central Palace automobile show. Of all things, he learned Elsie de Wolfe had designed the interior, which comprised rose-and-grey brocade. The Grand Central Palace exhibition hall on Lexington Avenue was a stroll for Vernon from the town house at 120 Lexington, which had been Dr Foote's medical practice and was their city base. He told Irene and her mother, who was living with them, that he was going to have a look. When he returned, he was energetic with excitement.

Irene knew the signs and sighed. 'How much did you pay for this little gem?'

'Five thousand dollars.'

It was a bankroll, a sum fit for a royal. Irene decided that Vernon required some strong economic advice and called in her terrifying Aunt Molly Bond. They trooped down the street to look at the low-slung car, with the attendant chauffeur Vernon had taken on, and Irene said the inside looked like a wallpapered jewel box. Aunt Molly gazed and gazed and sat in the driving seat. She led them back up the steps into the apartment building. Irene made drinks while she waited for Aunt Molly to lecture Vernon on his spendthrift nature, the need to conserve, to think about the future.

'You're very wise,' said Aunt Molly to Vernon. 'Spend it while you're young, while you can enjoy it. All my years in medical school I had to save every penny for my education so I formed a bad habit I could never break. Years later when I made money I had no fun out of it because I couldn't bring myself to spend it.'

Irene was in shock. Vernon thought he was the Governor of the Bank of England. They went off to spend the weekend at a friend's home at Manhasset, Long Island, which their friend had up for sale. Vernon, without a word to Irene, bought it. On the Monday he presented her with the deeds as a present. She was distraught. 'How much?'

'Just $85,000.'

'What?! Where did you get that money?'

'Oh, it's not real cash. I only put $5,000 down. We'll pay the rest at $1,000 a week.'

For Irene, 'exasperation' didn't cover it. Not even close. Cleverly, the live-now-pay-later Vernon convinced his wife that their new home would be much better for their growing number of dogs and animal menagerie. It had a private beach where swimming was good and safe. He'd bought it as is, the linen closets full, the library shelves stacked, the mahogany sideboards in the dining room packed with all required for entertaining. An economic coup, don't-cha-know. Irene had watched the tough producers of Broadway in negotiations, danced with acquisitive tycoons who peed ice water, mixed with those who'd really sold their grandmother's legacy and probably the good lady too, and regarded Vernon with an endearing smile. Vernon was sweet and lovable and totally useless with money. She loved him. Yet, if *he* was going to spend, *they* had to earn.

Life was a lively chequebook for Vernon Castle. Like the vigorous music they danced to, he couldn't stand still. Money was no object to his dreams of good times and happiness for Irene and himself. Their Long Island estate was a playpen; Castle House was business. Bessy Marbury had sat with friends including Almira Rockefeller and Marion 'Mamie' (Stuyvesant) Fish at lunch at the Ritz-Carlton Hotel opposite 26 East Forty-Sixth Street, which had been the premises of the dressmaker and Elsie de Wolfe's friend, Josefa Osborn. It had two mirrored, second-floor rooms which would be perfect for dancing. They were reached by two polished stairways, both with red tasselled ropes as handrails, so patrons could get their hands on something plush from the off. The ladies agreed to be the patrons (i.e. pay for) Castle House and 'bring dignity to the dance craze sweeping America'. Elsie de

Wolfe provided 'a highly tasteful interior appropriate to its ambitions'. Bessy Marbury banned booze to quieten anxiety that Castle House was going to promote any idea of immorality. What it offered for $2 a day, $3 on Fridays and Saturdays, was afternoon tea, happily served by ladies with dynastic surnames like Rockefeller and Vanderbilt, and dancing and dance lessons with Vernon and Irene Castle as the principal teachers. The Castles were the star attraction. They were vital: tea dances were abundant, available at every other hotel and restaurant. They were cheaper: hotels charged $1 admission which bought tea or a soft drink; cabarets were free entry and made their profit from selling booze and tea. It was an extraordinary expansion of places to dance; women going out to dance were an added attraction. One business pamphlet, *The Craftsman*, complained: 'Suddenly, in the midst of this money-getting, machine-made age, we throw all caution to the wind; we give up some of our business hours, and we do not only dance in the evening, but in the afternoon and in the morning.'

Vogue magazine was more welcoming and reported: 'The charming walls of Castle House became a setting within which one might take tea and twirl or be taught to dance at its courtliest and smartest artistic best.'

Pamphlets were issued on all manners of 'good form', like this one reproduced in their book *Modern Dancing*:

CASTLE HOUSE SUGGESTIONS FOR CORRECT DANCING

Do not wriggle the shoulders.
Do not shake the hips.
Do not twist the body.
Do not flounce the elbows.

Do not pump the arms.

Do not hop – glide instead.

Avoid low, fantastic, and acrobatic dips.

Stand far enough away from each other to allow free movement of the body in order to dance gracefully and comfortably.

The gentleman should rest his hand lightly against the lady's back, touching her with the fingertips and wrist only, or, if preferred, with the inside of the wrist and the back of the thumb.

The gent leman's left hand and forearm should be held up in the air parallel with his body, with the hand extended, holding the lady's hand lightly on his palm. The arm should never be straightened out.

Remember you are at a social gathering, and not in a gymnasium.

Drop the Turkey Trot, the Grizzly Bear, the Bunny Hug, etc. These dances are ugly, ungraceful, and out of fashion.

Vernon was as natural a teacher as he was a dancer. He enjoyed showing off and found equal pleasure when a pupil 'got the rag and went for it'. Irene was always impressed by his patience and ability to make even the most unlikely partner look good. Irene preferred to dance only with Vernon – the exception being William Randolph Hearst. He was the only one she had fun teaching to dance. The media tycoon would send his chauffeur to collect Vernon and Irene for dinner before their lesson for him and his wife Millicent began. Then, the floor would be cleared and Vernon would show Millicent Hearst the steps and Irene would instruct the man she called W. R. H. Few had good things to say about the avaricious Hearst but Irene praised his mind and ability to be shown a dance step once and retain it. She also offered the salutation that provokes an unlikely image: 'He also had that spring in his knees that is vital to a good dancer.'

As one, Vernon was being run off his feet. The profits of which were paying many times for his indulgences. Dance classes had brought him $1 a minute but he was now charging a minimum of $100 an hour – and half of that was taken up with hellos and goodbyes. Possibly, an invited, marketing fondle.

Lessons were provided at Castle House before lunch and were given by teachers, imported by Bessy Marbury and monitored by Vernon and Irene. The society ladies with their tea and lemonade and cake – and most of all their names – gave cachet to the establishment, while the $2 entrance fee provided its own obstacle to hordes of 'Texas Tommy' fanatics traipsing up the marble entranceway. Bessy Marbury said this was to allow youngsters, including Arthur Murray, to be taught to dance 'without being exposed to discredited elements', to protect the Castle brand and not frighten the gentlefolk. That view was validated by the emancipated intent of the dancing emporium.

Castle House was successful from the first morning it opened its doors on East Forty-Sixth Street, at the corner of Madison Avenue, in the pre-debutante grand ball season in the weeks before Christmas 1913 – allowing ladies of fine families, escorted by their inquisitive mothers, to prepare for their coming out. 'We did a thundering business,' said Irene, who also admitted that their clients only had a 'slim chance' of dancing with either her or Vernon, but 'for this price they had their choices of two orchestras, a chance to be served tea by real society women, and an opportunity to see the Castles.'

All while dancing to the music of James Reese Europe and his orchestra, which rivalled Alexander's as 'the best band in the land'.

It was with his friend James Europe that Vernon turned the frivolity of making music and entertainment into making history. It was fifty years, and it seemed no time at all, since Abraham Lincoln had issued the Emancipation Proclamation on 1 January 1863, freeing all slaves in America. It was a landmark clarification of Government policy if not a practical undoing of the chains. By 1913, racial barriers had been breached but not demolished; there was segregation in federal government, indiscriminate lynching of black people and 'nigger' and 'coon' were part of everyday language. You could argue racial barriers remained.

It was with the help of Mamie Fish that the Englishman and the musician from Mobile, Alabama, knocked another couple of those barriers down. Mamie Fish ruled over the social set in Newport, Rhode Island, as well as influencing the influential in New York. She was an addicted prankster and legendary hostess much indulged by her husband Stuyvesant, who had pioneered steam trains across the United States. When Grand Duke Boris Vladimirovich of Russia visited Newport, Mrs Fish issued invitations for a dinner and ball in his honour; on the night of the ball the Duke was detained by Mrs Ogden Goelet, who was a fierce social rival. Mary Wilson Goelet annoyed Mamie Fish with her high-handed manner. Her daughter May Goelet (with a dowry of $20 million) had married Henry Innes-Ker, the eighth Duke of Roxburghe, and her mother wouldn't stop boasting about the family union with a Scottish peer. With Grand Duke Boris off the guest list, Mamie Fish stole guests from her rival by announcing her new guest was the Tsar of Russia. When all her guests were at dinner, including some of society's greatest movers and shakers, the dining-room doors swung open and His Imperial Majesty, robed, wearing the Imperial Crown and carrying a sceptre, strode in. All were silent, heads bowed, until, to huge applause and laughter, the 'Tsar' was revealed as playboy Harry Lehr.

In Newport, Mamie Fish ran Crossways – the family's neo-Georgian house – where every August she staged the Harvest Festival Ball; the last dance, as it were, of the Newport social season. Vernon and Irene were there with Bessy Marbury on 22 August 1913, when the musical entertainment was provided by James Europe and his orchestra. Black bands had been providing ragtime to the gentry but now, with a bow to the magnificent Mamie Fish, they were playing for ballroom dancing. She had circulated how good 'James Reese Europe's Society Orchestra' was for dancing and entertaining at dinners and receptions. She liked their music and their style. Vernon loved it.

With his unstoppable enthusiasm, he believed he'd discovered 'the best dancing music in the world'. James Europe, the son of a slave freed following Reconstruction, was taken by the enthusiasm of Vernon and his openness; there was no side to Vernon, no oblique motives. Europe thought him 'one white absolutely without prejudice'. The only thing Vernon hated was bad dancing; which was difficult to the music of James Europe, who was a driving force for finding status and work for black musicians. Europe helped formed the Clef Club, a social organisation and professional guild; he developed a symphony orchestra composed of more than 100 Clef Club members, to promote their composers and performers. The Clef Club Symphony Orchestra was wonderful and, following many recitals in New York, staged all–original work in *A Concert of Negro Music* at Carnegie Hall on 2 May 1912. It was a major moment. The *New York Times* review said: 'These composers are beginning to form an art form of their own.' It was noted by the musician, jazz scholar and historian Gunther Schuller in his 2011 autobiography that James Europe 'had stormed the bastion of the white establishment and made many members of New York's cultural elite aware of Negro music for the first time'.

It wasn't all five-star reviews. When *Musical American* suggested the orchestra 'give its attention to a movement or two of a Haydn symphony', James Europe was prickly: 'We have developed a kind of symphony music that, no matter what else you think, is different and distinctive, and that lends itself to the playing of the peculiar compositions of our race. My success has come from a realisation of the advantages of sticking to the music of my own people. We coloured people have our own music that is part of us. It's the product of our souls; it's been created by the sufferings and miseries of our race.'

It was happiness which brought James Europe and his band – Vernon called all groups of music-makers 'bands' – and the Castles together. They were a remarkable combination, innovators charging at the Establishment. Bessy Marbury was canny not to charge *too* hard. She instigated the hiring of James Europe to provide the music at Castle House from 15 December 1913. She also hedged against any anxious alarm from patrons by engaging Henry Lodge, a white musician and composer of ragtime anthems. There were two ballrooms, two sets of music to choose from, as much as there were the sandwiches and cake (lemon drizzle for Vernon).

Like cake, for Vernon, there was only kind of music to dance to. He knew it was as important how you played as what you played. James Reese Europe and his orchestra supplied electrifying music, what Vernon described to Irene as 'infectiously danceable rhythms'. One of which Europe and his fellow bandleader and the band's principal pianist, Ford Dabney, turned into the music for 'The Castle Walk'.

Vernon and Irene's signature dance, the modified one-step created at Elsie Janis's birthday bash, was their only collaboration with Europe where the dance steps originated before the music. With 'Castle House Rag' and 'Congratulations/Castles Lame Duck' the music-makers and the dancers worked together. For them, James Europe created a turkey-trot one-step, from 'You're Here and I'm Here', which was written by Jerome Kern, the great and prolific composer who had been with Vernon on his first voyage to America seven years earlier. What a breathless rush it had been.

The secret of the partnership of Vernon and Irene with James Europe was that they liked each other: the music working with the dancing, and the other way around, was a neat bonus. Vernon and the orchestra leader were easy friends, laughing and enjoying what they were about. They couldn't imagine why anyone would trouble them. They were tearing up the rule book as well as the dance floor.

The *New York Times* music critic, a Mr H. E. Krehbiel, had a rant at them: 'In this year of our Lord, 1913, the ragtime dances are threatening to force grace, decorum, and decency out of the ballrooms of America.'

In his thesis 'Castles and Europe: Race Relations in Ragtime' (2005), the academic Christopher Martin didn't agree: 'The racial politics of the Progressive Era were repugnant, but the Castles were, within the constraints of their time, acting as agents of racial uplift for black Americans. I had expected to find them simply profiting from their relationship with black artists, treating them as invisible accoutrements to their success. After all, the Castles operated in a society that thoroughly ignored, marginalised, and exploited African-Americans. Instead, I discovered artists who were sensitive to the concerns of the black community, valued in both word and action the dignity of their associates regardless of race, and acted to raise the visibility of black artists.'

Of course, in that Progressive Era, Vernon and Irene, with the foot-stamping, stomping sound of James Europe's Society Orchestra, were ranting with full-blown ragtime right back at Mr H. E. Krehbiel and other soldiers of the doomwatch brigade. They were official partners: the Castle House Orchestra. The big sound blast back was endorsed when the Society Orchestra was given a recording contract by the Victor Machine Company on 28 December 1913: it was one of the first deals made with a black musician; the first ever with a black orchestra. The next day the Society Orchestra began recording 'The Castle Walk' and the 'Castle House Rag One-Step' and a string of other ragtime songs and tunes, with clarinets and pianos making merry together in a combination that some of the orchestra were calling 'jass'. Vernon called it very good news.

Which he also had for his friend James and the Society Orchestra. They had a new prospect. Vernon had been visited, discreetly, in his upstairs office at Castle House by Jules Ensaldi, an ambitious head waiter from the Café Louis Martin. His scheme was that Vernon and Irene – and, of course, himself – would do far better with their own supper club than being on salaries. Ensaldi, trained and with heavyweight social connections, would manage the restaurant-cabaret. All was agreed and all that was required was a location.

Vernon and his new business partner, Ensaldi, found one of the most unpopular spots underneath Times Square. It was a huge, square room protected from above by metal pillars and from the immediate next-door subway system by a thin, timber wall. It was, Vernon told Irene, a white-painted timber wall. The premises had been used as clubs and cafes but, being Times Square, a neon New

York landmark, it was a haven for business girls off-duty showing tourists other wonders of the city. A place, as Irene put it, for a busy girl to 'rest her feet and have a quick glass of sherry or port'.

Irene was not keen on launching an upmarket venture under the pavement at Forty-Second Street and Broadway. However, she said Vernon had four convincing words: 'The rent is cheap.' Irene, if not convinced, was persuaded. Elsie de Wolfe 'did' the interior design. Her own New York home had no electricity and was known as the 'House of a Thousand Candles', all of which produced a flattering effect.

The complexions of the patrons of Sans Souci underneath that corner of Broadway and Forty-Second Street also benefitted from the 'glow' of the lighting Elsie de Wolfe supplied to show off her rose-and-grey painted interiors. Elsie liked colour and, for the moment, and maybe in a tribute to Whistler, was wearing her hair dyed a sky blue.

She was at Sans Souci with Vernon and Irene and Bessy Marbury in those opening evenings of January 1914, when entry tickets were $100 each. Cornelius Vanderbilt hosted a party of eight. Diamond Jim Brady, in chunky jewellery, hosted his stomach and its gargantuan appetite. Irene wrote about Brady – she thought he was much too vulgar with the yellow diamonds, the size and amount of them – and her and Vernon's business ventures in 1918, when her memory was still full of the happenings; the fun of the dance if not the commercial involvement. For Sans Souci was just the start of it. The Castles franchised their name and also made a commitment to perform at the venues. They also introduced linoleum, which they'd danced on in Paris, as the prime choice for dance floors in America and it was their ideas, not management skills, which they bartered. Dancing, not business, as Irene repeated, was Vernon's skill. As was drumming, which he learned with great delight and time from Buddy Gilmore, the drummer in the Society Orchestra, while they played at the Sans Souci.

For a time, the Sans Souci was highly profitable for all concerned. But soon the city heat, a problem with fire regulations (there were no fire exits), Ensaldi's accounting and the pressure of other commitments shut down what Irene thought of as their 'little goldmine'. Ensaldi, with a desk of unpaid bills in his office, ran off to Paris with his pot of gold and was never heard off again. All illusions dissolved as fast as good sense in a Gin Fizz. They'd called the new enterprise 'Sans Souci, which freely translates 'Without Worry' Understandably, Irene found that most inappropriate.

'Inappropriate' is also what many social commentators called the arrangements between Vernon and Irene and the Society Orchestra. The Castles' immediate challenge against the shadow of intolerance happened swiftly and by chance. Vernon's lack of organisation had landed him, yet again, up the Swanee. He had accepted $2,000 a week to play at the rooftop club of William Hammerstein's Victoria Theatre in Times Square from the week of 12 January 1914. When he was offered $2,000 a week by Charles Dillingham to appear at the Palace in Times Square, he did not hesitate to sign a contract. That booking also began on 12 January 1914. 'Oops' wasn't enough to get out of that, don't-cha-know. Our learned friends decided out of court that Vernon and Irene could make amends, as would James Europe and the Society Orchestra, by appearing twice a day at each venue: four shows a day. Exhausting, but also a lucrative solution for, after legal fees, they had doubled their money. Vernon and Irene always insisted on playing with 'their' band which did not have one white member: 'Coloured musicians are better qualified to play music for our style of dancing.' The ironically titled Integrated Musicians'

Union promised thunderbolts of trouble if black musicians were allowed where they had never been before – the orchestra pits of the theatres of Broadway.

The clever solution was that James Europe and the orchestra were set up *on* the stage. Technically, it kept the union activists in place but all others accepted the arrangement as a breakthrough in race relations.

The *New York Age* pointed out: 'The barrier against black orchestras playing in first-class theatres for white artists was broken.' No one remarked that there was not one black dancer on stage. That a 'person of colour' was even in the theatre was considered an amazement and progressive. It was a far from perfect arrangement but it worked, for Vernon and Irene and their growing number of followers. Everybody wanted a part of that band. As long as Vernon and Irene were part of the deal. In 1914, around the world, they were as famous as the famous could be. What they did, how they looked, mattered. Very much.

Irene's aggressively short hair, her bob, her clip, was for so many a contribution to the female revolution. Women didn't have to conform to a stereotype and retain demure and flowing tresses built high on the head, towers of curls themselves topped by hats as elaborately fashioned. That style, like a sailing ship on the far horizon, faded away. It almost totally vanished, with Irene's appendix, when she had the latter removed in 1914 at the Women's Hospital in New York. When news was released that Irene had her appendix removed, it was claimed that it was dancing which had brought on her appendicitis. Irene angrily said it was quite the opposite; dancing had helped her body much more easily endure the surgery by exercising. Dancers danced themselves fit and healthy. The debate over her appendix bored quickly – the world wanted to know about her shorty hairstyle.

She'd prepared for her hospital stay by standing in front of a three-way mirror and with honed, sharp scissors trimmed her hair down severely. Minus her appendix and much hair, she went home to Long Island to recuperate by resting and swimming. After turns in the water, she hosed out the salt water and let her hair dry in the sun. Vernon praised the look but Irene was shy of presenting herself in public. She was persuaded to present her even more bobbed look by a dinner invitation from Elsie Janis and 'Ma'. They were entertaining Irving Berlin at the Knickerbocker Hotel. Irene organised a ribbon-and-pearl necklace affair into the size of her head and slipped it over, like a crown, to keep her hair in place. It was, of course, all very much part of being Irene Castle, aged twenty-one, and a very big deal indeed. She walked, head held high, into the Knickerbocker Hotel for dinner with Irving Berlin. No one much recalls what Mr Berlin had to say in his rolling, soft voice. Irene was conspicuous by her presence. The following week, 250 'Castle bobs' were styled; the next week it was ten times that number; and from then on fashionable women bob, bob, bobbed along. Cartoons appeared of men dressed as women to get a haircut in barbershops packed with women. Hairpins and headbands sold out. Cecil Beaton weighed in again praising Mrs Vernon Castle as a 'modern young lady of fashion whom we admire so much today, the first to cut her hair into the curly locks of a bob'. Newspapers bannered: 'IRENE CASTLE CUTS HER HAIR!'

The press adored Vernon and Irene. He was a hero of the dance; she the world's pin-up. It was a marriage made for newsprint.

There was a furious eloquence about it. Change was so swift. They were charging through the public psyche. For all women striving to be unfettered from the past, the rush was towards emancipation or, perhaps, another great party. They all shared an edgy ambition. Anything *did* go. Irene Castle was the First Lady of Style, all grown up, the twentieth century in short trousers. Societies, like kids, can be understood by their amusements This social landscape, and these kids, were the new ones on the block. They were so popular that when Irene wore a rose in her hair, the florists sold out of whatever colour and variety she had chosen. Versions of her Dutch bonnet (the 'Dutch cap', with its contraceptive connotation in Britain, was dropped in advertising) were worn by tens of thousands of women. When she went on stage as a 'Red Indian' maiden, Indian headbands sold out. She went with Vernon to boxing matches, formerly an all-male preserve, and announced to the *Boston Traveller*: 'I am most enthusiastic about all forms of sport. I really understand the finer points of our great games and believe women should be more interested in them.' In turn the magazine said: 'Mrs Castle has established a type of American girl. Now, girls in the United States diet, exercise and practise to become tall, dainty, slim and willowy. They shear their locks and call it the "Castle Clip."'

Irene Castle was pursuing an equal-opportunity enjoyment: life like a man. Happily, she didn't realise what a heretic she was. The social politics deep within the flash and dazzle were breathtaking.

She had no awareness of her audacity. The look, the world Irene created and wafted about herself, became an indispensable statement for women of her generation and all those frantically flapping after her.

The much-celebrated Gloria Swanson was aged fifteen in 1914, and she made the silent movie *The Misjudged Mr Hartley*, the first of many films, a year later. She worked with Valentino and Charlie Chaplin and Cecil B. DeMille, and – as a typical teenager – on her fashion. 'My mother loved to dress me up,' she wrote in her superb autobiography, explaining: 'I loved to show off the outfits she made for me. We started buying patterns and doing fittings every day. Mother stitched frantically. When I really wanted to impress I put on one of the new outfits I was dying to wear – an Irene Castle, a black-and-white checkered skirt with a slit in the front and a black cutaway jacket with a green waistcoat. I wore a perky little Knox felt hat with it.'

Debbie Reynolds, veteran of Hollywood musicals (her first significant outing was *Three Little Words* in 1950 with Fred Astaire; her breakthrough two years later with Gene Kelly and Donald O'Connor in *Singin' In the Rain*), said that Vernon and Irene retained an influence on style and dance when her career was blossoming. Evergreen at eighty-two, in 2014 she said: 'Fred Astaire had grown up with them as dancing stars so they were always a point of reference. That respect for their work was handed down to us by Fred and others who knew them or their work. They looked so wonderful and so glamorous.'

Vernon was debonair. He appeared to walk nimbly on an air of imperturbability. Irene was the champion of women on the verge, with the edgy ambition of craving more than marriage and motherhood. They shared a halo, a crusader crown: one that sat snugly on them, if a little tight and uncomfortably for the middle-minded Establishment.

Irene was called, in one newspaper report, 'the physical ideal of countless numbers of young women, who must now be as slender as one can be and still cast a shadow.' It was a neat point. Irene was a sportswoman and when she slipped into jodhpurs to make riding more comfortable, it was seen as another triumph in the fledgeling skirmish of the sexes. Silk hats didn't quite sail into the skies peered at through lorgnettes, but Vernon and Irene were very much part of change. They had no understanding of the enormity of it. They were having such a good time it was a challenge to catch their breath. They were living in and helping create a society which was more brazen, more obvious and urgent in its impulses. Sex, restrained under Victorian convention, yards of petticoat, and possible personality disorders, was on the dance floor. It was this sexual awareness that terrified and fired up the melting pot, the Church and City Hall, the Ku Klux Klan and the federal government, all of whom could not control and, for myriad reasons, despised what was happening, while many others delighted in it. Including Irene's recent dinner companion Irving Berlin, who celebrated ragtime and dancing with his latest song and its – much-intended – double-entendre title:

Ev'rybody's doin' it
Doin' it, doin' it
Ev'rybody's doin' it
Doin' it, doin' it

Irene adamantly endorsed Irving Berlin: 'Dancing is the language of the body.'

Not everyone got the joke. Yet as trendsetters, and with such a high profile, Vernon and Irene had to accept jealous sniping with their triumphs. They were in fact resoundingly carefree about criticism. that year, Vernon and Irene starred in a newsreel, *Social and Theatrical Dancing*, accompanied as ever by their old friend James Europe. Vernon insisted that Europe's dance rhythms, the syncopations, were so much more 'with the beat' than the music played by white orchestras.

It made, of course, commercial sense to elevate ragtime to the mainstream. Vernon and Irene took out a syndicated advertisement announcing: 'Mr and Mrs Vernon Castle have awarded Victor Records the exclusive services of the Castle House Orchestra for the making of dance records.' From that first recording session by the Society Orchestra on 29 December1913, Victor Talking Machine Company began endorsing the real McCoy, Bessie and beyond. More sessions followed, including one, on 10 February 1914, which nailed 'Castle House Rag' and Cecil Macklin's '*Très Moutarde*', which many music historians credit as serious groundwork for the significant sounds of the next one hundred years.

Most enduring of James Europe's partnership with Vernon and Irene are the eight Victor Talking Machine Company records made and released between December 1913, and May 1914. It's repetitive but makes the point: the recordings were the first by a black American instrumental group playing indigenous black music by black American composers. The Victor Talking Machine Company avidly marketed the records as 'dance music for the home'. The company felt obliged to put labels on the original recordings to make it clear the music was 'For Dancing'. Notes explain to record-buyers: 'The Tango, Maxixe, Turkey Trot, Hesitation, Boston, One-Step, Two-Step – all are represented, and the selections are those now most in demand in dancing circles.'

The promotional material raves on: 'Europe's Society Orchestra of Negro musicians has become very popular in society circles and has played for social affairs in the homes of wealthy New Yorkers and at functions at the Tuxedo Club, Hotel Biltmore, Plaza, Sherry's, Delmonico's, the Astor and others. Mrs R. W. Hawksworth, the famous purveyor of amusements for society, used the Europe players regularly and they have recently been engaged to play for Mr Vernon Castle, the popular teacher and exponent of modern dances. The success of this organisation is due to the admirable rhythm sustained throughout every number, whether waltz, turkey trot or tango; to the original interpretation of each number and to the unique instrumentation, which consists of banjos, mandolins, violins, clarinet, coronet, traps and drums.' The Victor Talking Machine Company's biggest James Europe hit was the 'Castle House Rag One-Step' with the B-side 'Congratulations Waltz' (the record was released under the reference Victor 35372). The company normally issued non-classical music on 10-inch discs but this one was produced on 12-inch format, giving couples those extra moments of dancing.

The recordings were historic but the purpose was for one thing only. Vernon's drumming teacher, Buddy Gilmore, was sure of that: 'Anyone with dancing blood in his system has got to dance when he hears this music.' There were so many steps to take to the linoleum floors: the turkey trot, the camel walk, the bear hug, and following, like a cavalry charge, came the Castle Innovation Waltz, the Castle Lame Duck Waltz, the Castle Half-and-Half, the Castle Innovation Tango, the Castle Maxixe, and the big one, the Castle House Rag. They were all popular dances 'refined' for society and ballroom dancing. One study reported that more than one hundred different dances were introduced to 'fashionable ballrooms' from 1912 to 1914. Music publisher Edward Marks told the *New York Times* in 1914: 'The public of the 1890s had asked for tunes to sing. The public of the turn of the century had been content to whistle. The public from 1910 on demanded tunes to dance to.'

The dance compositions arrived, and were received energetically, indeed with a ferocity that staggered even the writers of them, James Europe and his partner Ford Dabney. By May 1914, the Joseph Stearns publishing house was selling so much sheet music produced by Europe and Dabney that the writers resorted to a pseudonym, and not a very good one; they mingled their names and spelled backward to get 'Eporue Yenbad' to provide variety.

There was, as ever, a demand for the *new*. This *new*, and their patrons wanting an exclusive extra for their grand events, was always at Vernon and Irene's heels. The *new* had won them acclaim with Parisian society and contracts with Louis Martin. It also brought them social pressure.

The estimable Mamie Fish was never above impressing. When she entered into a lucrative negotiation with Bessy Marbury for Vernon and Irene's entertainment at a party for some grand visitors (they were always grand) from Europe, the deal was that a new dance routine would be revealed for the first time. The snag was no one told Vernon and Irene, who in the previous weeks had brought in three new numbers – which was their menu for that evening. Mamie Fish, with whom, Irene said, the US Army would not want to engage in hand-to-hand combat, had alerted the press; she'd announced 'new' dances by the fabulous Mr and Mrs Vernon Castle. She then told Irene: 'Oh, well, never mind. Maybe he can just lead you around into something a little different.' They didn't bother with too different and followed their rehearsed routine with a one-step they were developing and had already performed but not named. 'That evening, we didn't dance one new step, and nobody, *nobody*, noticed,' said Irene. Their dance did get a name. Mamie Fish and her guests were thrilled and the newspapers reported on this new phenomenon, the 'Fish Walk', which was absolutely perfect sycophantic syncopation. Ripe, too, for evolution.

The tremendous desire for all things dance, the intricate details and, most of all, the how-to-do-it like Vernon and Irene Castle, was overwhelming. The Castles responded with a beautifully produced and illustrated book, the 176-page hardback *Modern Dancing* 'by Mr and Mrs Vernon Castle', published in March 1914, which was one of the first and most successful how-to manuals. The Foreword read as follows:

Foreword

We feel that this book will serve a double purpose. In the first place, it aims to explain in a clear and simple manner the fundamentals of modern dancing. In the second place, it shows that dancing, properly executed, is neither vulgar nor immodest, but, on the contrary, the personification of refinement, grace, and modesty.

Our aim is to uplift dancing, purify it, and place it before the public in its proper light. When this has been done, we feel convinced that no objection can possibly be urged against it on the grounds of impropriety, but rather that social reformers will join with the medical profession in the view that dancing is not only a rejuvenator of good health and spirits, but a means of preserving youth, prolonging life, and acquiring grace, elegance, and beauty.

Irene and Vernon Castle

This was followed by a pointed introduction from Elisabeth Marbury which amounted to social instruction:

In a recent address by the poet Jean Richepin before the members of the French Academy, the evolution of modern dances was convincingly traced from the tombs of Thebes, from Orient to Occident, and down through ancient Rome. M. Richepin protested against the vulgarisation of these dances when performed by inartistic and ignorant exponents, but argued that centres should promptly be established in every capital of the world where the grace and beauty and classic rhythm to which the modem dance so naturally lends itself should be developed and emphasised. With this aim in view,

Castle House in New York was started, and the services of Mr and Mrs Vernon Castle were secured by me to conduct and superintend the dancing there. Mr and Mrs Castle stand preeminent today as the best exponents of modern dancing.

In Europe as well as in America it has been universally conceded that as teachers they are unequalled. Refinement is the keynote of their method; under their direction Castle House became the model school of modern dancing; through its influence the spirit of beauty and of art is allied to the legitimate physical need of healthy exercise and of honest enjoyment.

The One-Step as taught at Castle House eliminates all hoppings, all contortions of the body, all flouncing of the elbows, all twisting of the arms, and, above everything else, all fantastic dips. This One-Step bears no relation or resemblance to the once-popular Turkey Trot, Bunny Hug, or Grizzly Bear. In it is introduced the sliding and poetical Castle Walk. The Hesitation Waltz is a charming and stately glide, measured and modest.

The much-misunderstood Tango becomes an evolution of the eighteenth-century Minuet. There is in it no strenuous clasping of partners, no hideous gyrations of the limbs, no abnormal twistings, no vicious angles. Mr Castle affirms that when the Tango degenerates into an acrobatic display or into salacious suggestion it is the fault of the dancers and not of the dance. The Castle Tango is courtly and artistic, and this is the only Tango taught by the Castle House instructors.

As for the Maxixe, it is a development of the most attractive kind of folk dancing. Both Mr and Mrs Castle have made a specialty of the Maxixe as an exquisite expression of joyousness and of youthful spontaneity.

The Half-and-Half is an original drawing-room dance invented by Mr Castle. It combines the best steps of the Hesitation and the Maxixe, but the tempo is entirely new.

In this book, Mr Castle has explained in detail, and with the aid of some excellent photographs, exactly how to dance these modern dances – and so clearly and simply that anyone reading the text can follow their explanations, and by attention and practice learn to dance with ease and grace. We have here, then, the authoritative book on dancing, written by the foremost exponents in America, the inventors of the famous and popular Castle Walk.

Perhaps in view of the widespread criticism of some of the modern dances I may be permitted to add a word concerning dancing itself. If we bar dancing from the world we bar one of the supreme human expressions of happiness and exultation. The tiny child skips for joy and prances to the music of the hand organ long before it knows the difference between happiness and sorrow. In times of festival in many countries dancing is the keynote of the gathering. The attempt to start a moral campaign against all modern dancing is destructive rather than constructive, unless we offer something better in its place, unless we go forward to newer dances – that appeal to the moral sense as well as to the eye. All work and no play dulls both Jack and Jill. If young working men and women dance, they fling off morbid introspection; they become alert, alive, full of the zest of life. For the moment they forget the grey and sordid influences, thanks to the buoyancy of our American temperament; therefore I say that the best course in the interest of morals is to encourage dancing as a healthful exercise and as a fitting recreation.

I may be wrong, but it seems to me very improbable that the majority of boys and girls who go to public dances are guilty of harbouring and of fostering the thoughts that are imputed to them by those who proclaim against dancing. I believe that only a small number of them dance vulgar steps, some perhaps impulsively, but chiefly because they do not know any better. They want to dance; they want pleasure and excitement, and they take it as it comes to them, the bad with the good. It is our duty to eliminate the bad and encourage the good. Surely there cannot be as great a moral danger in dancing as there is in sitting huddled close in the darkness of a sensational moving-picture show or in following with feverish interest the suggestive sex-problem dramas.

Nor from my point of view is there as much harm in dancing as in sitting home in some dreary little hall bedroom, beneath the flaring gas, reading with avidity the latest erotic novel or the story which paints vice in alluring colours under the guise of describing life as it really is.

The Maxixe and the Tango are only two of the so-called modern dances. The Innovation, introduced at a ball recently given by Mrs Stuyvesant Fish, is in my opinion more graceful, as it is a dance where the partners need not even touch hands in certain of its steps. In the One-Step the man must hold his partner loosely if he does the pretty measure where he steps to one side of her as they dip; and in the Hesitation Waltz the steps require that the man and the woman be slightly apart. The Turkey Trot was a dance which deserved much of the abuse it received; but it died a natural death, because more attractive dances were offered in its place. So will the objectionable features of all modern dances be thrust aside as the statelier and more graceful steps are danced.

I believe dancing to be a useful as well as a beautiful art, and I think that the women of every city should open properly conducted dancing halls for young people where they can dance to good music under refined supervision.

Give them clean fun to offset the hard work of the day. Give them exercise for tired muscles; give them instructors to teach them, without charge, the correct positions and the correct steps for the popular dances, and every girl and boy you teach in this fashion will teach their friends, until by constructive elimination we have done away with what is vulgar by giving our young people something better.

We are planning now to have classes for girls who work, under the direction of volunteer teachers from Castle House, and I feel that it is a venture whose success is assured, and one which will be copied by men and women of leisure all over the country. It is easy to make the young happy and easy to rob them of joy. It is our privilege, as experienced, responsible guardians, to put within their reach every means of innocent amusement. Otherwise they will fill the void in their lives by amusements of a more questionable character.

The child of the tenement would be delighted if put into a beautiful, clean and airy playroom; so will be the men and women of all ages when we show them how to dance the modern dances gracefully and modestly. I may be a very gullible person, but I have talked to hundreds of girls about their dancing, and they have put into my hand the golden key to the situation by saying with a puzzled smile and questioning eye: 'We're dancing wrong? Well, maybe; but we don't know any other way to dance. Do you?'

We do, and we can teach them. That is really the situation in a nutshell. They must dance. The lure of the rhythm, the sense of flinging aside the weariness of the working day, is as strong in the heart of the girl behind the counter as in that of the girl in the private ballroom. The man who labours in the humbler callings is as interested in his girlfriend and as anxious to dance with her as the young man in what we call 'society.' And what is more, I do not and will not believe that all those young persons, the fathers and mothers of tomorrow, who are working and striving to earn honest livings and to rise in the world, connect their moments of recreation with suggestive ideas and unworthy ideals.

To them dancing means a stretching of the mental muscles as well as those which are physical. It means something different from the dull daily round; it is almost as natural as the desire for food and sleep. The forbidding of the modern dances in public centrer is dangerous. It sets that alluring sign 'forbidden fruit' upon what otherwise would arouse no prurient curiosity. We are told that the new dances encourage too much freedom, and, while 'all right if properly danced', are all wrong in a public dancing-room. These would-be reformers never see that they are tacitly admitting that it is ignorance of the dances, not knowledge of them, that does the harm.

It is not difficult to find the explanation of some of the undesirable dancing. A working man and girl go to a musical comedy. From their stuffy seats high up under the roof they look down upon the dancers on the stage. These are – so the programme tells them – doing modern ballroom dancing. The man on the stage flings his partner about with Apache wildness; she clutches him around the neck and is swung off her feet. They spin swiftly or undulate slowly across the stage, and the programme calls it a "Tango". The man and girl go away and talk of those 'ballroom dances'. They try the steps; they are novel and often difficult; they have aroused their interest. The result is that we find scores of young people dancing under the name of 'One-Step' or 'Tango' the eccentric dances thus exaggerated and elaborated to excite the jaded audiences of a roof garden or a music hall.

There is no one to tell those young people that they are mistaken in their choice of the steps, that 'society' does not do those dances. They hear hundreds of men and women denouncing the scandalous modern dances, and in their ignorance think that these are the only dances.

Let us, therefore, have dance halls that are properly run, with instructors to teach the new dances, with a good floor and good music and a welcome for everyone.

Let us have places of amusement where the fathers and mothers and even the little ones can come with the young people, and where they can look on and enjoy the healthy relaxation of their children.

Let the dance halls become decent social centres where families can gather in sympathy and in understanding. There teach that it is better to dance correctly than to undulate round and round in a narrow circle and in a close embrace, misnaming this a Hesitation Waltz.

The One-Step, the Hesitation, the Lame Duck, the Innovation, the Half-and-Half – all the new dances, in fact – have enough pretty steps to delight the hearts of girls and boys who want to show off. They are easy enough for even the awkward girl to learn, and they are good exercise and clean exercise for every boy.

I am delighted to find that the public schools are taking up dancing, and I believe that if every woman's club would give a free dance for the young people of the neighbourhood once a week, with an instructor and a chaperon present, that they would do more good to the race than by discussing eugenics or by indulging in a flippant study of social economics. Dancing is first and foremost a healthful exercise; it is pleasure; and it is an art that brings to the front courtesy, ease of manner, grace of body, and happiness of mind. It is for us to set this standard.

Many prominent citizens and some of our clergy have recently denounced modern dancing, believing in all sincerity that certain vulgar dances which they have witnessed are the models upon which general dancing must be based. Unfortunately, this is a case of the innocent suffering for the guilty, and it is our business and pleasure to prove that any sweeping condemnation of dancing as a pastime is not founded upon fact and that many have erred through ignorance rather than through intent. Let us, therefore, cooperate with our guardians of civic decency and aid them constructively in the elimination of the coarse, the uncouth, the vulgar, and the vicious.

Let us establish once and for all a standard of modern dancing which will demonstrate that these dances can be made graceful, artistic, charming, and, above all, refined.

Elisabeth Marbury
New York, March 1914

The commercial intent was always present, but Vernon and Irene had inadvertently won a place, and one of authority, on the right way of behaving. They were looked on for advice, as an example, of how to have it all, a marriage and a his-and-her career. It was far removed from dancing: it was the impact of their personal code which had rewritten what was and was not acceptable. 'This is the way to live your life,' was the message. Arlene Louise Croce, the eminent dance critic, founder of *Ballet Review* and authority on the work of Astaire and Rogers (*The Fred Astaire & Ginger Rogers Book*, 1972), singles out Vernon and Irene from all others associated with the birth of modern dancing: 'They were, perhaps, the first large expression of modern mass society and its cult of good taste, its how-to lessons, its obsession with the Correct Thing.'

However, as with all how-to books, the missing factor in *Modern Dancing* is visual motion. Yes, there are wonderful still photographs, but you don't see the movement. The profitable result was that book sales soared and readers bought tickets, especially for the cabarets where dancing enthusiasts and the curious could get a close-up look at the Castles' high-steppin' shoes and the couple in them. Age set no parameters, a world of enthusiasts were restless to experiment, keen to emulate the easy style, the spontaneity of expression, and dance like Vernon and Irene.

There were no tickets available for the show involving Vernon and Irene and the dancing – though not in a 'refined' style – roller-skating bear. That was quite a performance; one of their truly great.

Chapter Seven
Animal Crackers

'All animals are equal, but some animals are more equal than others.'
George Orwell, *Animal Farm*, 1945

obby the brown bear wasn't a nuisance at all. He behaved like a gentleman in the backseat of the taxi with Irene. Granted, he was all over her but it was a squeeze and the driver of the yellow cab kept going late into turns, his head twisted around looking at his passengers. Vernon, shuttled in to Bobby's right on the backseat, promised a tip 'as big as the fare' if the driver would slow down a little. They had endured a spot of stress.

The Castles' home on Manhasset Bay, Long Island, the seaside of choice for Manhattan, was a sanctuary for animals, hangers-on who had a connection – often English actors – and any other breed requiring a free bed. Their hospitality was for all, their devotion reserved for the animals. Walter Ash calculated he grilled more rare-to-medium steak, sirloin not rump, for Vernon's collection of dogs than for any grand party. There wasn't often a stray animal left wandering after Vernon and Irene drove past.

Their generosity, the frenetic zeal and belief of their over-the-rainbow circle that the glory days would last for ever, was a poor partner for the reality of the upkeep of the rambling Manhasset Bay house, now boasting a houseboat, tennis courts, polo ponies, and the further accoutrements of living as fast as your fame. It was expensive. To meet their overheads the couple would go on the vaudeville circuit, which paid handsomely. They would only do it, Irene said, when they were short of ready cash. This, she explained, 'seemed to be quite often'. She nor Vernon never sought fact nor reason for that.

Which found them in the pre-Prohibition days of Chicago in the back of a cab racing down North Clark Street with Bobby who, when the fluffy and friendly bear cuddled in, they found should have been called Blossom. Vernon and Irene had contracted with the Orpheum Circuit, a San Francisco-based coast-to-coast chain of vaudeville theatres with all markets of venues and audiences. Neither of the dancing stars liked the vaudeville roundabout, but needs must. They danced through two shows a day but were increasingly upset and appalled at what was being done to animals in the shows. An animal-themed act would open or close most vaudeville shows. Even from the front stalls, it all appeared cute and kind. Children giggled and their parents found it charming as animals leaped through hoops and monkeys dressed as jockeys rode little dogs in 'races'. Backstage, the conditions for the animals were often horrific. Vernon and Irene became animal-rights crusaders because of what they witnessed on the vaudeville circuit (and in 2014, decades after it was established, Irene's Orphans of the Storm animal sanctuary is still in operation). George Orwell, making a political point, of course, wrote what inspired him to create *Animal Farm*: 'I saw a little boy, perhaps ten years old, driving a huge carthorse along a narrow path, whipping it whenever it tried to turn. It struck me that if only such animals became aware of their strength we should have no power over them, and that men exploit animals in much the same way as the rich exploit the proletariat.'

Vernon and Irene's experience was far more vivid and she shouted about it to the world: 'We saw dogs beaten unmercifully after the curtain fell and given the water cure in the alley, with the trainer holding a powerful hose close to the dog's nose and filling his lungs with water. We saw animals shocked with electricity, stuck with needles and starved except for the few titbits of reward which made them do the things they were afraid to do. There was little affection between the trainer and his animals. Affection might make the dog unpredictable on the stage. So, the animals were cowed, afraid to make the slightest mistake. We knew nothing of human organisations or how to go about having anyone punished for cruelty to animals. A humane officer came around once a week but apparently not to look at the animals. Instead, he went to the corner saloon with the trainer for a drink and a few laughs and if he ever sent in a report it was a whitewash. We learned only one way to correct it, a very inadequate method, but one that made us feel better. The minute we saw an animal beaten or punished in any way we said: "How much do you want for it?" Sometimes it was a monkey, more often it was a dog, but in any case the price was very high, which robbed us of any profit we hoped to make on a vaudeville tour.'

After their encounter with Bobby-Blossom the Bear at the Palace Theatre in Chicago, they refused ever again to appear on stage with an animal act; they had it written into their contracts and lost lucrative bookings because of it.

Vernon and Irene had been at the Palace Theatre for two days when they heard what they called plaintive wails from beneath the stage. Irene said she thought it was a sick child in the basement. When they went down the stairway to investigate they were met head-on by a trainer, Geraldini, leading a big brown bear up towards them. They back-stepped and the Italian trainer led Bobby-Blossom into the wings of the theatre. He pushed the bear into a chair and then shoved a Coca-Cola bottle filled with honey into a feeding muzzle. The hungry Bobby-Blossom gurgled down the honey but as he did so Geraldini rammed and clamped roller skates on to the bear's feet. A yelping poodle was shoved into the bear's arms and, with another big shove, the animal bundle was pushed onstage. Irene saw it all and was distressed but not as much as Bobby-Blossom. She and Vernon were charmed by the talented bear but appalled at the living conditions provided. One bottle of honey a day was the best of it. The rest of it was a cramped cage in a room used as a smoking parlour by the musicians. When Irene was involved in a photographic session for the show's publicity with the bear he was 'controlled' with a baseball bat by Geraldini. When the trainer cracked the bear with the bat it was all too much for Irene and Vernon, who was with her.

Irene looked at Vernon, who was off to her left. They both looked at Geraldini, back at each other, then turned and together said: 'How much do you want for the bear?'

Geraldini's English had monetary fluency: 'Nine hundred dollars.'

But the bear had to complete his Chicago engagement first. Irene said the bear slowly and groggily recovered, and shook his head – as if clearing it of stars – and was led away. She and Vernon owned him. What on earth were they going to do with him to guarantee a long and happy life? They went to dinner to discuss it.

The Bronx Zoo was close to Irene's family home in New

LOBBY—RECTOR'S RESTAURANT, Broadway at 48th Street, New York

ONE SECTION MAIN DINING ROOM, RECTOR'S, Broadway, at 48th Street, New York

RECTOR'S
BROADWAY
AT 48TH ST,
NEW YORK

© 1913 GEO. RECTOR, INC.

Top left and below: The lobster palaces of New York became legend but none more so or more magnificent than Rector's, which created a worldwide reputation – like Vernon and Irene – and enhanced it by being among the first to install proper dance floors. The advertisement dates from 1913, the year in which Rodolfo Guglielmi – later Rudolf Valentino – first saw the Castles dance.

Top right: Irene Castle loved to dress up for the occasion, this time as a Native American in an image she autographed and sent to fans on request.

Left: A time to dance: a poster for Flo Ziegfeld's *Follies* of 1911.

Right: A collector's item: the original edition of *Modern Dancing*, published in 1914, of which there are only a handful of copies left in the world.

Below: Irene was much sought after as a model by glossy magazines and fashion houses. She had both the figure and a natural grace, seen here on the cover of the fashion magazine *The Delineator* of November 1915.

Above: Another for the collector: the sheet music for the 'Castle Walk', with all the appropriate credits; originals are sought after by memorabilia hunters fascinated by the era.

According to Cecil Beaton, Irene was the 'modern young lady of fashion whom we admire so much today, the first to cut her hair into the curly locks of a bob'.　　(© *Getty*)

ADOLPH ZUKOR
PRESENTS

IRENE CASTLE
IN
"THE FIRING LINE"

By ROBERT W. CHAMBERS

A Paramount – Artcraft Special

SCENARIO BY CLARA BERANGER   DIRECTED BY CHARLES MAIGNE

© FAMOUS PLAYERS - LASKY CORPORATION-1919

Paramount Pictures

ARTCRAFT PICTURES

Morgan

It was in silent films where Irene's look gave her the headline advantage; she was the star of the show, the name above the title, as here in 1919's *The Firing Line*. Her co-star was the romantically named Antonio Moreno – in reality Glaswegian David Powell – who died half a dozen years later just as he, and the talkies, were taking off.

Left: This is what the well-dressed leading man was driving, and sometimes over the speed limit. Vernon liked the idea of a mile in fifty-one seconds (just over 70mph), but always tried his best to go much, much faster.

Right: Vernon made a sketch of his first combat attack and that was turned into a more realistic drawing to illustrate his dogfight over the Western Front.

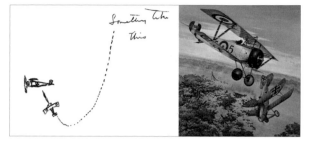

Left: Irene, in suitably military costume, photographed in 1917 – she is wearing the distinctive tunic, nicknamed the 'maternity jacket', and wings of her husband's service, the Royal Flying Corps.

Right: A coloured still from *The Story of Vernon and Irene Castle* (1939) showing Ginger Rogers dancing with Fred Astaire, who is wearing the studio's idea of RFC uniform.

(© *RKO/The Kobal Collection*)

Above: The poster said it all. William Randolph Hearst, Irene's dance pupil, propaganda specialist, champion of high headlines, gave his star incredible billing: 'Mrs Vernon Castle, America's Best Known and Best Dressed Woman,' in *Patria*, the fifteen-part moving-picture serial of all time. Irene was rarely off-screen – earning her $1,500 a week – and in Episode Four plays a lookalike character, Elaine. Based on the *The Last of the Fighting Channings* by Louis Joseph Vance – the novel was serialised in Hearst newspapers – the screenplay gave Irene opportunity to dance.

Below: By the time *The Hillcrest Mystery* was released in March 1918, she was a widow.

As the world would remember them: Vernon and Irene Castle dancing in 1913, before the war that would eventually separate them.

(©Everett Collection/REX)

Top left: Irene had made plans for her reunion with Vernon. She is buried alongside him at Woodlawn Cemetery: together again, gracefully prized in marble, bronze and time gone.

Top right: Her fame did not diminish, securing her top billing for this 1922 silent film, in which she played a cabaret dancer who ends up helping to run a logging camp.

(© *Everett Collection/REX*)

Below: RKO Studios in 1939, when they filmed *The Vernon and Irene and Castle Story,* believed 'Southerns certain to dislike coloured orchestra' so James Europe and Company were whitewashed from the picture. Walter Ash stayed, but played by white Walter Brennan (left), seen with Fred and Ginger as Vernon and Irene and the magnificent Lew Fields playing himself three decades on. (© *RKO/The Kobal Collection*)

Rochelle and they had big, comfortable bear cages. Irene sent them a telegram offer of their prize find. The zoo messaged back that they had more bears than they required; indeed, bear cubs were being sold for $15 each. The Rock Creek Zoo in Washington, DC had many brown bears; did Vernon and Irene have a black bear, or a grizzly? Irene asked why they'd ever think she could provide any animal a zoo was short of. By Saturday, the last performances at the Palace, there remained no place at a zoo for Bobby-Blossom. Vernon and Irene, anxious about their bear's prospects, pitched up at Chicago's Lincoln Park Zoo before their matinée show. The zoo's man in charge, Cy DeVry, disappointed: there was no accommodation available.

Irene was in tears and then DeVry told her: 'We have an old black bear that's been here for years and if you don't mind taking a chance with yours, you can put your bear in with him. The pen's large and maybe they'll get along all right.' Irene put away her handkerchief.

They told Cy DeVry that they would deliver Bobby-Blossom late on Sunday morning around 11 a.m. The curtain fell on Saturday night and they were given the key to the bear's cage; Geraldini left on the train for Kansas City. Now, that Sunday morning, they had to transport Bobby-Blossom to Lincoln Park Zoo. They rumbled through many options when Vernon, whom you have to adore, arrived at the obvious: they'd call a cab. They found a yellow cab outside their hotel and asked him to drive to the backstage area of the Palace Theatre, so they could pick up a friend. Now, this was pre-Prohibition Chicago so the previous evening at the end of the run the booze had flowed. The Castles were leaning into each other by the time they made it back to their hotel. That morning they had punishing hangovers. So, Bobby-Blossom wasn't the only one with a sore head. It is best to follow the following madcap scene while imagining flickering silent movie images and a jaunty Joplin piano soundtrack:

The nervous, sleepy couple creep slowly into the darkness of the basement to see if the great big bear will voluntarily retire from showbusiness. In the gloom they see a chain still hanging from Bobby-Blossom's collar. Irene swoons a little to distract the bear and slips her right arm into the cage to grab the chain. Vernon has the key to the cage. He turns it. The bear sees an open door and takes off up the iron stairs with Irene hanging on the chain and Vernon hanging on to her. Flying to freedom the bear quite remarkably does what is wanted to heads for the taxi and its open door. Coaxed a little by Vernon and Irene he gets into the middle of the back seat with Vernon holding the chain beside him. Irene wanders round the cab and gets in the other side. They have Bobby-Blossom surrounded. And the taxi driver terrified. He starts his engine and drives quite fast to the zoo. Then faster. And then very fast. He brakes abruptly to a halt at the zoo and Vernon eases out of the cab and sprints off to find the bear keepers. The taxi driver closes the connecting window with the back seat. Irene sits alone with her friend. They are both nervous. Irene's stomach rumbles and the bear growls in reply – and then the keeper appears and takes the chain and control. All head for the bear pen and, collar off, Bobby-Blossom meekly wanders into his new home. From the cave at the rear of the pen appears the black bear. It is a stand off. They raise themselves high on their hind legs and bellow their growls. Irene looks away so as not to witness a bloodbath. The taxi driver who has joined them starts laughing. So does Vernon. And the keeper. Irene turns.

Bobby-Blossom and the black bear are playing, happily rolling around like best of bear friends do. The keeper pushes in food. They're behaving like teddy bears. They picnic.

Vernon and Irene took the taxi back to their hotel and invited in the driver for glasses of champagne. There was something to celebrate. They had found a home for Bobby-Blossom and the taxi driver had his story for a lifetime. Who'd ever guess who — and what — he had had in the back of his cab?

Vernon and Irene were in the business of being sensational and they continued to be. This year of 1914, with Vernon twenty-seven and Irene twenty-one, was set to be eventful. At Manhasset, while Walter Ash ran the house and staff, Vernon devoted himself to polo and his ponies — but his increasing interest was in showing German shepherd dogs. He had kennels for more than two dozen and twelve at any one time, most of them highly trained police dogs. The pride of the kennels, following the death of Zowie earlier in the year (Vernon kept his ashes at home), was Tell von Flugerad, who won many field trials and Vernon's heart. Tell went everywhere with him. He was in the car when he and Irene drove around a corner and saw a donkey farm. What made them stop was a foal. It was love at first sight. A negotiation was completed with the owner and the foal went into the backseat. Vernon told Gladwyn MacDougal: 'It's surprising how difficult it is to make a donkey sit down in the backseat of an automobile.'

Or to stop Vernon's need for adventure and new larks. Irene sighed a great deal.

Dogs, donkeys, cows, ponies and motor cars. Vernon delighted in them all. Bessy Marbury despaired of them; that is the cars — and the Castles' spending. Waving a $1,500 receipt for a horse Irene had bought, she complained to Gladwyn MacDougal:

'Motor cars purchased with joyous carelessness... fur wraps fell upon Irene's lovely shoulders like manna from heaven. Their day was never complete unless they bought something.'

Which was why their manager sent them on the road, on what was to be 'The Whirlwind Tour' of America. It wasn't all about money. Bessy Marbury was also aware of a growing resentment against the Castles. The conservative accusation was that the majority of young people performing modern dances had not a clue about the 'refinements'. It was all very well for the swells of society but others were dancing their way into moral depravity. Buttoning their coats up against all this, the New York City Club Committee on Public Amusements and Morals singled out Vernon and Irene: 'The Castle Walk, one of the most popular dances of the day, requires the partners' feet to be placed in a position which, while it may be taken without bodily contact, usually results at the public dances of the city in an interlocking of the partners' lower limbs and continual rubbing together of the bodies.'

In this racial atmosphere of separate but equal and not quite sure – something Vernon had never witnessed in England – black community leaders were as concerned as their counterparts. Pastor Rev. Adam Clayton Powell of the Abyssinia Baptist Church in New York delivered a sermon titled 'The Negro Race is Dancing Itself to Death'. He thundered: 'Our young people are too frivolous because they feed on too much trash. You can see the effects of the tango and ragtime music not only in their conversations but in the movement of their bodies about the home and on the street. Grace and modesty are becoming rare virtues. In public dance halls girls pick up escorts, sit on men's laps and go for joyrides and dance in intimate contact.'

Again, Bessy Marbury calculated the social responsibility and business sense of spreading the cult of refinement. When they had decided a tour would happen, but not the details, she announced, on the doorsteps of the silent powers of America, to the *Worcester Telegram*, voice of central Massachusetts:

> Our plans are to spread this proper instruction in dancing, broadcast through every possible agency. That is one reason why the Castles are making this spring tour of thirty-two of the principal cities of the country. Not only will they dance the latest dances, but Mr Castle will illustrate the mistakes usually made by the average dancers, and will address the audience, telling them how the dances should be danced. I do not believe that many people dance in a vulgar way except through ignorance of the proper methods, and I believe this tour of the Castles will be a wonderful dance crusade that will elevate the standards of dancing all over the country. The modern dances cannot be banned. They have arrived, and they will remain. They are not at all objectionable except when they are danced by people who do not know how to do them.
>
> Mr Vernon Castle will teach everyone.

The Castles' book *Modern Dancing* was the handbook for the tour, which followed the success of a pivotal collaboration between Vernon and Irene and James Europe and the National Negro Orchestra on 8 April 1914 at the Manhattan Casino in Harlem. 'A Night in Tangoland, a Joyous Festival of Music and Dance' was arranged by James Europe's just-formed Tempo Club, an organisation Europe and Ford Dabney envisaged representing black entertainers everywhere. The dancers were enthusiastic supporters of the National Negro Orchestra. They had discussed appearing together that summer in Paris and London and doing an American tour before. The Harlem concert would be their first tryout.

Vernon and Irene plotted the dances and the music for 'A Night in Tangoland' and the projected four weeks of shouting the gospel of dance around thirty-two different cities with James Europe and Ford Dabney, two regular visitors to their Manhasset farm. This affable, friends-and-working connection was easy for Vernon and Irene; their tour of the East Coast and Midwest of America more of a challenge for race relations and racial tolerance. Vernon, of course, marched to his own drumbeat. He and James Europe's drummer Buddy Gilmore were like a couple of school kids around a drum kit. James Europe himself, tall at just more than six feet high, and a big man (heavy in weight but with it neatly spread around), had any hint of threat dismissed by his blinking eyes behind his metal-framed round spectacles. He looked like a friendly professor who'd serve tea during lectures. And in fact, one thing James Europe did deliver along with his band-standing music were lectures.

He was described by the *Saturday Evening Post*, after a Carnegie Hall concert on 13 March 1914, 'as one of the most remarkable men, not only of his race, but in the music world of this country. A composer of some note, some of his serious efforts were played the other night, and his dance music is known wherever the tango or turkey trot are danced. He is head of an organisation which practically controls the furnishing of music for the new dances, and at the same time, he is able to expend considerable energy upon the development of the Negro Symphony Orchestra. Unaided, he has been able to accomplish what white musicians said was impossible: the adaptation of Negro music and musicians to symphonic purposes.'

This 'professor' of music lectured back: 'The reason the Negro is in such demand by the wealthiest and most fashionable classes of white society is simply because he has an inimitable ear for time in dancing, is well trained, and is an instinctively good musician. The Negro plays as if it was a second nature to him, as it is. Our symphony orchestra never tries to play white folks' music. We should be foolish to attempt such a thing. We are no more fitted for that than a white orchestra is fitted to play our music. We have developed a kind of symphony music that, no matter what else you may think, is different and distinctive, and that lends itself to the playing of the peculiar compositions of our race.'

James Europe was always aware that it was Vernon and Irene who had insisted on his orchestra touring with them and who had broken down that barrier in vaudeville theatre. It was also important to say so publicly and it was. The Tempo Club issued a statement: 'Mr and Mrs Castle are the best friends of the coloured professional and while they are known for being artistic and exceptionally original in the terpsichorean art, they are also noted for their benevolence and congeniality. Race, colour, creed nor religion mark their lives.'

Europe was a man of true conviction, and of action. He spoke out for racial equality and expected discipline from his orchestra. In turn the musicians stuck to the rules, wearing formal black tie for performances, and precisely following the printed scores and their conductor's baton. This was a band to Vernon but an orchestra for everyone else. On 8 April 1914, at the Manhattan Casino, the concert was held to raise funds for the National Negro Symphony. The audience bulged to capacity at around 3,000 and there were a couple of hundred disappointed music and dance lovers who nevertheless hung around outside and didn't have to strain too much to hear the music, if not see Vernon and Irene dance.

Dance they did. They followed the Symphony Orchestra onstage and, with James Europe's 'band', a trimmed-down version of the National Negro Orchestra, did the Castle Walk, the Castle Maxixe, the Half-and-Half and the Tango. Those on the streets outside and around the corners of Harlem could hear the applause. On 9 April 1914, the New York newspapers reported in a gush of praise. The *Sun* was pleased, if a little aghast, that 'the Castles, wizards of the dance, who are to terpsichore what Edison is to electricity, chose to appear before one of the leading Negro organisations of the city'. The *New York News* had no reservations: 'The concert was perhaps the finest musical and dance programme ever given by and for coloured people, one that commanded such monstrous ovations it was impossible to say if the honours were bestowed on James Europe or his orchestra or upon the greatest dance artists of the day, Mr and Mrs Vernon Castle.' There was further comment about this evening of 'unique entertainment' and the upcoming 'Castle Tour' of America. The Castles, it was reported, would be performing with a 'very interesting orchestra composed of coloured men'. Well, said Vernon, it was a black band.

It was equally a tricky tightrope, freedom of the individual alongside social responsibility, and nothing was black or white. It was all a difficult grey. There were extremes on both sides. James Europe was accused of pandering to white taste by bleaching African music; the Castles of crass temerity for working with black musicians. In St Louis, birthplace of T. S. Eliot, ragtime and a non-linoleum dance floor, there could have been some expectations of what Vernon and Irene and James Europe were bringing to town. Yet, no, the *St Louis Post* made it clear for its readers what the upcoming show in May 1914 at the Odeon featured: 'The Vernon Castles Dance to the Music by African Band.' This 'African Band' was 'led by the Famous Europe'. It was a prize puzzle of marketing.

The Castle Tour was a revelation to Midwest audiences attuned to minstrel shows and 'coon shouters'; there was safety in that unthinking brashness, and they were wary. It was also a revelation for Vernon and Irene. Plans to go all the way out to the coast and play San Francisco and Los Angeles (where they had an invitation to visit William Randolph Hearst at the mansion he'd created across from the beach in Santa Monica) had changed, and they turned the tour around in Omaha, Nebraska. It remained at thirty-two cities in twenty-eight days, more of a tornado than a whirlwind.

Irene packed for all weathers. Unsegregated hotels and restaurants, places which would take the mix, had been arranged. It wasn't open range anywhere. The tour began at Grand Central Station in New York and in style. They had their own train; three Pullman cars had been reserved to take the tour city to city. As the porters struggled with Irene's trunks of clothes, all essential for the dance, and the steam engines belched and hissed, and the incessant rattle of the station echoed off that cavernous interior, tour manager Arthur Hopkins found places for them all: James Europe and an orchestra of eighteen in one car; the Castles and six dancers from Castle House, Gladwyn MacDougal and, for the first few venues, Bessy Marbury, in another; and the costumes in the third, which was also the dining car. Tell was there, and assorted other dogs. Vernon, patient and kindly, never embarrassed by his horde of pets, was in charge. The platform manager, all grey whiskers and importance, cried 'All aboard!', a whistle shrieked and the Castle Special steamed out of town on 27 April 1914.

It was an endeavour, a pioneer trip into unknown territory. At all the stops banners flew: 'The Castles Are Coming, Hooray, Hooray, Hooray!' Crowds, sometimes bewildered by the entourage, turned out to greet the Castle Special. The tour group had no black dancers, no white musicians, so no proper integration. However, they all worked happily and well together and – newspapers on the tour reported, as in a scoop – the black musicians were treated as almost the professional, if not social, equals of the dancers. They did travel in separate Pullman cars.

A wily commentator at the time pointed out that Vernon and Irene shared similar roles. It was true: she credited him with their fame and fortune (now $5,000 a week against the average $5-dollar working-man take-home – six cents a day for a plantation worker), and although she was a 'new woman', she remained the 'little woman': she was Mrs Vernon Castle. It said so on the billboards. It was topsy-turvy.

The Castle Tour presented the same show at every venue. The reception was different at every stop. The audiences welcomed and applauded. Many had never seen a black orchestra; some never a black entertainer. The newspaper critics, perhaps believing they reflected the feelings of their readers, regularly took umbrage about the prominent role of the all-black orchestra. The show began with a demonstration of exhibition dancing, Vernon and Irene tripping the light fantastic. The Castle House dancers would perform – a polka, a hesitation – while Irene changed her frock. Women in all the cities were as interested, if not more, in what Irene wore and how she looked, as in how she and Vernon danced. The orchestra would blast into superb instrumental numbers, Irene would change costume again, and Vernon would present a snappy patter on dancing to the audience, his 'dos' and 'don'ts' on the dance floor punctuated with off-the-cuff remarks.

He was a clever stand-up. Not so clever were some of the comments their show received.

The black singing quartet's offering during a break from the dancing is described by a Syracuse newspaper 'as being that of the palmetto tree and the watermelon patch, with faint suggestions of persimmons and the voodoo'.

When Vernon and Irene were half an hour late onstage in St Joseph, Missouri, the local newspaper said the audience used the time to discuss 'the varying shades of the chocolate hue in Europe's eighteen-piece orchestra and watched the manoeuvres of the drummer.' Buddy Gilmore was called 'particularly black and particularly busy'.

There were drum solos from Buddy Gilmore – he sat smack up on centre stage, being the core of the dance band's rhythm – and from Vernon, who added a touch of vaudeville, juggling his drumsticks in the air. Audiences were astonished by him; he was having such a good time, you could grate a carrot with his grin: a big, wide smile that brightened anywhere.

Yet, not the mood of Mr Butch Johnson, a former prizefighter and the culture critic of the *Minneapolis Journal*. Butch was a writer who was reputed to have a way with humour, especially when applied to society types. He didn't like the legs on the dancers: 'too skinny'. Vernon? Well, he couldn't understand his English accent. It was when Butch scribbled his pen towards the orchestra that it became unpleasant: 'Chocolate Joe is on the stage playing a base [*sic*] drum, a snare drum, cymbal, a whistle and one or two other instruments all at once, and no kid [*sic*], that's right. He plays with his feet, knees and teeth. A lot of darky musicians sit in the regular music-makers' places, and if it was a travelling medicine show I could sense it out, but what those society people are putting down good coin to see it for is what gets me.'

Unknown territory? It was more like outlaw country. Yet it appeared to be greeted with equanimity, especially by Vernon. William Elkins, an orchestra member, whose eloquent and trenchant memories of the tour were published by the *New York Age* on 28 September 1948, said Vernon could deal with anything: 'Nothing ever fazed him, there was no situation which he was not the master of, with his quiet, dignified manner.'

Dignified... unless, of course, he was playing the drums, solo or with Buddy Gilmore. Then he was all drumsticks, arms and feet flailing around like rioting spaghetti. There were other views of Vernon's talents. 'He produced such a hellish noise as Tartar band ever could equal, drowning even the music of the orchestra, to the great delight of the audience,' thought the *Boston Transcript* newspaper.

The second part of their show involved a dance contest, with the winning couple getting the Castle Cup and a chance to compete in a dance-contest final at Madison Square Garden on 23 May 23 1914. Irene had been doubtful about the appeal of the contest but got it wrong. Dozens and dozens of couples took to the stage desperate to win the Castle Cup, very good and very bad dancers aged from eight to eighty years old; she chose the winner with varying criteria which always involved the need to catch their midnight train on to the next show.

Although tired, by the time they climbed aboard the Castle Special the minds of the concert company were always alive with a buzz following performances. Mixed relationships between artists of different races were rare in 1914 but this crowd got together most nights to enjoy themselves and enforce the rules and behaviour of the tour. They staged mock trials in the musicians' car, which could be haphazard depending on champagne's connection with the natural post-production high spirits. William Elkins, a wizard on the banjo, was the judge, James Europe the prosecutor and Gladwyn MacDougal the perfect defender; he liked everybody. There were all manner of misdeeds which could get you in the dock: mismatched socks, brown shoes with blue suits, drinking before a show, whistling in the dressing room, being late, chewing gum onstage and, for Vernon (who picked the jury) and Irene, any missteps on stage. The Castles' most regular misdemeanour was being late for the Castle Special. They were always ordered to 'pay your debt to society' by buying champagne for all. The rest of the guilty – no one was ever innocent, despite Gladwyn MacDougal's emotive pleas for the 'poor wretch' – bought beer. William Elkins, who was seventy-six when he spoke in 1948, recalled the Castle company of the tour as 'one of the most perfectly disciplined organisations and one in which everyone enjoyed themselves'.

Yet this rattling ragtime period of fabulous wealth and the most demeaning poverty, of Empire attitudes retained alongside incredible and racing change, continued to berate harmony. Vernon demanded respect for and from every member of the company but he was no bully about it; he was ever the diplomat. He had to be with the fragility of race relations, no matter the bonds formed. William Elkins gave his best example:

One of the white dancers, talking to a local stagehand, was overheard by one of the members of our troupe to use the word 'nigger'. The case was reported for trial. Well, that was the first of such an instance and I thought it best to speak with Mr and Mrs Castle before taking such a touchy subject up, for fear of how the offender might take it and knowing what could develop. But Mr Castle spoke up, right away, and told me to bring him up in court and fine him fifty dollars.

The case was called and the prisoner pleaded guilty. Instead of fining him fifty dollars cash, the fine was champagne, sandwiches, and refreshments for the whole troupe that cost him at least fifty dollars. The victim objected, but Mr Castle, who was standing in the door looking on, warned the offender that if he did not pay the jury composed of the musicians might be a little rough. Needless to say, he bought the refreshments and on our special train that night, Mr and Mrs Castle, the offender, and the whole company had a wonderful party and after that there were never any other insulting remarks.

From his previous experience, William Elkins said he wouldn't have been surprised if the Castles had sided with the white dancer. It was the easy way. That was the status quo, the general way of thinking. The offending word was in daily and casual use. '[Yet] Mr and Mrs Castle are the finest people I have ever had the pleasure of working with in my whole career.' The Castles, white dancers, had made Negro dances 'acceptable' for white audiences. In turn, James Europe and his orchestra and teams of black musicians had achieved a superb reputation with white audiences by their association with Vernon and Irene. Black dancers could never have taught 'proper dancing' to white people, that was threatening; in Harlem cabaret clubs Vernon and Irene were rare, often the only, white faces before, nearly a decade later, it became daring and fashionable at the Cotton Club.

With his English upbringing, Vernon couldn't understand why there had to be a fuss. He said that if you made a noise about something you made it more than it ever needed to be. Irene, with an altogether different background, the New Rochelle romantic rather than the realistic view of the world, could casually use language which was commonplace. There is an undated article (most likely from 1916) from the *Dancing Times*, which is available in the Castle archive at the New York Public Library, in which Irene writes about turning black dance into something for white society: 'We get our new dances from the Barbary Coast. Of course, they reach New York in a very primitive condition, and have to be considerably toned down before they can be used in the drawing room. There is one just arrived now – it is still very, very crude – and it is called "Shaking the Shimmy". It's a nigger dance, of course, and it appears to be a slow walk with a frequent twitching of the shoulders. The teachers may try to make something of it.'

Vernon and Irene and the Castle Special passengers were in a primitive condition when they too arrived back in New York for the dance-off championship at Madison Square Garden. The finale on 23 May 1914 was packed with paying fans who were not fazed by how far off the dancers were or how difficult it was to hear the orchestra properly. They cheered when Vernon and Irene danced onstage and kept on applauding until late in the evening when Mr and Mrs Sailing Baruch, a middle-aged couple from New York, were acclaimed the first national dancing champions.

It was a reflection of how democratic dancing had become that Mr Baruch's brother Bernard was in the audience. Bernard Baruch was a powerful figure in American finance and politics and in 1916 he would advise President Woodrow Wilson on US national defence. That summer, as he watched his brother and sister-in-law Leona do the Castle Walk at Madison Square Garden, there were growing signs of the forthcoming need for that advice.

Book III
Wartime

'Four slows steps forward (in closed position).
Four quick steps forward.
Four quick steps, turning right.
One slow step forward.
One slow step, crossing in back.
Four quick steps forward.
Four slow steps forward, turning right.'
Oscar Duryea, 'Instructions for the Foxtrot', Imperial Society
of Teachers of Dancing, London, 1914

Chapter Eight
Kiss and Tell

'You must keep your mind on the objective, not on the obstacle.'
William Randolph Hearst, 1913

When the Archduke Franz Ferdinand, heir presumptive to the Austro-Hungarian throne, and his matronly wife Sophie, Duchess of Hohenberg, were shot dead on 28 June 1914 in the Bosnian capital of Sarajevo by the Serbian nationalist Gavrilo Princip, Vernon and Irene were having tea at the Ritz-Carlton opposite the Castle House with Bessy Marbury, and talking about getting away from it all. They needed a holiday. They were arranging to meet in France, where all three planned to be in a couple of weeks. Across town, James Europe was trying to choose an effective costume to lead the grand march for the black theatrical fraternity 'Frolic of the Frogs' annual parade through Harlem. He picked a red circus master's outfit.

Vernon and Irene, along with her mother, Vernon's German shepherd Tell von Flugerad and Irene's Belgian griffon, tiny Kiki, chose to travel to Europe on 18 July, while Austria was making repercussive and humiliating demands on Serbia, including the dismissal of all anti-Austrian elements within the Serb Government and military. They sailed first class from New York on the SS *Imperator*, a smart German three-deck liner which, unusually, sported a figurehead: a crowned eagle with grasping claws. They were entertained at the captain's table by Captain Theo Kier and spent good-weather days in happy ignorance by the two-deck-high Pompeiian-style swimming pool. Irene's mother was going to stay in Paris while Vernon and Irene danced at the Casino de Deauville and earned cash to pay for two months of more relaxing in the sun, including a visit to Bessy Marbury and Elsie de Wolfe in Versailles. As they sailed the Atlantic on the Hamburg-registered liner, Serbia bowed to all Austria's demands – but that was not enough as Germany, seeking their 'place in the sun', urged aggression by their Austrian allies. The Prussian military were an arrogant and angry bunch, jealous of the British Empire, and needing an excuse to flaunt their potency, to deflate Slavic influence and force a Teutonic dominance in the Balkans. The abrupt and horrid death of a married couple, whose gloved hands failed to stop the bullets, as an excuse was quickly put aside by the Great Powers, much as were the newspapers carrying sensational news of the assassination by Vernon and Irene and a majority of others. It was all so *foreign*; the reactions so much puff and wind. If anything happened it would be over quickly; such things were. But like much else, war was changing: horses still gave armies their mobility but cavalry charges were as good as a pub dart against artillery and men with machine guns crouching in trenches surrounded by barbed wire. Few were prepared.

Vernon and Irene decided to stay with Mrs Foote in Paris and do some dancing at the Café de Paris for their 'Papa Louis'. None of them was prepared for the sullen atmosphere in the French capital, the anxiety and the suspicion and the whispers. There were rumours about runs on banks, gold bars and people being smuggled over borders. Not knowing what was true and what was false made it all more terrifying. Vernon and Irene saw familiar faces from England and America when they went to dance at supper. The society word from England was that children were fashionably playing war games with tin soldiers and that was as close to fighting as it would get; indeed, if there was trouble it would be like the Boer War, not something to fuss over. Talk was more of the Russian season and Caruso at Covent Garden, of Diaghilev's quarrel with Nijinsky rather than the one between Serbia and Austria.

In France, Irene said the gaiety had drained out of the Café de Paris. It had also gone from people's faces. Louis Barraya was reassuring but did not totally convince her. Armed with much insider knowledge, he told her Austria was carrying on as if it were dancing, going around in circles.

It was a writhing dance, around and around in circles, which belied the aggression, and did make many wonder, despite the evidence, if Germany really was on the rampage.

The evidence grew. Austria, with Germany's guns to their shoulder, played with Serbia and rejected all the concessions made. Which allowed Russia, always willing to venture into the Balkans and gain Mediterranean access, an opportunity to race to the aid of its loyal Slavic ally. That mobilisation in this 'family' of nations – all heads of state and many of their advisers were, it appeared, related – started the defence alliance with France. Even France, still smarting from the defeat by Bismarck's battering in 1870, was willing to agree with Serbia and Russia and, with Britain as the go-between, eager to find a compromise.

Vernon had been doing much better with his writing home. He'd spent at least fifteen minutes each day during the voyage on his correspondence, before becoming restless, but that was time enough to scribble out some news for Norwich. In return there were letters waiting for him and Irene care of the Café de Paris. The diplomatic manoeuvres of states had not penetrated East Anglia; doom, impending or otherwise, was unheard of.

There were names in the newspapers of people Vernon and Irene had talked about. It was the end of the 1914 season: Henley, Wimbledon, Ascot and the Harrow vs. Eton cricket match at Lord's were finished. It would soon be time for the grouse, for the guns to come out on the moors. The German Army commanders had a plan, rolled up and ready for many months, to make France powerless by attacking towards Paris through Belgium, whose neutrality was promised by British guarantee.

As the Whitehall mandarins deciphered diplomatic cables, Vernon read new letters from Norwich to Irene over dinner with Mrs Foote at their 'good luck' table by the dance floor of the Café de Paris. Irene recalled the other tables during their two weeks there having a stillness, a quiet chatter, patrons being more interested in conversation than the music or dancing.

One Friday evening, on 31 July, the night before they took the noon train to Deauville, they had a goodbye drink with 'Papa Louis'.

'Is there going to be a war?' Vernon asked him.

'*Je ne sais quoi*,' he replied with his usual shrug.

Vernon stayed jolly; there would be no problems. It would all be fun in Deauville. Irene wasn't sure, but she knew her husband trusted his luck. She remembered their last engagement at the Grand Casino in Normandy, when her mother had bankrolled some of Vernon's gambling: 'He was such a child about gambling, as in everything else. He never won anything in his life but he never lost faith in his luck.'

Mrs Foote stayed in Paris while Vernon and Irene, with Tell in the baggage car and Kiki yapping on Irene's lap, sat that Saturday afternoon of 1 August 1914 in a pleasant carriage, as Germany declared war on Russia. They arrived at the Hotel Normandy in Deauville and were met in the lobby of the hotel by their friend Will Stewart. It was a scene of confusion, guests and employees not knowing what was happening, what to do. Irene saw actress and singer Lillian Russell, the longtime companion of Diamond Jim Brady, 'lost' in a corner of the lobby but then she was gone, out the front of the hotel. She saw none of the usual society figures.

At the reception desk, instead of the August crush to get into the hotel, guests were trying to get out. Quickly, Vernon and Irene wanted to follow them. They did, but not before witnessing a remarkable scene in the great hall of the casino which for the first time was open to all. There were scores of country workers, men and women from the fields, singing the 'Marseillaise' which the Hotel Normandy's orchestra was playing as if their lives depended on it – which arguably they did. Everyone knew war was at their heels. All contracts were cancelled. That was the best of it.

On Monday 3 August, Germany declared war on France. On 4 August, German troops went into Belgium and Britain's ultimatum, that a state of war would exist between them if Belgian territory were violated, expired at 11 p.m. that day. With no German withdrawal, King George V, in Council, declared war. The Colonies and the Dominions were not consulted but their viceroys and governors-general duplicated the action. Tsar Nicholas II and King George appealed to their cousin, the Kaiser, but he ignored them. His Chancellor, von Bethmann-Hollweg, said the treaty guaranteeing Belgian neutrality was 'a scrap of paper'. He admitted Germany had breached international law. All hell was loosed.

The diplomatic days were over: in the corridors of power, and at the transport points of Europe. With Will Stewart, the dogs, and the time of a boat leaving from Trouville (the Channel port across the Touques estuary from Deauville), the Castles prepared to flee the Grand Casino and France and make for England. There was a refugee ship sailing that night from Le Havre. Vernon cashed American Express traveller's cheques and took the only currency going, Belgian francs, worth little more than the time of that particular day. It was a panic, the story of which Irene told shortly afterwards. She started with the essentials and that was that the baggage men had run off and they had to load their own 'trunks and hatboxes' on to an old horse and older cab and make for a boat.

The boat at Trouville was the first shock. So was the man in charge. The boat, a side-wheeler, had a tiny cabin and there were people all over it. The sneered-at Belgian francs turned the 'captain' into Pontius Pilate, but even that currency, in big enough bundles, made him dry his hands and help all of them, the dogs and hatboxes, aboard. The crossing to Le Havre was rough and crowded and long. Le Havre was a mess; everyone was going somewhere fast and because of that mostly going nowhere at all. Some were stumbling about in army boots too big for them, tripping over new uniform trousers pooled around their ankles. Will Stewart went to find tickets for England while Vernon and Irene guarded the baggage and dogs. He got the last of the transit papers but there was one proviso: no dogs on a refugee ship. They also had no quarantine paperwork for the animals. But Vernon was going nowhere without Tell.

'We'll wait for the next boat, that's all there is to it,' Vernon told Irene and Will Stewart.

There was no next boat scheduled. France was at war. There might never be another sailing to England. Who knew?

Vernon wouldn't let go of Tell's collar. Irene was going to smuggle Kiki under her cloak. Will Stewart kept consulting his watch. Vernon spotted a horse and cab and decided to take Tell to kennels, where he could leave the German shepherd temporarily. Irene raced around with him. It was frantic as they desperately rushed about Le Havre until Vernon found a vet who would, in return for promised cash, keep Tell safe until Vernon returned for him. Vernon checked the vet was too old to be conscripted and had plenty of supplies to feed Tell and the other animals in his kennels. He pointed to a straw-filled kennel and told Tell to get in. The he kissed the dog goodbye, shed a tear, and nobody spoke as he, Irene and Will Stewart headed for the refugee boat, which had little space on board. Passengers – at 600, double the capacity – rested where they could and many huddled on the decks. Irene kept Kiki under her coat and cloak when she found a bench in the smoking room. It was a perilous trip: destroyers and coastguard vessels checked and double-checked passengers and the boat's movements, sending it around and around to avoid areas of the Channel they believed had been mined by German forces. There was no food, no water or anything else to drink. It took seventeen hours to reach England. They found seats on a train for London and on board used newspaper to create a toilet for Kiki. Irene said Kiki was 'too immaculate' to go until they arrived at the St John's Wood home of Vernon's sister, Coralie, and Kiki ran into the garden.

In Britain, they found that people believed the war would be over by Christmas. The country thought that Russia and France, with some help from the British Army, would take care of Germany and Austria-Hungary on land while the Royal Navy would easily blockade the North Sea. Swiftly, combat on the *new* scale came as a devastating shock to Britain and its troops; also the realisation that Germany was technically more advanced in warfare. This war was to be the Great War. Vernon, in his desperation to rescue Tell, saw the signs earlier than most.

That evening at his sister's, he explained to Lawrence Grossmith his plan to return almost immediately to France. Grossmith was doubtful about that. He and Coralie, constantly sought after for musical-comedy roles, were wary of their own planned trip across the Atlantic to appear on Broadway in Paul Rubens and Guy Bolton's *Nobody Home*. It had music by Jerome Kern and was sure to be a success, but no one knew who would be at war with whom in a few days, never mind a few months. Germany was already on France's doorstep. Britain was at war with Germany.

Vernon could not be dissuaded. He said that he and Irene were more concerned about the dog than her mother. Mrs Foote was fluent in French, had been to school in Paris and had many friends there to help her arrange her return to America. Tell had no one to help him. All the society friends and contacts of Vernon's sister and brother-in-law, the young bloods, were trying to use any influence they or their families had to get a post with a cavalry unit at the front. That's where glory and heroes were made — or so the thinking went, two years before armoured tanks rolled into battle and all over the already destroyed 1914 preconceptions. It was these contacts, through Lawrence Grossmith, which did get Vernon an interview with the correct person at the Board of Agriculture in Whitehall. He left Irene in bed and went off first thing; by the afternoon he had permits to bring Tell back from France and into England, where he would be kept in quarantine kennels. Vernon's own kindness returned to help him when Elsie Janis, on stage in London, and her 'Ma' learned of his problem. 'Ma' was shrewd and had exchanged most of her paper money for gold coin. She gave Vernon a pocketful to buy his way back to France. It was tricky, as travel paperwork was kept for troops on the move, but charming Vernon talked his way on to a boat train. He was a happy man when he bounced off the Channel boat in France. Then, he was asked for his passport.

Yes, he had Tell's papers, but nothing to identify himself. He made a joke of having left his passport in some luggage and went off to the customs–immigration line. Vernon 'borrowed' a passport from another English traveller who went through officialdom first and then, through a chain-link fence, handed it back to Vernon. The document switch was risky, but in the pandemonium of the place he got away with it.

On the French coast, he found there was no direct boat to Le Havre. He'd have to go to Paris and travel on but escaping Paris was not simple: trains were reserved for troops and civilians needed a permit get to get on board. Vernon the actor took over and he talked himself into a permit and on to a departing train for Le Havre. The next problem arrived there with him: he couldn't recall the location of the vet – and Tell.

Which led to something of a French farce. Vernon galloped around Le Havre in a horse cab visiting vet after vet. He triumphed at his fifth attempt. With his faltering French delivered through a huge grin he explained that he had come to collect Tell, his dog. *His* dog? But it had been the other gentleman who had instructed him to treat the dog as a child and to give him to *no one else*. Vernon, frustrated and sensing Tell at the far end of the run of big cages, attempted to explain that Will Stewart was only translating what he, Vernon, had ordered. It was a poor go, not convincing.

The vet did agree to allow Vernon to see Tell. The dog bundled out of his cage, glad to be free of constraint, and leaped into Vernon's arms. That sealed the deal. Vernon bought a stiff metal leash from the vet and hooked it around his wrist; no one was taking Tell from him again. The impressive Board of Agriculture paperwork, gold coins and determination got them on the way to London and an arranged meeting with quarantine authorities at Victoria Station. No officials turned up, so Vernon and Tell took a taxi to St John's Wood.

It was a little victory for Vernon, but he began to think what more he could achieve; the world was in a mess. Many he'd talked to on his trip were enlisting. Irene said he was never quite the same after he returned from France with Tell: more restless – if that was possible – hating to sit still other than for meals and short bursts of animated conversations. He resented being pushed about. While he was in France, a cabled contract had arrived from New York, from the clever and wily producer Charlie Dillingham. Irving Berlin was writing the music and lyrics for a new show, his first fully scored Broadway musical; it was to be called *Watch Your Step* and Vernon and Irene were wanted to headline. Rehearsals began in late September.

Irving Berlin was a master of popular song, a bestseller of sheet music and records like 'Alexander's Ragtime Band' and 'Everybody's Doin' It', both important to Vernon and Irene, but this time his job was to supply dance numbers, upbeat rhythms and melodies, love songs, waltzes and, of course, ragtime, the beat to which all was happening. There would be instrumentals too. A couple of songs were ready, the risqué 'Lock Me in Your Harem

And Throw Away the Key' and 'Tango Tea'. Charlie Dillingham had enlisted the prolific and much-admired *Ziegfeld Follies* veteran Harry B. Smith to write the book for the show. The story, an excuse for Berlin songs and dancing by Vernon and Irene, was a trifle about a $2 million inheritance offered to any relative who has never been in love. Temptation is flourished before the only two claimants who, of course, fall in love.

Perfect material, all round, for the Castles. Yet Vernon, surprisingly, wasn't enthusiastic. If they were to accept the offer, they had to return quickly to America for rehearsals. Stephen Menken, who pulled strings with the shipping companies, had, together with his wife Alice, hosted soirées at which Vernon and Irene had danced. Even in such difficult circumstances, he was able to get reservations for them, Irene's mother, and Tell and Kiki, on the luxury Belfast-built liner the RMS *Olympic*. The ship's status as the largest ocean liner in the world had been taken only briefly by the *Titanic*. Mrs Foote cabled that she had arranged to meet them in Liverpool for sailing.

Before they took the train north, Vernon and Irene let the dogs loose in Coralie's garden for a run around. Irene said Vernon had been fussing around during those drawing daylight days of mid-August 1914, and now he came out with it.

'I've been thinking about this war business, darling. I think it's my duty to enlist.'

In Irene's most thoughtful published remembrance of that moment, she says: 'I looked at him standing there. I could almost see him lying dead or wounded on a muddy field with no one to look after him, all because he had insisted on going to war. Vernon was very serious. He so wanted to enlist. I fear I was responsible for his not doing so.

'It wasn't our fight and he was more American than he was

English, and Huns couldn't last in an all-out war, everybody knew that.

'I cried bitterly and tried to persuade him to think it over before he made such a serious decision… I prevailed, but my victory in this matter was only for a short time. He was resolved to go to war from the time he came back from France with Tell… I don't think my logic even touched him.

'Yet, he was devoted to me. He could not stand to see my cry. He, finally, agreed to sail for America…'

Chapter Nine
Dressed to Kill

'Over there, over there,
Send the word, send the word over there
That the Yanks are coming, the Yanks are coming
The drums rum-tumming everywhere.
So prepare, say a prayer,
Send the word, send the word to beware
We'll be over, we're coming over,
And we won't come back till it's over, over there.'
George M. Cohan, 'Over There', 1917

Vernon wanted to be over there. He was distraught. With his
European summer in the sun rudely interrupted by Kaiser
Bill, exposing him to so much emotional turmoil, he became a
misery. He was torn by patriotism and the thought of forsaking
Irene for the front line. For once, he was a busy man who couldn't
be busy. His concentration would not settle to provide a solution.
Nothing seemed to help.

Irene did. When they sailed back to America on the *Olympic*,
Irene and her mother had arranged to switch Vernon's thinking
away from war and back to the dance floor. There was much
distress and many passengers were ill at ease. War in Europe had

been declared; the *Olympic* was only the greatest liner in the world because the *Titanic* had sunk sailing the very route they were at this moment on. There was a need for distraction. A gala dance on 27 August 1914, held on the high seas in a palm-tree-decorated room off the Grand Staircase, along from the Café Veranda, was their answer.

It was a success and brought some life and humour back to Vernon, who delighted the passengers with his antics and his dancing. As did the plans for *Watch Your Step*. Charles Dillingham had a strong sense of the popular and wanted to blend ragtime and the dancing mania into a Broadway show. He'd been at work for months. Clearly, Vernon and Irene, the lord and lady of the dance, were a major marketing coup, an insurance against the work of the Broadway newcomer, Irving Berlin. Yet it was a slow process and rehearsal dates were endlessly pushed back. Irene saw Vernon getting edgy and employed the tactic that had worked on the *Olympic*. It brought a smile beneath his straw boater. They would make some big spending money doing a few weeks of vaudeville. They signed with Keith-Albee Corporation and there was little time to dwell on war. They danced the tango, the maxixe, the one-step, the polka – and the foxtrot.

Vernon and Irene gave ongoing life to the foxtrot and with it the basics of an endless parade of dances and the easy rhythm of popular songs. Also, although much argued, it was a vital part in the birth of the blues. The foxtrot was essentially the steps they had danced for Mrs Stuyvesant Fish and, to her enduring happiness, named the 'Fish Walk'. It developed during the Whirlwind Tour when James Europe, experimenting at the piano, liked the slower rhythms of 'Memphis Blues' created by William 'W. C.' Handy, the influential 'father of the blues'. It was the first blues song Handy had written and he said James Europe, who believed in it as dance music, was the first band leader to play it.

Europe played it for Vernon and Irene as they toured America. He asked Vernon if it worked as a dance, despite its contrast to the faster Castle Walk and one-step. Vernon wasn't convinced the public wanted a slow tempo; the demand then was for 'staccato music'. Yet Vernon worked with Irene and he created some movements: when they danced them at private parties, the compilation of steps was a hit. It was also significant in that it proved again that Vernon and Irene's ragtime dancing speeded the acceptance of black music by white Americans and Europeans. The 'Fish Walk', with new breaks in rhythm, was now the foxtrot. The earliest version worked on music which had a 4/4 rhythm at about forty bars to the minute; half the tempo of the one-step. Sixteen bars was normal but the foxtrot worked on twelve and twenty bars and the unlikely breaks.

Vernon put it in less technical terms for readers of *Ladies' Home Journal*. In a social-barrier-breaking how-to-dance series of three two-page articles, published in October, November and December 1914, and written specifically for the austere – and previously ragtime-resistant – national magazine, his words were illustrated by drawings of dance steps:

If you will play an ordinary 'rag' half as fast as you would play it for the one-step, you will have a pretty good idea of the music and the tempo. Once you listened to the music you will find absolutely no difficulty in dancing to it, but the natural inclination is either to dance very fast steps double time to the music or very slow steps with it. It's best to combine the two, alternating between two and four steps to the bar. By doing so you not only make the dance comfortable but you also make it possible to do a great variety of easy and amusing steps.

The dance had two slow steps – a glide, stride or drag – and four fast – hop, kick and stop – and Vernon explained: 'This drag is a very old Negro step, often called "Get over, Sal".'

It took the sensitive readers of *Ladies' Home Journal* on the hop. Some wrote in about the need for smelling salts, to get over these sensational revelations about modern dancing. Their distress, however, had eased Vernon's. The work on the foxtrot occupied him. He was rightly convinced that this was a dance that would last. The more he was asked about it, the more he gave credit to James Europe for the creation he and Irene had originally named the 'Bunny Hug'. In turn, the orchestra leader was quizzed by newspapers (for dancing news was headline material) about the origins of this foxtrot. No one gave much notice to vaudeville comedian Harry Fox's claim to the dance, but all listened to James Europe when he spoke to the *New York Tribune* at the end of November 1914. He had an academic authority about him:

There is much interest in the growth of the modern dances in the fact that they were all danced and played by us Negroes long before the whites took them up. One of my own musicians, William Tyres, wrote the first tango in America as far back as the Spanish–American War. They were the essentially Negro dances, played and danced by Negroes alone. The same may be said of the foxtrot, this season the most popular of dances. Mr Castle has generously given me credit for the foxtrot, yet the credit, as I have said, really belongs to Mr Handy. You see, then, that both the tango and the foxtrot are Negro dances, as is the one-step. The one-step is the national dance of the Negro, the Negro is always walking in his dances.

The foxtrot was immediately included in the *Watch Your Step* programme, with Irving Berlin delivering popularity in songs for the dances, such as 'Show Us How to Do the Foxtrot', 'The Syncopated Walk' – this *was* the first syncopated musical – and many others, including the waltz number, 'What Is Love?' What, indeed?

Berlin was a wonderful romantic and was present for many rehearsals of *Watch Your Step*. Musical historians say he was captured by Vernon and Irene's 'Hesitation Waltz' – it suspends the second beat – and he used the effect a decade later, when much else had changed, for 'What'll I Do, What'll I Do'. The hesitation on the third beat is credited with giving the song everlasting charm, an epistle to loss and uncertainty.

What was a definite during the long rehearsals and out-of-town tryouts of *Watch Your Step* was that the troublesome behaviour of one William Claude Dukenfield, a.k.a. W. C. Fields, could not go on; he was, it seems, continually mixing his metaphors with his martinis. His comic turn, among many vaudeville acts conjured into the music, drama and dance, were taken out of the production. Which gave more time for dancing. Irene (on the posters as Mrs Vernon Castle) danced the foxtrot playing herself, Vernon was 'The Dancing Instructor', who with an inside joke was the man 'who invented the steps you watch'.

It was not their choice but the show marked their first appearances without the back-up of James Europe and his orchestra. Still, they found time to be the star attraction – 'The Most Famous Couple in America' – when their friend staged a grand display of dancing and music, once again at the Manhattan

Casino in Harlem. James Europe's orchestra continued to provide the music for the dance classes at Castle House, so when Vernon and Irene went into another club venture negotiated by Bessy Marbury, it was his twenty-piece orchestra that was onstage.

The new venture was on the top floor of the Shubert Brothers' Forty-Fourth Street Theatre and they called it 'Castles in the Air'. To complement the rooftop venue there was the Castle Club in the basement, a prototype speakeasy, and the haunt of thirsty youth-about-town like Scott Fitzgerald. Vernon and Irene (for their $1,500 a week) were required to make appearances at the clubs after the theatre. Luckily, they had the energy to live up to their billing as the most celebrated couple this side of the moon. Their stars were soaring. With *Watch Your Step*, the Castles got the audiences in; their dancing and Irving Berlin's music had them returning repeatedly. Charles Dillingham's production of dance and ragtime opened at the New Amsterdam Theatre on Forty-Second Street, walking distance from Castles in the Air, on 8 December 1914.

We can only puzzle what sort of Christmas that Irving Berlin was dreaming about – but his first Broadway show was a present, a big one, for Broadway. It broke box-office records from opening night. It ran and ran and ran. Many gave the credit to Vernon and the foxtrot, others to Irving Berlin's remarkable talents, but Irene would acknowledge no other theory than her own: it was her dress that was the killer, that won the audience. 'The costume I wore opening night was probably the loveliest costume the world has ever seen.'

Well, no equivocation there. This creation was the work of Lucile Duff Gordon and was a marvel which Elsie de Wolfe compared to a Fragonard. The material – twelve yards of it went around the bottom – was chiffon in blue-grey and there was silver brocade and grey fox and a cloak and emerald and green satin; it was quite a bundle of fashion. When she wore it, Irene believed she was in heaven.

The costume, which became part of the New York Metropolitan Museum's permanent collection, was as remarkable as it was theatrical. It did cause a fuss. The next morning when Lady Duff Gordon arrived at the premises of Lucile she found a queue of women waiting for her. They all ordered copies of the dress. Within days, orders had arrived from all over the country; within weeks Irene said that when she danced at Castles in the Air after the theatre, there would be at least half a dozen women wearing the dress in different colours. Irene bowed to the genius of Lucile: 'Even if she had never done another thing, she would have been remembered for that one beautiful dress, a masterpiece which was to influence style for a long time.'

Irene herself was in huge demand as a model. There were photographic sessions, with sets of pictures of Irene in Lucile's gowns appearing in *Vogue* and *Harper's Bazaar* and *Town and Country*. The stout, full-figured Edwardian look was disdained. Narrow hips, flat chests, a slim silhouette: that was what was chic. Cigarette sales increased; smoking quelled the appetite, or so the tobacco impresarios implied. 'Cures' were introduced for dieting. Slimming pills appeared over the counter and on the black market and, along with cocaine, were constantly on offer. Lucile, whom Hearst was now paying more for her columns, aimed at a slender style; the former 20 square yards of fabric for every dress now scaled to a little more than half that. Irene, without help, was *the* image for it all: graceful and gamine.

That year, in 1915, the American cosmetic companies spent $1.5 million on advertising. That sum quickly soared by ten and more times, along with the demand of modern women like Irene. For the first time, women were being told they could look beautiful, and that it was as acceptable for ordinary women to aspire to and to enjoy being lovely, as it was to dance. They found it was a contentment which required compromise. The 1907 innovation of French chemist Eugène Paul Louis Schueller's permanent hair dye, Oréale, was now generally acceptable and the catalyst for the fortunes of the world's leading beauty company, L'Oréal.

Vernon was a bit of a wardrobe himself: with his straw boater, blue blazers and white ducks, his brown-and-white boardwalk shoes, the spats and the smile, the pearl-handled cane and any combination of the previous, his tailless dancing suits, the image of a man lifted with aimless abandon above it all... ah, he *appeared* in paradise.

Admirably, he never disclosed any personal turmoil to anyone but Irene. She saw how restless he was when they returned to 120 Lexington Avenue each evening after their obligations were complete. Exhausted, she would soon be asleep in bed. Vernon would sit in his study and work his way through the newspapers, piled as high as his desk chair, and read, sometimes until dawn, the news from Europe, the news of the Great War. Yet he was still making the news himself. The *Dramatic Mirror* offered the popular outside view of them as the winter of 1915 rushed on: 'Vernon and Irene Castle are our supreme ballroom artists, possessing distinction, intelligence, delicacy of dance, and what is termed in the varieties – class.'

Vernon and Irene had other, even more ardent, admirers. Vernon enthralled women. While cards were arriving in Irene's dressing room with gentlemen pleading to take her to dinner, Vernon was the subject of endless infatuations and flirtations. Irene, in a practical moment, saw Vernon's ladies as good for business.

Vernon was often stalked. Women would turn up at the theatre or the Long Island house claiming they wanted to discuss dancing; his fans ranged from debutantes to dowagers. Irene suspected the 'great beauty', *Follies* showgirl Olive Thomas, had her hooks in Vernon. He took his mind off war and the women by playing polo, for Irene explained: 'Deep down, Vernon and I had a devotion for each other which no amount of outside interference or momentary piques of jealousy could destroy.'

A welcome visitor was the cowboy and vaudevillian Will Rogers, who regularly joined other friends of Vernon's for a polo match at a field close to the Manhasset house. The amiable Rogers was much taken by Vernon. He mentions him and his own first polo-playing appearance in his memoirs: 'I will tell you how I knew Vernon was game. He had a polo team and had been playing quite a while. At least, he knew the rules. The first day I played I didn't know a polo ball from Bolo Pasha. I could ride but I couldn't hit the ball with a rake. I was in everybody's way, missing the ball farther each lick.

'Finally, I came a-tearing across at right angles at Castle, thinking I would scare the dancer off the ball. It was a foul, as I was crossing him.

'The Englishman didn't scare worth a darn, he kept a-coming at me too.

'We hit, and there were dancers, horses and rope-throwers scattered over all of Long Island. What did he say when we got up? "That's all right. I did that too, when I was learning."

'We all had many a tilt at him and he never flinched.'

Rogers's vaudeville rope trick act and down-home humour started him on a glorious career but 'Oklahoma's Favorite Son' didn't make *Laughing Bill Hyde*, his first, silent, film, until 1918. Vernon and Irene, however, débuted at the movies some three years earlier than that. Vernon was a wonderful leading man, Irene a screen siren, in *The Whirl of Life*, Vernon's dramatisation of their own life. It was made a year after Pearl White survived the *Perils of Pauline* and such make-believe adventure, black-hatted villains with evil moustaches and intent, was written with relish into the story. Vernon's friends James Europe and Buddy Gilmore had roles along with Walter Ash and a string of Broadway actors. The other leading man was Tell, the German shepherd, with whom Vernon rescues the kidnapped Irene in the final reels. Of course, the big finale was Vernon and Irene, resplendent in evening dress – white tie and another above-the-ankles Lucile gown – dancing. Animated, their attraction whirls out, as the title intends, on the flickering screen, and they look even younger than they were, which was not too far into adulthood. They were a brand name and now they were dancers *and* actors on stage and screen.

The Whirl of Life received good reviews (especially from Mr Hearst's newspapers) and played at cinemas throughout America, including in the South where film distributors had no control over casting. Progress would sort that.

Irene did everything she could to keep Vernon's mind occupied. They danced benefits for animal charities – collecting more 'little friends' every time – went horse racing... and to all those outside of their inner circle appeared content. Yet Vernon was becoming more detached. He was disturbed by the sinking of the *Lusitania*, torpedoed off the Irish coast by a German submarine on 7 May 1915, while sailing to Liverpool from New York City; a familiar and regular route for Vernon and Irene.

He read every detail in the newspapers: the *Lusitania* had started to list dramatically on one side, and went down in eighteen minutes; 1,198 passengers and crew died. There was no death list at first and it was Charles Dillingham who told him that Charles

Frohman, their producer from *The Sunshine Girl* and Dillingham's close friend, had perished at sea. Vernon sought increasingly more detail about North Atlantic submarine warfare and Germany's declaration of a warzone around Britain. He was angry that the German Embassy in Washington, DC had had the temerity to place an advertisement – 'an advertisement!' – in American newspapers warning potential passengers on the *Lusitania* to stay away. It was ridiculous. President Woodrow Wilson had promised the United States would not get involved with a war in Europe; Vernon had no time for Wilson.

Letters from home were arriving all the time. They were full of detail of the zeppelin attacks in Norfolk and Suffolk and his father gave news of the UFOs, the ugly flying objects, over Norwich. The first zeppelin raid on Britain was on 19 January 1915, and was spotted early from the village of Hingham, seventeen miles from Norwich. The 'zeppo' turned towards Great Yarmouth and delivered nine high-explosive bombs, killing two people and doing massive damage; it delivered more destruction on King's Lynn.

Vernon was getting the local details from his family. With each letter there was more information of zeppelin-inflicted death and destruction near Norwich or the surrounding area. The UFOs were also all over Suffolk, and American newspapers recounted the raids, reporting this letter from a woman in Woodbridge. The chatty banality makes the message terrifying. It spooked people like Vernon. He could see his family under attack. The remains of Mrs Rose's letter to her brother, as written, reads:

I have been trying to get a photo of the damage caused by the terrible zeppelin raid here, but no one was allowed to take them, though I know there have been 'snaps' taken by private individuals and if I can happen with one I'll send it to you. I'll try and detail it as far as I can remember.

I went down the town about 9' o'clock that evening, and heard the soldiers had all been called out, and people seemed rather concerned, although there had been false alarms before. Somehow it seemed different and we came back home again. Soon after, another batch of soldiers marched by with rifles – all so quiet and dark. We waited till nearly 10 o'clock and then, as there seemed no trouble, I felt tired out and decided I'd go to bed.

Walter was listening at the front bedroom window, as he felt there was something 'brewing', and just after, he came in and said he thought I ought not to get into bed as he could hear a zeppelin in the distance. I waited a minute and then he ran in again and said we had to get downstairs at once. I scrambled on some clothes and down we came, groping in the dark. It was a horrid experience. When we got to the bottom of the stairs, Walter said he'd just run to the door, and see if he could locate the sound, as the soldiers had all started firing their rifles.

When he got to the door and looked out he darted back in a hurry, for the zeppelin appeared just going over the corner of the house, and we made for the cellar; but before we could get to the door there was a very brilliant flash and then a terrific explosion. How we got down the cellar steps I can't say. We stood there huddled up, praying to be kept safe. The din was simply indescribable, what with the guns crackling all round, the row of the zeppelin and explosions and the falling of masonry, etc. No one could possibly imagine the awful feeling of a raid. The experience is simply unimaginable. The agonising suspense, and never knowing where the next bomb will drop.

Well, the worst damage was done on St John's Hill. The bomb here dropped on the pavement in front of Mr Welton's front door. The house was completely wrecked, but with the exception of Lily and Mrs Welton being slightly cut and bruised, none of the others were hurt; but Mr and Mrs Tyler (bootmaker), who lived opposite, were both killed outright, and their house absolutely smashed up; also the one on the other side, and all that side of the corner house (the front of which looks out into St John's Hill). Clarke's shaving saloon on the opposite corner was smashed up, and the little houses that run along New Street, opposite St John's Hill, were likewise smashed considerably. As for glass; well, there wasn't a window left – not a whole pane left anywhere. Five persons were killed here and several injured.

When the zep moved on it dropped another bomb up Castle Street in Whitbread's garden, but it fell into an apple tree, which it rooted up in fragments and made a round hole about 16 ft. in diameter. The apples were sent many yards away. Another bomb (incendiary) fell in Stett's garden, and set fire to his greenhouse and pigstys [sic], and the pigs were roasted alive. This was eventually put out. Next was dropped on the stables of the Wagon and Horses, which were reduced to bricks and dust, and a pony was killed. The zep then altered its course, and went along over the Ipswich roadway. An incendiary bomb was dropped just outside the house where the Smiths of Melton now live; it's that new house, and they were away at the time. The next-door neighbour ran in and put it out, or the house would have caught. Another was dropped right down through the middle of a new house being built, all finished but the roof. After that they made for Ipswich, but big guns were fired on them and they altered their course.

As Vernon read the reports, he believed he must alter course too – but there was Irene and his responsibilities to consider. He had to organise and then take his place in combat.

More immediate, financially, was the need for Vernon and Irene to get back onstage with *Watch Your Step*. The show was such a hit Charles Dillingham signed new contracts guaranteeing them more than $100,000 a year. They had the Long Island home and Lexington Avenue to look after and an expanding family. A casual count of their animals – most of whom travelled with them – was astonishing. Their tour managers had to give early warning to the railways of the Castles' 'livestock'. Manager J. Clyde Rigby's list from 1915 reads exactly like this: 'Nine monkeys, 3 German sheep (police) dogs, 2 Belgian griffons, 11 bulldogs (10 full English and Boston and 1 French), 1 Russian wolfhound, 7 parrots, 2 Angora and 2 Persian cats, 4 (small Florida) alligators, 5 cockatoos, 1 black bear, 7 guinea pigs, 27 canaries, a large assortment of rabbits, and any number of white mice and rats.'

That didn't count Rastus. The round-faced French Guinea was Irene's favourite monkey and went everywhere in her arms. Pullman, first class. When Irene applied her stage make-up the ever-present Rastus applied lipstick, eye pencil and rouge to his cheeks.

The Castles' stars were soaring so high: this was their walking-on-water moment. As it was for many in London – as society circles behaved excessively; excessive as the war. Monkeys were very favourite. Affluent hipsters like those in Lady Diana Cooper's set struggled to be the most unorthodox. A phenomenon was the Italian lost soul, Luisa, Marchesa Casati Stampa di Soncino, who went to parties with charlatans-about-town, boa constrictors and albino blackbirds – and always, always, mauve monkeys. Rastus stuck to primary colours. Irene busied herself with lesser decorated animals when the Castle circus went on the road with *Watch Your Step* to Boston and then Chicago, where they appeared at the original Rector's for supper shows.

Vernon had his eye on the money and the newspapers. He was so aware that he had not been in the war from the first. This guilt was continually clacking around in his brain, syncopated, like a rag he had to dance to. He had danced with Irene to raise funds for Belgian relief and other wartime charities but that was nothing. He had been in America for nearly a decade, he was married to an American, he liked Americans and living there but: he was an Englishman. He owed all his loyalty to Britain. The show was moving on to Philadelphia, but before it did Vernon asked Charles Dillingham for a quiet drink. He explained. The producer, still hurting from the loss of his friend on the *Lusitania*, understood. Vernon said he would leave when a replacement was found and ready to perform. Irene was quiet as she heard the news. She later said she knew by then not to argue.

His decision made, Vernon's irritability vanished. By taking on a purpose he had purpose. Vernon wanted to be a pilot, which had all the adulation and glamour, the flying gear and the clever kit, the romance... and a life expectancy, on average, of three weeks. There was always a demand for qualified pilots. He enlisted with the Imperial Royal Flying Corps (IRFC) and joined the Canadian 84th Squadron. Flying machines were, like machine guns and underwater boats, all *new* tools of destruction and despair. Military leaders had regarded planes as information gatherers: perfect for reconnaissance, not for warfare. The Great War was beginning to make flying practical and pilots into heroes, flying helmets fashionable; goggles loose around the neck the chic accoutrement. Admirers would buy the airmen a drink and offer the bar; girls a shy kiss and the honeymoon suite. These fliers, these pilots, were going where few had gone before.

Adventures above the clouds, piloting wood and fabric strung together with piano wire, attracted the cavalier and talented and often added to the stars in the sky. The odds were against Vernon, aged twenty-eight, being one: he was tall for a cockpit, past the optimum age for a fighter pilot, reflexes start to go in your teens; he beat them like he did his drums, with an exceptional athleticism and dedication.

It took time. He arranged to pay for his own flying lessons, allowing him to offset his opsimathy and 'jump the queue into the air' when he got to England. With a pilot's licence, he could avoid the parade ground and be off to fight in France. He didn't need Kitchener; he was planning his own war. He did need the licence. Irene had her own private funds and said she'd 'buy' his Minerva car for $1,000 and keep it for his return. He'd given away two polo ponies; she'd look after the others and the rest of their menagerie. A dog-lover friend was 'buying' Tell for $1,000 but that was all gesture, the dog was too old to be prized by money; for the buyer, Ben Throop, it was a way to help out Vernon. He had many friends who supported him. He kissed Irene goodbye in their hotel room. She felt 'too desolate' to go to the train station with him.

He began training on twenty acres of tract land east of Newport News, Virginia, on 10 December 1915, the opening day of the Atlantic Coast Aeronautical Station and its flying school. Glenn Hammond Curtiss, the barnstorming aviation pioneer and a founder of America's aircraft industry, chose Newport News as it offered the most equitable climate, winter and summer, on the Atlantic coast. His work was experimental, including the development of a 'hydro-aeroplane' (these would come to be known as flying boats and seaplanes); his base a legendary source of amazing flying machines and exploits – and daring pilots like Vernon Castle.

Chapter Ten

Dancing on Air

'What'll I do
When you are far away
And I am blue
What'll I do?'
Irving Berlin, 'What'll I Do?', 1924

Vernon was going too fast. He was in a hurry but that was no mitigation for Patrolman Walter Smith of the Newport News Police Department (Traffic Control). These flying boys might be a big deal in the sky but down here on God's earth, on the roads of Virginia, they had to obey the law of Nature and, of course, the state. Mr Castle was driving unnaturally fast in his 1914 Mercer Raceabout on 21 January 1916. The police officer made that clear to the court. It was 'unnatural'. The speed limit was 15 mph. Mr Castle was driving at nearly 30 mph.

This vehicular misdemeanour meant a $2 speeding ticket for Vernon and a front-page story for the *Daily Press*: 'Vernon Castle, dancer and aeronautical student, yesterday was summoned to appear in the police court this morning on a charge of exceeding the speed limit in his automobile. Patrolman Smith, who is responsible for his predicament, avers that the dancer was rushing down Jefferson Avenue to the municipal small-boat harbour in a racing car at a speed of something like 30 miles an hour.'

It was celebrity journalism. Vernon's run from the Chamberlin Hotel at Old Point Comfort in Hampton to the airfield and training was a daily cat-and-mouse game with the traffic police; he was always polite and always paid his traffic ticket. Shoved further back in the newspaper was the arrival at the airfield of Steve MacGordon, one of the most renowned of fliers; he held the world record for looping the loop: twenty-one loops in eighteen minutes. For Vernon and the war effort, that was much more important news.

MacGordon was joining test pilot Victor Carlstrom, a former Wyoming cowboy, in flight instruction. Carlstrom was an intuitive instructor and Vernon his perfect pupil. With MacGordon leading classes, the cowboy-flier was hands-on teaching Vernon and the flamboyant flyboy Harold Marcellus 'Buck' Gallop.

These testosterone-packed characters were more interested in taking on the Red Baron than Patrolman Smith. There were thousands of young men like Vernon and Buck Gallop throughout America and Canada who wanted into the war and they were drawn to Newport News by Curtiss and his adviser, Captain Thomas Scott Baldwin: this was the man who had the final word on experiments, be it the planes or the pilots who flew them. Every day newspapers reported the exploits of the Red Baron, Rittmeister Manfred, Freiherr von Richthofen, and his partner, the younger and almost as deadly Oberleutnant Ernst Udet. Hauptmann Oswald Boelcke trumped all the aces. The creator of air-warfare tactics, Boelcke had won the Iron Cross – the Blue Max would follow – before Vernon was allowed in a cockpit.

The more the flying-school pupils read about the exploits of the German airmen, the quicker they wanted to fight them. Vernon had no concerns about taking on these already experienced forces. He, and very few did, had barely any conception of it. Kaiser Bill's favourite, Boelcke, a graduate of *Flieger-Abteilung 13* (Aviation Section 13), was an influence on all fighter pilots. Vernon and the others had to learn how to stay alive in the skies. Strangely, Boelcke helped them. As they trained in early 1916, he published 'rules' known as *Dicta Boelcke*:

Try to secure the upper hand before attacking. If possible, keep the sun behind you.

Always continue with an attack you have begun.

Only fire at close range, and then only when the opponent is properly in your sights.

You should always try to keep your eye on your opponent, and never let yourself be deceived by ruses.

In any type of attack, it is essential to assail your opponent from behind.

If your opponent dives on you, do not try to get around his attack, but fly to meet it.

When over the enemy's lines, never forget your own line of retreat.

Tip for Squadrons: In principle, it is better to attack in groups of four or six. Avoid two aircraft attacking the same opponent.

Suddenly, it was all so much more real for all the pupils: 'Over There' was a lot closer. There were thirty would-be aviators in the first intake: twenty-eight Canadians, American Buck Gallop, and Vernon, who had paid $800 to be part of it. Their instruction was aboard an aircraft designed by Glenn Curtiss, the JN-4D 'Jenny', which was a two-seater biplane of no notable technical brilliance, other than it stayed up in the air. It was a dependable training plane (95 per cent of American and Canadian wartime pilots learned to fly on it) and instruction was intensive and strict.

Vernon and Irene wrote back and forth. Nevertheless, she admitted: 'I've no idea what might be happening to my husband down in Virginia.' She toured with *Watch Your Step* as he worked to complete fifty hours of flight instruction. The course ran from six to eight weeks and began with the trainee in the front seat and, depending on how good the pupil was, four to ten hours of dual-control instruction. The instructors did not always follow the seating procedure but wherever their location, they had to yell instructions and were often muted by the whistling air and the impolite roars of the engine. When it was time for Vernon to fly solo, he was moved to the back seat; the Jenny was always flown solo from the back seat. Vernon had to complete twenty-four hours of solo flight and then a further sixteen hours of cross-country flying before he qualified for his 'wings'. The schedule was pressed harder as the war, which they said would be but a trifle, persisted in its overall damnation.

Vernon loved being in the skies. There was a freedom, a mastering of your own destiny. Up to a point. The 'headmaster' of the flying school was Captain Tom Baldwin, who said the theatrical star was his star pupil: 'Some men simply never could learn to fly, while others take to it at once. He is a born airman for he has the touch in his hands. That is essential, and he is one of the most apt pupils I have ever seen.' Vernon had all the bravado, the theatricality of his profession, of his life, with his goggles dangling from his neck so everyone knew he was a flier; he backed up that superficial, easy stuff with a gift for flying, for navigation and control of the 'craft, for barrel rolls and loops, for

– as Vic Carlstrom described it – being so graceful, for dancing *on* the air. Vernon even learned how to make an Immelmann turn, a dogfight tactic named after German pilot Max Immelmann: an aerobatic looping which swiftly repositions an aircraft at a higher altitude.

All candidates were required to do a final flight test: complete ten figure-eights, one successful dead-stick landing from an altitude of 1,000 feet, and a landing within 150 feet of a predetermined spot; dead-stick landings are performed with the engine switched off. It makes it trickier but it's good to know you can do it if you've got the Red Baron on your tail. Enrico Caruso recorded 'O Sole Mio' – on a 12-inch disc – for the Victor Talking Machine Company on 5 February 1916, the same day Vernon completed a perfect dead-stick approach and landing – and his instruction. He received his graduation certificate from the Atlantic Coast Aeronautic School on 9 February 1916. Irene had the Caruso record for him, a present, when they met for a farewell night which had been complex to arrange. *Watch Your Step* was playing in Indianapolis and if they were to meet, it had to be there – and briefly; Irene had to play St Louis the next night.

The future dominated their conversation, what they would do when war ended and mostly it involved children and acres of land and horses and more children and a farm and animals on that farm which the children they'd never had time for would play with. The dreams gushed lavishly out shadowed by the unsaid dark questions of what might happen until show time arrived. Vernon found a corner in a box to watch but was spotted by Irene's co-star and his friend, the vaudeville comic Frank Tinney. He grabbed Vernon on to the stage and the audience went wild, pleading for the Castles to dance for them. It was difficult for

Irene with her upset over the next day's farewell in St Louis. But dance they did, to the adoration of the cast and crew and the audience who stood with admiring applause, which rather embarrassed Vernon. Irene had resolved to help Vernon be brave. They went on to St Louis and the next day at the city's station, on a wet Monday morning, they said goodbye in such a dither they fumbled the words they had both rehearsed for the moment. It made it easier and, of course, harder. Irene admitted she gave the worst performance of her life at the theatre that evening. Her thoughts, unlike the show, were not entertaining. She felt lonely and lost in what was an ever more turbulent world. She had her pride in Vernon to help. But he wasn't there to hold her.

Charles Dillingham, the consummate showman, had witnessed the audience reaction to this 'goodbye dance'. He was dominated by commercial considerations but did have sentimental aspirations: he could make money and help Vernon. He made enquiries and then offered Vernon and Irene an idea and a deal: a farewell show at the Hippodrome in New York with 'The Stars and Stripes Forever' composer John Philip Sousa conducting the music. It was a bonus: cash for Vernon to take with him to war, and a little more time together. The only downside was marching-band man Sousa, who didn't quite have the ragtime cachet of James Europe. Or the beat. Contracts signed, Charles Dillingham hired the extravagantly sized New York Hippodrome Theatre for the Vernon and Irene farewell.

The rest was a tactical operation. Vernon would speed, he travelled no other way, from Newport News, while Irene took the train east while another stood by, with one carriage for her, through the colonnades and vast architectural splendour of Pennsylvania Station, ready to take her from New York in time for Monday's opening night of *Watch Your Step* in Pittsburg. The show, wherever it was happening, had to go on. Newspaper reports from early 1916 of the one in Europe indicated that the armies of all the nations at war were bleeding to death. There was also an urgent push to establish supremacy in the air: part of Vernon's mission.

At the Hippodrome, with seats for 5,300 and a stage stretching 100 by 200 feet, their appearance was also part of a propaganda drive. British diplomats and their sympathetic US counterparts had encouraged the fanfare farewell, a celebration of courage, a not-too-subliminal appeal for support. Woodrow Wilson was attempting to stay in the Oval Office by keeping America out of international conflict, but he was on the cusp, he had to be, of taking on Pancho Villa and the revolution in Mexico. Charles Dillingham, who had an ongoing association with the Hippodrome on Sixth Avenue, simply wanted to put on a show. The reception of Vernon and Irene was astonishing, even to him. They really were the most famous couple in the world. Everybody wanted to see them dance. All the seats were sold and nearly 600 fans and friends were allowed to sit on the stage. Vernon pleaded with a grand smile that he and Irene had not been left enough room to dance. They would try to manage, he said. They did.

Irene described what she wore: 'a full grey chiffon skirt; a navy-blue braided bodice with the IRFC wings sewn on to it; a Scotch cap tilted over one eye, because it most resembled a Flying Corps cap.' She admitted to some nerves 'at the thought of dancing with him to that packed house without the slightest hint of rehearsal' but happily added: 'There was no need for nervousness. As we swept out on to the stage we were one again and we flowed into our old dances without the slightest miscue or hesitation.'

All accounts hold up this box-office-record-breaking evening in mid-Manhattan as a flag-waving curtain-up for many Americans regarding the fighting in Europe. There was most certainly no ambivalence where or why Vernon Castle was going. Irene, her tension angry at itself, complained that John Philip Sousa was conducting a military march, not a ragtime dance. Vernon held her closer, told her it was of no consequence, and whispered 'I love you' in her ear. At that, she admitted: 'It didn't matter. Nothing did for the moment. We had each other and we were dancing.'

The crowd were as emotional as Vernon and Irene. They whistled and shouted and clapped and cheered. Many cried and cried. Flowers in eloquently gathered floral tributes were handed over the footlights for Irene. Vernon was given an aeroplane of flowers made just for him.

The audience, so many of them young, teens with parents, groups in their twenties, crowded at the stage door, a scene public relations people lie in bed dreaming about. Even the weather, cold, but crisp, making the overcoat finery and the dresses flirting the tops of shoes, the fur wraps huddled at the neck, romantic in gaslight, was wonderful: mystical PR. For Vernon and Irene the crowd was another challenge to conquer. Excitement whooshed them through it and she said neither of them could believe the adoration. It was the biggest crowd they'd ever performed for, an audience which had exclusively come to see them dance. At Pennsylvania Station Irene's train was ready to depart leaving no time for emotional farewells. It was one kiss and Irene was sitting back in her private carriage revelling in the privilege, feeling like a Queen.

While Irene enjoyed her enchantment, it was late that evening when Vernon arrived in Harlem, where James Europe and Buddy Gilmore were playing. He apologised again for Sousa working the Hippodrome but Charles Dillingham had contractual obligations. Europe's 'Castles in the Air' band remained in demand and they talked about business; James Europe had been sending many of his orchestra members to play in London and Paris to feed the shortage of musicians caused by the war, their other main conversation topic. Black troops were going down to face Pancho Villa in Mexico. Vernon was off to England and then France. James Europe was making his own arrangements. They made plans for a concert when this other 'bother' was resolved.

The visit also repaired fences. Four days before he'd gone off to Newport News, Vernon had taken Irene to meet up with James Europe and piano man and composer, 'I'm Just Wild About Harry', Eubie Blake. The musician George Carter told the story in the *New York Age* on 9 December 1915: 'One night Eubie and Jim Europe were out with Vernon and Irene Castle, taking them on a tour of all the nice black clubs in Harlem. The Castles wanted to see the dancing. It was an enjoyable evening until they got to Leroy's place [Leroy Wilkins, brother of Baron Wilkins; they both ran clubs] and discovered he wouldn't let them in. Eubie was stunned, because as well as he knew Leroy, he never before realised that he refused to allow whites into his club. Angry and embarrassed, Jim and Eubie stood outside the door and begged Leroy to let them in. "You know me, Leroy," said Jim. "You know I wouldn't bring anybody in your place that wasn't all right. Why, this is the famous, the great Mr and Mrs Vernon Castle." Jim was probably the best-known man in Harlem and his feelings were hurt. "Jim," said Leroy, "I know you're all right, and I respect you. But I don't care who they are. They're white and they can't come in here. That's my policy and I'm sticking to it." And he wouldn't let them in.'

It seemed everyone was testing their limits. Elsie Janis and her 'Ma' were still in England. Elsie was a sensation in London, the most popular American actress on the British stage. Elsie could bring audiences to tears and to laughter; her Sarah Bernhardt impressions won applause from Bernhardt herself. Elsie was not devoted to her success but to Basil Hallam, who starred with her in *The Passing Show* at the Palace Theatre and thereafter never left her side on- or offstage. The war complicated that situation. She and Basil Hallam Radford – the man who invented the phenomenon of 'Gilbert the Filbert', who was enlisted by his true surname in the Royal Flying Corps as Captain Radford – were planning to marry when he returned from the war. She understood how Irene felt with Vernon's departure for England and told her: 'Strange how peaceful ones managed to go while the more truculent ones were still getting ready. Vernon was no more of a natural fighter than Basil.'

In a memoir Elsie wrote of the day Basil went to war: 'I left him standing on the platform of Euston Station, chin up, blue eyes clear and fearless. In my hand I held a photograph he had posed for at the last moment in uniform and on it he wrote: "If we still love those we lose, can we ever quite lose those we love?"'

Irene had reached her limit with the financial burden of the rambling Manhasset estate bought on impulse by Vernon. It was costing $1,000 a week in mortgage payments, as well as requiring a mass of money to care for the house and grounds. A speculator took over the $49,500 mortgage of the Long Island estate, which was worth at least five times that. Irene, correctly, thought she needed a business adviser. She hired a male secretary who said he was a whiz at finance. On his first day, he stole $5,000 and ran off to join the army. Irene believed she had the Midas touch, in reverse. Maybe so.

She was touring with *Watch Your Step* when she got notification of Vernon's sendoff. It was in the newspapers, picked up nationally from the *New York Journal* of 20 February 1916, and was less romantic, for her, than that of Basil Hallam's leaving of Elsie Janis. The *Journal* reported: 'Speeded by the cheers and tears of hundreds of friends, Vernon Castle, the dancer, today is on his way to England. He boarded the White Star Liner *Adriatic* amid a tumultuous waving of flags. Just as the gangplank was about to be drawn up, a handsome and fashionably clad young woman brushed her way through the crowd. She practically fought her way to the dancer's side. She threw her arms around him. Five times, onlookers say, she kissed him. Castle blushed profusely.'

Ah, Vernon. At least he had the delicacy to blush.

It was more confusing than embarrassing when he arrived at British customs at the devil's hour, 3 a.m., on 26 February 1916. There was no Vernon Castle as stamped in his passport; his father's name was Blyth. Vernon charmed his way into his homeland.

He had his military enlistment papers: the Royal Flying Corps was part of the British Army and the fliers were aerial support, running artillery back-up and photographic reconnaissance for the British Expeditionary Force (BEF). The dogfights and bombing became part of the job description. Vernon still had to earn his 'wings' – to be assigned to a squadron. Before he set about his war, he checked into the Savoy, London WC2, across the Strand from theatreland. He had planned his tactics. He knew his strengths. He required an HQ. He had to organise a commission and his military training. He read that, on average, twenty-five would-be fliers were being killed in training every week. Every day raw recruits who survived were sent to the front, and most often the same fate.

Tomorrow, for Vernon, was always another day. He was lucky. Typically, he was more concerned with how Tell and Rastus were doing without him than how he was without them.

Chapter Eleven

What'll We Do?

'The reason birds can fly and we can't is simply because they
have perfect faith, for to have faith is to have wings.'
J. M. Barrie, *The Little White Bird*, 1902

London was the same but different. Vernon wandered down the
stairway from his third-floor room at the Savoy and took
a right into the lobby. He hadn't known what to expect but
hadn't imagined this bustling atmosphere and he desperately
wanted to join these people; they were going somewhere. All
around him, men were in uniform and he felt as if he'd turned up
at one of Mrs Stuyvesant Fish's receptions in dungarees. It was his
best suit, his shirt with rounded collar and a sober tie, a grey stripe,
neatly and tightly tied. He felt it was choking him with all these
army boys about. He was out of place like the short-legged girl
in the *Watch Your Step* chorus. He'd grow a moustache; that would
give him a more military look.

He walked down to the Thames, along the Embankment and
back around to Trafalgar Square, and then along the Strand to the
Savoy. There were no messages and he went to lunch. Back in his

room, he began his first letter to Irene. For her, he detailed over the days to follow his life in England; the first time he was truly far apart from her. His letters are an insight into him and his relationship with Irene – and the world. They shine so much they vividly reflect a distant time that could still, with eyes squeezed together and mind open, be yesterday. As Joplin might suggest, they are best read slowly. The letters, presented as written, become richer as time passes, as does Vernon's experience of the Great War.

Savoy Hotel, London
26 February 1916

We landed safely this morning at about 3 a.m., after a great deal of delay with the customs, and the people who question everyone who comes into England now. They have to be so careful, and I had an extra difficulty with my name. You see I came over with my passport as Castle, but as Father's name is Blyth it was very hard for me to explain. You see I should probably have come as Vernon Blyth, but I thought there would immediately be terrible difficulty with my mail and everything, because Vernon Castle has been my name for ten years. My life insurance is Castle, and there are a thousand reasons why I couldn't go back to my old name, but I had a great deal of hard work trying to explain it to the officer in charge. He said I should change my name legally by 'letters patent', whatever that means.

Well, darling, on arriving in London I went to this hotel, where I shall stay for a day or two until I know what my plans are going to be, and had a bath, etc., and went across to the Gaiety to see George Grossmith. He seemed delighted to see me, and he knows several people of influence in the Flying Service and immediately got in touch with a man in the Admiralty, who is going to see me at twelve o'clock tomorrow. He said that there should be no difficulty in my getting in at once, as I had already received my pilot's licence. I'm quite excited about it, as believe me one feels an awful mutt in this place without a uniform.

London is very surprising. I expected everyone to be very sad and the theatres empty, but on the contrary the show business is better than it's been in years; the place is simply packed with soldiers, who look splendid. Of course it's pitch dark at night, all the lights are either put out or dimmed to the extreme, and the sidewalks are whitewashed so that you can see them in the dark. The town is practically on the wagon, except for a few hours each day, from 6.00 to 9.00 at night, and you are not allowed to buy anybody a drink; everybody must pay for their own, even the women. In George's dressing room I found Raymond Hitchcock; he is going to play in a show here. He invited me to Ciro's, which is open until one, but no drinks. Our original band of Tuck and Johnson were there... As they turned us out at one, Hitchy and I had to come home. God! How the people dance! Five years behind the times. Oh darling, if you were only here to show them how to dance and dress. There are no chic women to speak of, but the men are awfully smart, and it makes one feel very proud to see the way they take this war, it makes you feel awfully patriotic and sure of winning.

I'm very tired, sweetheart, so I shall close now. I hope to have good news in my next letter. I can't tell you any war news, as the censor won't allow it... I could cry I'm so lonely sometimes, and everything reminds me of the time when we were here together. Johnson's band played all our old favourites tonight, and brought tears to my eyes. We did have such wonderful times, didn't we, darling?...

I'm a good boy about writing, aren't I, darling? I hope it keeps up. Kiss all the pets for me, dear, and tell Rastus his daddy loves him.

Savoy, London 29 February 1916

I'm sorry not to have been able to have written you Sunday and yesterday, but I have been to Norwich and I didn't get a moment to myself. Grannie is a dear, she asked all about you, and sent her love. She isn't very well, poor dear, but she is frightfully intelligent. Most people when they get old seem to get sort of silly, but she is so very sensible. Norwich is alive with soldiers, they have always had soldiers stationed there, but now there are very few civilians. All my old school friends have gone, and some of them unfortunately have been killed.

I went to the Admiralty, and I think I will get my commission next Tuesday if all goes well. I also went to the War Office to see a friend of George's who has a lot of influence, but he was out, so I am going again tomorrow. There is an awful lot of waiting around to be done. I feel like a bad actor trying to see Shubert for a job.

Hitchcock phoned and asked me to dinner and theatre with some people named Joel tonight, and I accepted. We had a very nice dinner at the Carlton, and after we went to a corking play in which were Gladys Cooper and Chas Hawtrey. They are both simply wonderful, and I loved the piece. After, we went to Ciro's and had something to eat. The few ladies were fat and didn't dance, thank God! So I played the drums and watched the crowd, which is always amusing.

It's when I get home that I feel so terribly lonely. I haven't even got a dog to talk to, but I guess I shouldn't grumble, especially to

Left: A star is born: Vernon, stylish at age nineteen, posed with a wary look for his first publicity front-of-house theatre photograph in New York.

Right: The teenaged Irene Foote's love rival, the diamond-loving stage actress turned silent-screen star Kathleen Clifford, here in a scene from *Kick In*, a 1922 crime drama.　　　　(© *Getty*)

Left: Irene in 1915, four years after she and Vernon married: 'her "look" – the "Castle Bob" – was a gift to the press'.

It was Irene who brought a smile to Vernon's face as they displayed the steps which made them famous around the world. Everyone wanted a sprinkle of their stardust. And there was much magic to go round, with an extraordinary number of steps and combinations, but even flamboyance had to be elegant. *(© Everett Collection/REX)*

Left: Vernon and Irene Castle giving an exhibition dance in 1916 at the invitation of the legendary hostess Mamie (Mrs Stuyvesant) Fish.

(© *Everett Collection/REX*)

Right: And here at an early display for the Vanderbilt family, their dress and tone more formal than when they began classes at Castle House.

(© *Getty*)

Above: Vernon and Irene practised their routines with great care before these were presented to their students at Castle House. The treat for the dancing pupils was to receive a 'surprise' visit from the Castles, who would dance for and with them. It was a huge attraction, and their young student-teacher, Arthur Murray, recognised the potential.

(© *Getty*)

Below: The glossy couple: the Castles tried to escape attention at home in Manhasset, Long Island, but a magazine photographer persuaded them to 'sit' for him in 1915. As Vernon gazes at Irene at the piano, her sister Elroy looks out from a family photograph next to a bronze of a polo player.

(© *Everett Collection/REX*)

Above: Fashion icon: Irene modelling creations by Lucile Duff Gordon. Left to right: dressed by Lucile for *Watch Your Step*, and 'summer' and 'winter' costumes.

Below left: 'Lucile' – Lucy, Lady Duff Gordon – the British aristocrat who survived both the sinking of the *Titanic* and scandal. One of the most influential designers of the early years of the last century, she was Irene Castle's fashion adviser and confidante.

Below right: Irene with Tell, after Vernon had joined the Royal Flying Corps. She is wearing an RFC tunic and the 'wings' sent to her by Vernon from the Western Front. She posed 'in uniform' as part of her wartime fund-raising efforts.

Right: Irene riding – sidesaddle, no less – with Grand Duke Dmitry Pavlovich, the exiled cousin of the ill-fated Tsar of Russia. Vernon joked: 'He's a Russian bear but he won't get my honey.'

Below right and inset: James Europe's musical and racial barrier-breaking Society Orchestra, who were helped and inspired by Vernon and Irene into making some of the most popular music of the early twentieth century. Their collected, foot-tapping, hip-swirling recordings remain available. The sheet-music cover for 'On Patrol in No Man's Land' highlights Europe's service in the US Army during the Great War, when he led the 'Hellfighters' Band.

Below: It was a Hollywood public-relations dream: Irene was starring as 'Sylvia of the Secret Service' when real-life hero Vernon visited the leading lady on location. Tell completed the family photograph, which was taken at the Pathé studios.

On Patrol in No Man's Land

ADDISON AMUSEMENTS Inc. *Presents*
Lieut. JAMES REESE EUROPE
AND HIS FAMOUS
369 *th* U.S. INFANTRY "HELL FIGHTERS" BAND

GOOD NIGHT AN[...]
ON PATROL IN N[...]

M. Witmar[...]

MRS. VERNON CASTLE
AND HER SOLDIER HUSBAND
AT PATHE STUDIO

Capt. Vernon Castle's favorite 'bus.

Note 'Castle' on Rudder.

How this brave man met his death.

Pinned under engine on front seat.

Top left: This Curtiss JN-4 two-seat trainer was Vernon's favourite 'bus', and the groundcrew and his fellow pilots loved the bespoke touch – a castle chess piece painted on the rudder.

Top right: Vernon was always confident around flying machines, although never casual in his dealings with them or the men around him. But he was not invincible, nor immune to the vagaries of fate. This photograph of his crashed 'Jenny' was captioned 'How this brave man died.'

Below: The sorrow and shock of Vernon Castle's death is etched into the hunched posture and on the face of Walter Ash (far right) as he stands by the wreckage of Vernon's crashed aircraft, his deep grief understood and shared by squadron members themselves emotionally punished by the abrupt casualty. The depth of the bereavement spread like a fever over the Texas base.

19 February 1918: draped in the Union flag and carried on the shoulders of his RFC comrades, Vernon's coffin is carried into New York's 'Little Church Around the Corner', followed by senior British and American officers. Irene, in full widow's weeds, is third from right in the foreground, with her mother behind her, both escorted to their left by Vernon's brother-in-law, Lawrence Grossmith. Despite the damage to the photographic plate, the crowd of well-wishers can be seen in the background.

you, my darling, but at the same time I want you to know that I miss you too frightfully for words, dear, and I haven't even started to do any work yet. Oh, but we will have a wonderful time when I do get back. Won't we, darling? I haven't heard a word from you, up to the present. It must take a long while for mail to get to or from America now, what with the censor and the few boats running. By the time you get this, all the news will be old, and I will, I hope, be in uniform.

Give my regards to everyone we know, won't you, dear?

Savoy, London
4 March 1916

I missed writing to you again last night, but I had had a rather strenuous day, and I really felt too tired when I got home. Yesterday I was invited to a lunch party at the Royal Navy Yacht Club, and at the table sitting next to me was a man named Captain Lorraine. He used to be on the stage, but is now in the Flying Corps, and early in the war did some wonderful work and got the Military Cross. I was of course delighted to meet him, and I told him of my intention to go in the Naval Air Service, and he told me that they were really the inferior branch, and that they were not doing any real fighting like the Army, and he offered to take me to the War Office after lunch, and do what he could for me if I wanted to join the Army, so of course I accepted, and after the meal was over we marched off to the War Office, and he took me up to the very head man there, who was quite a friend of his, and a major. The major, after looking at an enormous book in which there were hundreds of names before mine, said, 'Well, if he can fly, and you vouch for him, Lorraine, he can go right in.' And so, dear, I have got a commission, and am now a 2nd Lieutenant, RFC [Royal Flying Corps], on probation. The rank is not so high, but it is remarkable considering the fact that I have been here only a week, and they usually have to wait months and months before getting anything at all, and commissions are not as easy to get now as at the beginning of the war. Lorraine says I shall only be in England two months, and then I shall be sent right out to France.

My training camp is in a place called North Fleet, which is in Kent, and I expect to go out there about Wednesday. I've been shopping all morning, getting my uniform and kit made. I'll have my photo taken as soon as I get my uniform. One thing I have to be careful about, and that is not to get my name in the papers, over here; it is considered the height of bad form to go in for any kind of publicity or advertising. I shall be glad for them to know in America that I really am in the RFC, because I'm sure a lot of the people still think I'm bluffing, especially 'Jim Jam Jems'.

How is the show going, and how much longer do you stay out? Be sure and tell me all the news, dear. I do so long to hear from you, darling, and no letter ever comes for me. Oh, if you only knew how miserable I feel sometimes you would feel very sorry for me. Sometimes the orchestras play your number, 'Dancing teacher, show me how to do the foxtrot', and I feel so homesick. Everything seems so very long ago, as though it were in a different life. If I would only get a letter from you it would help an awful lot...

Norwich
8 March 1916

I received four lovely letters from you last night, and it was such a relief. You don't know what it means not to have heard from you in so long. It takes so long to get a letter now. I am expecting any day to be called to duty, but haven't heard yet. I tried on my uniform which is not quite finished. I'll have my photo taken when it is done and send it to you. I'm simply crazy about the little poem you sent me. I wish I could send you one, but somehow my words don't rhyme...

You're in Dayton today. Poor darling, it's such a rotten town.

Savoy, London
10 March 1916

I got back from Norwich this evening in time to have dinner here, and the first person I saw as I walked into the Grill Room was Ernest Lambert; he looked just the same except that he had grown a moustache. I, of course, thought he was 'somewhere in France'.

I've got my uniform now, and I look just like Rastus in it. I wear one of those little monkey caps on the side of the head. I am leaving on Tuesday, and have to report for duty Wednesday. I don't think it will be a very pleasant place, as I have orders to appear with a camp-kit which consists of a folding cot, canvas bath, waterproof sheets! And a lot of things that seem to say I'm going to sleep in a tent or something. However, I shall be very glad to get started anyway.

I went to a society party tonight. They had some coons, and the dancing was fine. Everybody there was over fifty; I asked where the younger element was, and was told that the young women all worked in the hospitals, and didn't go out at night as a rule, so getting wounded has its compensations. I hear some Americans have just got in from New York, so perhaps I shall get some mail. I look forward to your letters more than anything on earth, darling. I hope you will write me often; if you don't I'll write you a lot, and make you feel ashamed.

I'm not going to write a very long letter tonight, dear, as I must be up early and do my shopping...

RFC Rinsly's, England
20 March 1916

I'm afraid it's days since I wrote to you, but, sweetie, you must forgive me because I've had so much to do I absolutely haven't had a single minute to myself, except when I have to go to bed, and also I've been quite sick for the past few days. I had to be inoculated for typhoid, and for a day or two after it makes you feel quite ill. I have to be done again in a day or two, and also vaccinated. I guess if people in America could see me now they would never think it was me. My uniform makes me look much taller, and I have a small moustache. I haven't been able to get my photo taken because I can never get into town. I get every other Sunday off, but then the laces are closed. The following is a schedule of the day:

6.00 a.m.   Early morning flying
7.30   Breakfast
9.00   Flying and mechanics
11.30   Glass of milk and cake!
11.45   Attend lecture
1.00 p.m.   Lunch
2.00   Drill and parade
2.30   Flying, etc
4.30   Tea
5.30   Lecture

6.30	Wireless telegraphy and signalling
7.30	Dinner

After dinner, study for tomorrow's lecture. You will see by this, dear, that there is 'nothing to do 'til tomorrow'.

The weather has been frightful, it hasn't stopped raining all week, and so the flying which we do in all weathers has been very bad. Of course we don't fly so much as on fine days, but we have to stand by the machines, unless we are given jobs to do. It all seems so strange and different to what I am used to that sometimes I think I am dreaming. Yesterday (my day off) I went to Norwich for a few hours. I arrived there 1.39 and left 6.15, but Father wanted to see my uniform; he was very proud, and cried. He got a lot of fun walking with me to Grannie's house because all non-commissioned soldiers have to salute me, which is of course very thrilling!

The meals here are very plain, but quite good. They wouldn't suit you, sweetie, as we never get chicken, and we have to go up to the chef, plate in hand, and get our own food, which is somewhat of a scramble sometimes. They have apple pie every day, which rather pleases me. I hope you won't get the impression, sweetie, that I am kicking about my fate, because I'm not. It's what I expected and I enjoy it all but the weather.

I expect to be here, dear, for two months, and then I will take an examination, and – if fortunate – be decorated with a pair of wings, and sent to the front, which will be about 1 June. You speak in your letter, darling, of coming here to see me; if you did this before I went to the front, I'm sure I could arrange to get a week off, to spend with you alone. It seems too good to be true, I shan't think about it or I'll cry. I'd give my right eye to have you with me for a little while... Send me some photos, darling, I haven't any of you but my pocket ones, and the red leather frame I used to have in my dressing room.

I must go to bed now, darling, as I have to get up so early in the morning. Give my love to all our nice friends. Kiss my Rastus boy for me – bless his little heart. I bet he's cute with his little wardrobe trunk. God bless you, my sweetie...

Savoy Hotel, London, England
7 April 1916

It's ages since I wrote you, but I've been terribly busy, and then sick, and I simply haven't had time. At the moment I am on sick leave with influenza. I've been in bed three days, but I'm better now and I am going back at 6.30 a.m. tomorrow morning...

One of our chaps got killed the other night. He was going up after a zep and I guess he over-controlled in the dark, and fell. He fell quite close to me, and made me feel awfully sick.

I was out all night in charge of some flares (they are bonfires for lighting up the field at night) and I guess I must have caught my cold then. The zeps are pretty busy lately, but we manage to keep them away from London, and they don't seem to worry anybody... If you have any new photos I wish you'd send me one or two, darling. I came away without any and all I have is what I cut out of magazines.

There isn't much news that interests you, sweetheart. I went to Raymond Hitchcock's opening night last week. He was a big success. I also went to a party afterwards given by a flying officer who was just leaving for the front. I saw Pito there so he wasn't killed after all. I also heard from Tim, and he gets a week's leave soon, and I am going to meet him in town. Lionel Walsh is a major out at the front, and quite a big nut.

I must close now, dear. I won't keep you waiting so long for a letter in the future.

Rinsly's, Middlesex, England
14 April 1916

Here is the proof of my photo. I'm afraid it's not very good. I shall go and have it taken again when I can. It's rather hard as we are not allowed out of barracks in the daytime. This was taken when I was on sick leave, and it looks it. I hope Rastus likes it – he looks like his daddy.

There's no news, dear. I'm improving in my flying, faster than anyone here, and I'm now flying the big machines they use for fighting. They are perfectly wonderful and much easier to fly than the small powered machines, just as a big car is better than a small one.

I'll write a regular letter tonight, dear – it's lunchtime now...

The loving letters were an energiser for Irene, who found life on the road with *Watch Your Step* and without Vernon to be a chore. The show had been a huge celebration of dance and Irving Berlin's songs, but when it closed that April of 1916, she was desperate to be with her husband: 'I fled to Vernon to spend six days with him before he went to the front.'

The time was brief because she had signed for $1,500 a week to star in a propaganda film, *Patria*, which like the popular *Pearls of Pauline* and *Pearl of the Army* was to be told in the popular serial reels: cliffhanger endings, often literally, brought audiences back week after week. *Patria* was to be filmed around Ithaca, New York, and then in Hollywood. With Irene's dancing pupil William Randolph Hearst at the helm, it had a simple theme: evil foreigners are defeated the all-American way.

Hearst put much faith in Irene, who was a supreme social tightrope walker. A year earlier, the tycoon had become besotted by showgirl and future industry starlet Marion Davies, whom he would dream of and build monuments to; Irene befriended her and, remarkably, still stayed on wonderful terms with Hearst's wife Millicent. Now, he was investing in Irene's popularity in his first truly serious venture in the fledgeling film industry. While she waited for the *Patria* script of movieland derring-do to be completed and her leading man to be cast, she sailed to see the real thing, Second Lieutenant Vernon Castle of the Imperial Royal Flying Corps.

Although Vernon Castle's letters are intact, those written by Irene to her husband have never been seen; they may have been lost in the chaos of wartime or simply the chaos of Vernon's rushed and slapdash living arrangements. Irene did write separately in 1918 of her visit to London. As ever, her writing is a remarkable reminder of the attitude and language of the time and, most of all, of her love for Vernon. The story of Vernon and Irene is a love story; the war and other bothers of life were intemperate interruptions. She went to England immediately the run of *Watch Your Step* ended on a six-day visit. The *St Louis* was about to dock – Irene was in her cabin adding some final touches of make-up – when a passenger told her Vernon was there. Indeed, he was but on a tender boat bobbing around beside the ocean liner. He was in his uniform. He wore his 'wings'. It was the first time Irene had seen him in fighting-boy bloom. They leaped about waving at each other and when a gangplank linked the tender to the *St Louis* he all but flew into Irene's arms. It stayed like that in London as they tripped around theatres, dinners and parties. They danced every night till early the early hours. The evening before Irene sailed back to America they went to Pusey, Oxfordshire, where Vernon had to report before his posting. They spent the night in the village put and it was a tearful time. They tried to laugh and have fun but couldn't at this last supper

before who knew what. Irene said it was painful. It got worse. She
boarded he train and opened the carriage window to wave goodbye.
Vernon, in uniform, was standing at attention. Saluting. Irene sobbed
for most of her journey. She also wrote a poem on a scrap of paper
and later Vernon attached it to a watch chain and wore it around his
neck. It was to fly with him again and again over the Western Front:

Almighty God, if thou art there,
Listen to my humble prayer
And keep him safe.
Keep him in your care always –
Watch o'er him through this weary day
And keep him safe.
Make him feel my love and sorrow.
Bring him back some near tomorrow
And keep him safe.

Chapter Twelve

A Life in Letters

'*I have loved the stars too fondly to be fearful of the night.*'
Sarah Williams, 'The Old Astronomer to His Pupil', *c*.1860

While Irene went off to become a movie star and battle with Louis Vane's screenplay for *Patria*, the menacing and evil Japanese villain, Baron Huroki, and a carnival of Hearst-inspired foreign-looking henchmen, her husband was put on readiness for action. Irene was welcomed back to America with a two-foot-high silver loving cup, heralding her as the 'most popular motion-picture actress of 1916' for *The Whirl of Life*. The honour, from a Hearst readers' poll, was presented as the marketing for *Patria* began. The tact was in what was and was not acknowledged.

In his letters, Vernon innocently reveals the censorship gap between officers and their men. His writing also highlights how those at and flying above the front dealt with the hell of it, of Verdun and then the Battle of the Somme, of the loss of more than 1 million combatants over no man's land around a river in northern France. It was his own acute history lesson. Irene had left London and he was soon to be on his way to France:

Central Flying School, Upavon, Wiltshire, England
13 May 1916

How sad it is to have you leave me so soon! I can't realise it yet. It seems as though I have had a very beautiful dream and that you haven't really been here at all.

This is a rotten day. Poor child, I do hope you get better weather; it will be such a rotten trip anyway.

I hear that the flight I am posted to is to be moved to a place called Gosport, which is on the south of England coast, and more out of the way than this. I shall be sorry if they send me with it, because, although it's not very lovely here, they have a squash court, and I have very comfortable quarters. If I move, I'll cable you.

The machine I am to fly is called the Morane Monoplane. It is a very small machine and very fast.

Thank you for sending me fruit, darling. I haven't received it yet but I expect it tonight...

Central Flying School, Upavon
14 May 1916

I haven't smiled yet. I feel so lonesome and blue. It's just terrible, having your mate snatched away. I received your sweet letter this morning. It was so good hearing from you and now I guess I shall have to wait a long while before I hear again. Your little prayer was too adorable, sweet. I am going to tie a string to it and wear it around my neck until after the war; God will surely listen to such a pretty prayer.

It has been raining all day here, and I have only done twenty minutes flying. The hours here are a little trying. We have to get up at 4.30 and start flying at 5 a.m., and only stop at 8 p.m. I get very tired after dinner and am quite ready to go to bed at 9.30. We are supposed to dress for dinner, so I have written Foster and asked him to send me my bag with my dress clothes.

Central Flying School, Upavon
17 May 1916

... I am sick in bed with a slight attack of tonsillitis. Yesterday at 5 a.m. I had to fly a machine to Gosport and bring an old one back. On the way back a valve in the engine broke, and I was forced to descend in the middle of Salisbury Plain, in the rain and miles away from the nearest village, and there I had to stay for fourteen hours, before help arrived. The result is a bad cold and sore throat which the doctor calls tonsillitis, but it isn't anything like as serious as when you get it. I am staying in bed all day and I expect to be all right in the morning.

I haven't heard how long I am to stay here, but I don't think very long. I shall be glad to go as it is very miserable here.

The fruit came last night, darling. Thanks ever so much. It's perfectly delicious. It's going to be terrible, waiting for a letter from you, dear, but when they do come I'll get a lot, won't I? How is the boy Rastus? I hope he will keep warm...

Fort Grange, Gosport
26 May 1916

I wonder how you are and what you are doing. It seems ages since you went away, and it is only two weeks today. The time passes awfully slowly here. The days are so long, and this new daylight-saving scheme of putting the clocks forward an hour makes them all the longer... Our anniversary is the day after tomorrow, isn't it, darling? I forget if we were married on the 28th or 29th, but I am taking a chance on the 28th. Oh dear, I hope we are together on the next....

Fort Grange, Gosport
27 May 1916

Today I have a little something to write about. I am afraid I can't make a whole lot of it. When I went up for my flight this morning on a Bleriot monoplane, I took up a sergeant with me who wanted a ride, and when we were up about ten miles from the aerodrome, an inlet valve broke, which means you have to turn off your petrol and come down at once, as your machine is apt to catch fire. Well, I managed to spot a young wheat field and manoeuvred to land in it quite respectfully. Of course we were surrounded by the usual crowd of school children and farm hands, who see machines in the air every day, but never see them closely. Presently the owner of the field came along in a motorbike and sidecar, and he very kindly offered to take me to his farm where I could telephone. So I left the sergeant in charge and went off with the farmer. He was quite young and very clever. He has the cutest farm, darling, I have ever seen. Six dogs of different sizes and breeds, little ducks in a pond, and ever so many cows in a dairy, little colts, and everything in the world that goes with a farm.

The loveliest old farm home in the world, with modern bathrooms. He lives there all alone and makes his living as a farmer.

Oh darling, I do wish you had been there with me. He must have thought I was a fool. I was so tickled with his dogs, and the little ducks, only a day old, swimming about, not caring a darn about their chicken mother. He gave me a peach of a lunch and I returned to my plane and found that it had been fixed, so I said goodbye, and sailed away. The field was so much more difficult to get out of than in. I managed to dodge the trees and so ended a very pleasant little diversion. I guess I've bored you stiff, sweetheart. I should have written this letter to Mother, as she likes descriptions.

It's awfully hard to write when nothing happens to write about. This evening I flew the machine (the first time) that I'm going to fly at the front, namely a Morane monoplane. It's an awfully nice machine, and I enjoyed it very much...

Give my love to all at home and a big kiss for the boy from me.

Fort Grange, Gosport, England
30 May 1916

... I've now got to a point where I simply can't write. There isn't a thing to write about. All I do is suck my pen and vainly try to think of something to tell you...

I'm taking a machine to Northolt tomorrow, which will be rather nice as I shall see [name redacted]. Do you remember him? Poor old [so-and-so], the one you offered to give a dancing lesson to at the party, has lost his nerve as a result of his crash. He's too nervous to fly again, so he is being transferred to a balloon section. I'm awfully sorry because he was a peach of a pilot...

Well, darling, goodbye till tomorrow. I hope you're happy, sweetie, but I hope you miss me...

Savoy Hotel, London
3 June 1916

I was sent here this morning to report to the War Office for service overseas and I am to go to join a squadron in France this week. They couldn't tell me what day I was to leave, but I am to report to Gosport on Monday morning and be ready to leave when I am told, which, I imagine, will be about Wednesday.

I'm awfully excited about it, of course. I don't care much about staying here if I can't be with you and I'd much rather be fighting...

Savoy Hotel, London
4 June 1916

This is only going to be a short note because I have to get up early tomorrow in order to be at Gosport. I went out with the [name redacted] in the Rolls this afternoon, to Maidenhead on Thames, and we had tea at a hotel near the river. I had a very nice time although the weather was very bad. We went to Ciro's again for dinner. It was too crowded to dance. I played the drums most of the time.

By the time you get this, sweetie, I think I shall be in France. I wonder if I shall get any letters from you before I leave England. I do hope so – it will cheer me up ever so much if I do.

I'm enclosing a picture of you, dear, which came out in the *Daily Mirror*. I've got your little prayer chained to my neck on the watch chain you gave me last Xmas. I have worn it ever since I received it, and I shall keep it on till I come back to you, darling...

Savoy Hotel, London
6 June 1916

...This is my last night in London as I leave for France tomorrow. I haven't been told yet what squadron I'm going to, but I shall cable you tomorrow and let you know. I feel awfully blue. I wish you were with me tonight, darling. We have just heard the news of the loss of Lord Kitchener, and it has sort of depressed everybody. Another thing that worries me is that I haven't had any letters from you. I suppose the censor is holding them up, but I do want them before I leave. I am sending my motorbike to Norwich to be stored. I was sent away so suddenly I didn't get time to even try to sell it...

Well, darling, I must close now. I shall still try and write you every day even if the letters are short and dull... Don't worry about me. Everything will come out all right and 'we'll live happily ever after'. I shall be thinking of you every minute no matter where I am...

France
9 June 1916

Darling:
I have just arrived in France, and I leave for my squadron in a little while. I have thought of you all day, sweetheart. I hope you won't worry about me.

Everything here in France is very thrilling and sometimes a little sad. I am very happy, darling...

I have just arrived here. 'Here' is a little village in France, and I am quartered in a funny little cottage, kept by an old French woman. I have to walk over a manure pile to get to my room. It's horribly dirty outside – but quite clean in.

I've been travelling all night without sleep so I am going to rest for a few hours now. Five of your pictures are hanging on the walls – such beautiful things look very strange amid such dowdy surroundings...

France
13 June 1916

... It's just a month today since you sailed from England. I can hardly realise it – it seems to me quite a year. Time passes quite quickly here, but somehow it seems such ages since I had you with me.

The weather has been simply appalling and there has been very little activity. We are expecting a big drive all along the front, in which we hope to gain a lot of ground. When this will take place I don't know, but I don't think it will be many weeks now. I hope not anyway. I'm sick of this place and the only relief is being up in the air. The village is terrible, and the food we get isn't a bit nice. If we were only near a town where one could get a decent dinner, it would be all right, but we're out of bounds from anywhere decent...

Forgive me for grumbling, won't you, darling? I have no one else to tell my troubles to, and it's done me lots of good to tell my mate. Don't worry about me, darling, though I didn't expect to find this a picnic. All leave has been stopped so there isn't much chance of my being in England for some time. When you come back though we must try and arrange for me to get some leave, or a job in England... I guess I shall have earned my leave by then.

Every day I look in vain for a letter from you. Perhaps I'll get one tomorrow...

Somehow, even with the chaos of war, letters to and from the Western Front found a way over and around the confusion, which was a mitigating normality amid the atrocity and horror. For Vernon, as for thousands of others, letters provided a link with what appeared a safer and saner world, something always of debate in the trenches where all seemed madness. He often included drawings, little sketches on his letters, like this one (below) showing his 'attack' bombs still attached to his aircraft when he had to make an emergency return to base. On the page with the drawing he told Irene: 'I landed, but not without a great deal of fear, because I still had under the machine the bombs that I was supposed to drop on the railroad… as they explode by contact, you will see that it was no fun landing with them.' (The aircraft is a two-seater, probably a Nieuport 20.)

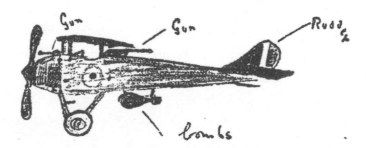

British Army in the field, France
16 June 1916

… I received three more letters from you today, and some music, and a letter from Mother. Gee! It's been a great day for me.

I haven't missed a day writing to you, sweetie. My letters have been pretty punk, but I always send an envelope. Your letter prayer is always round my neck. It's getting a little 'grubby' now. I can only get a bath twice a week, but that's considered very often here in France.

I'm so glad you've got the black pony. Did you have to write twice for him? Perhaps one of your letters has gone astray. I hope not, but I guess it can't be helped if any of them do.

Gee! I wish you had got Rastus's younger brother, but of course the boy would not have liked it, so it couldn't be done.

Gee! I wish I could go with you to hear the coons play. Remember me to Tracy and Buddy, and the boys if you see them.

Thanks ever so much, sweet, for the music. It's awfully good of you to think of it.

I haven't done any fighting yet, but things are going to be very busy soon. The General was here today and told all the pilots to learn all the positions of the various places along the front. We've got a nice day today, for the first time since I've been here.

Well, darling, I've got to go and fly now.

Vernon's letters, through wartime censorship, lose their locations, or exact locations, from time to time as he operated between France and Belgium.

18 June 1916

... We had a very exciting day today. The German aeroplanes made a raid and dropped a lot of bombs around without doing a terrible lot of damage fortunately. Five of their machines did not return and were brought down by ours. I was up in a little machine but did not see any of the Hun machines, but in the evening, just before I went to dinner, in fact, directly I went out after writing you, I saw a duel in the air in which the German machine was shot down. It fell at a tremendous rate, nose first, for the pilot managed to right himself at the last moment. His observer was shot in the knee, but the pilot wasn't hit at all, but was obliged to come down on account of his petrol pipes being shot away.

The squadron got him and entertained him at supper before sending him to a detention camp. We have the machine with us here. It's a 'peach', and there are a lot of things about it which we would do well to copy if they only will.

The chief thing about their machines is that they are comfortable. Their seats are upholstered and roomy, and you can sit in them for hours and not get tired, while ours are small and make your back ache after half an hour's flight. I hope this doesn't bore you, darling. You know I haven't many subjects to talk about.

Today hasn't been very good. The weather is cold and rainy. Oh, I nearly forgot to tell you. I've got a girl puppy. It's a sort of black-and-tan, and awfully cute. It was lost, and they were going to destroy it because the men aren't allowed to have dogs. I saw it and rescued it and it's terribly sweet, and as lively as anything. Trust a mutt for being clever. I don't think it's more than two months or ten weeks old, but it barks at tramps and can jump off a table with ease. I call it 'Lizzie'. This is her paw, [above an inked pawprint].

France
19 June 1916

Your letter of the 31st received this morning and also a little gold aeroplane. Thank you ever so much, sweetheart, it's so good of you. The Kewpie [toy] soldier and the Victor records I haven't received yet. Of course, darling, lots of things go astray, but it can't be helped. I got all, or nearly all, of your cables, eventually. The censor delays everything considerably, but it's very necessary as nearly all the spy's communications come or go through America.

Lizzie is such a nice little pup and so clean. I get quite a lot of fun out of her and she follows me everywhere...

I wish I could send you some snapshots, but it's absolutely forbidden to have a camera, here. I have to go flying now, dear, so I must close. I'll try and write you a better letter next time. Lizzie sends Rastus a kiss.

France
21 June 1916

I wasn't able to write you yesterday I had so much to do all day, and in the evening, just when I was sitting down to write, a lost French aviator came down in our aerodrome. I was the only officer here who could speak any kind of French at all, so I had to look after him and get him some dinner and a place to sleep.

We are just about to commence hostilities, I think. The guns have been going off pretty regularly now and we are all getting very busy.

I had a letter from you today, sweetheart. Cables are very expensive here so I can't wire often. Number one is considered the 'crack' squadron of the Flying Corps, and I am proud to be on it...

23 June 1916

... I've just arrived here at my new squadron where I shall no doubt remain for the next six months. This place is quite near the firing line, and I shall be over the German lines every day, but I will be as careful as possible, and with your little prayer around my neck, come back safe and sound...

24 June 1916

Just a little line to say goodnight. I've been awfully busy all day learning the wireless signals, and about the machine guns, etc.... The Germans are certainly busy about here, and you get plenty of 'Archies'. I suppose you must have read about 'Archie'. He is a big German gun that does nothing but shoot at aeroplanes. They say one gets quite fond of him after a while...

25 June 1916

I wonder how, and where, you are today? On account of my moving I haven't had any letters from you for four days, and I feel so lonely. I don't feel so far away when I have a letter from you ...

It's very exciting here. There is so much more to do, and it's a corking squadron. Today I went to a small village a few miles from here that has been under fire for a long time. I was going to tell you why I went there, but I guess it would be indiscreet in the eyes of the censor, even if I didn't mention the name of the village. But I will have a lot to tell you when it is all over, and when I get old I shall be able to tell our children all about the Great War, and bore them to tears.

Most of the villages around here are more or less shot to pieces, and the inhabitants moved to more peaceful spots, but in some cases, old people insist upon sticking to their homes, and when a piece of shell carries away a corner of the cottage, they go to work and patch it up again. It's very hard to make them understand my French, as the majority of them speak Flemish.

26 June 1916

... I can't write a long letter, sweet. I've been in the air for three hours and been potted at by German anti-aircraft guns. It's quite easy to zigzag and dodge them, but it's frightfully tiring and one feels awfully lazy when one gets down safely...

28 June 1916

I am snatching a moment now to write you in case I don't have another chance today.

We only do two or three hours in the air, a day – it doesn't sound much, but after two hours flying and being under fire the whole time, you feel a wreck. But it's better than being in the trenches. From the air it looks like a very old piece of Stilton cheese.

... Don't worry about me here. The best-looking girl I've seen here looks like this [he had included a drawing], and had her last bath several epochs before the war.

In the field, France
29 June 1916

... There is a gramophone here playing all of the *Watch Your Step* music, and it makes me so homesick...

Lizzie is all right, as she takes care of herself, but we are under orders to be prepared to move on six hours' notice with only 35 pounds of baggage. Lunch is ready, darling.

France
30 June 1916

Oh, I am so happy today, darling. I have received all your mail. It came this morning – eight letters! I wanted to save some for tomorrow, but I just couldn't wait. It would have been worse than not looking at your presents till Xmas, so I simply went away all by myself and devoured them all. You don't know how I've waited and longed for just a word from you. I almost cry all the time I'm reading the sweet things you say to me...

I took a machine over the firing line today and had a perfectly wonderful time. I left it at No. 3 squadron and had tea with them. They are such a decent bunch.

As soon as the big flight starts I shall be moved up, so I don't worry much. Now I've got your letters nothing could make me unhappy. At No. 3 they have two little raggy dogs – twins – named Push and Pull. The only way you can tell which is which is to blow in their faces. If he puts his tongue out at you, it's Push. If he doesn't, it's Pull – isn't that cute?

Darling, I'm so proud of you winning that cup, and I'm so interested in your work. I know you will be a great success, and I shall be more tickled than a mother. I wish I were there to help you. Not that you need it, but I could kid myself along that I was of some use.

I'm sorry, sweetie, that I haven't any snapshots for you. I sent you one yesterday. We don't have cameras at the front much, except special ones for photographing gun positions, etc. Gee, the guns look so large. I never realised they were so enormous, and they are all painted with green and brown spots so as to be indistinguishable against the ground.

I must close now, darling – you must excuse the pencil because

I've only got one fountain pen full of ink, and I'm saving that for the envelopes...

I say my prayers every night to God and you, love. Don't worry about me, precious. I'm very careful always. Kiss little Rastus for his daddy. Don't forget to send me newspaper clippings and anything from you that will go in an envelope. I feel so far away sometimes.

France
1 July 1916

I wasn't able to write you yesterday. This is the first day I've missed since I've been out here, so you must forgive me, precious.

I was terribly busy yesterday.

I had twenty-five photographs to take over the German lines, and what with taking them, developing them, etc., I was going from 7 a.m. till night, and I couldn't have written a letter to save my life. This photography is the worst job one can get because they have to be taken very low and one is well in range. I had my plane hit three times with pieces of shell, and the concussion you get makes you think the machine is blown in half. I don't mind telling you, darling, that I was sick with fright and jolly glad to get back home, only to find the wretched cameraman had put the plates in wrong and that I had to go up and take them all over again. I got them all finished but one, yesterday evening. I shall take that one today. But one is easy, because I can dart down over the spot, 'snap it', and beetle off home before the Archie guns get a range on me. I hope I don't frighten you, sweetie. Perhaps I shouldn't tell you all this, but one doesn't get these jobs often, and they are really not as bad as they seem.

I received three letters from you today, sweetheart, written on May 22nd, 23rd and 24th. They had gone first to Central [Flying] School and from there to Gosport, then to the Savoy Hotel, where they were sent to Northolt. Then they were put into a fresh envelope and sent to C. F. S. again; – back to headquarters in England and lastly here to France...

I have also traced the Victor records. They are detained by the customs who want the shipper's original in voice. There is no further news, my love. Things are pretty much the same here, but I hope something is done one way or another, before the cold weather sets in. Goodbye for the present, little wife. God bless you and keep you safe and happy always.

France (near Ypres)
3 July 1916

The weather has been very fine lately and so there has been a great deal of aerial activity. Gee! I'll have so many tales to tell when I get home. I suppose that everything in America is prepared in mess and everyone will be joining summer camps.

I'm so glad you're fond of my boy [Rastus], tell him I think of him an awful lot and wish he were with me, but I'm thankful he's not as I like to think of him with you.

I suppose you have read in the papers that we have made some progress in the war. I only hope we keep all the ground won. I sent you a postcard the other day. It is the nearest town to us here and gives you a rough idea of what it looks like around these parts.

God bless you, and all the animals around you...

France
4 July 1916

... Two sweet letters from you today. It's so lovely to hear from you all the time... I love the snapshots you sent me. I've got them pinned up all around my tent. I think B. Drew is awfully nice and Lou is a peach. I am resting today because I had a spill yesterday. My machine turned turtle on landing. The engine went 'fut' and I couldn't quite make the aerodrome. I'm not hurt a bit, but they seem to think that a day's rest after a spill is good for the nerves. I haven't suffered from 'nerves' yet so I really didn't need it.

We have gas helmets here on account of German gas attacks. They make you look like 'ghostesses' ...

5 July 1916

... I could get such wonderful snapshots, but it's absolutely forbidden, and a court-martial offence. The French Army are all allowed to have cameras.

We are doing wonderful things just at present. Gee! I hope it will last. The Flying Corps has had rather bad luck. They lost fifteen machines this last week. I hear today that poor Coats – the boy who gave the party with us – was shot down. I didn't hear any details, but I hope he wasn't killed, or better still, that it was a mistake.

Anyway, if we keep on as we are going now and don't lose any ground, I think there is a chance of our having peace this winter. Wouldn't it be wonderful!

I hope you don't mind my writing in pencil, darling, but I don't get much time, and I can write quicker this way.

How is Mother? Give her my fond love. I would like to write

her, but I'm awfully bad at writing, and I only have time to write to you, darling.

Lizzie sends her love to Tell. She is a great joy to me, and to most of the officers here. They all love her.

There is a hospital next to us here, and there are an awful lot of wounded come in. It's extraordinary how happy some of them are because they have been wounded and are going to get a rest; and if they get a good wound, they get what they call a 'Blighty' – which means they get to England. It seems the height of good fortune to get a 'Blighty'.

The Marmon looks splendid in the photos you sent me. I would give anything for a ride in it. I haven't driven a car for nearly six months.

Vernon's letters reflect his carefree personality – like the Castle Walk he wanted to go *up* on the beat for Irene – but in the long moments before and after combat and tragedy there would clearly be other emotions. Those find a way into the letters. It is the dwelling on details which makes it all so more disconcerting. The normality cursed by the necessity of war in which the only definitive factor is death itself.

France
9 July 1916

I received three sweet letters from you yesterday. They came just at the right moment. I was feeling very depressed having just got back from a funeral.

I shall have to stop this letter in the middle because I am due to go over and drop bombs on a Hun railway in a few minutes. Now I must leave you for a while and go and do my bit...

Back again, darling – German aircraft seem to be very busy today. They were over here when I started out, but when I got up to 12,000 feet, I couldn't see any. I saw one machine which I thought might be a Hun so I turned to meet it, but discovered it was only one of ours, after all; but the pilot didn't notice me until I was quite close, and when he did see me he thought it was a German machine, so he fell about 2,000 feet out of fright. I was awfully sorry I scared him, but it's always hard to tell German from English or French, until one gets close enough to see their marks.

I am sending you my cap today, sweetie. You left it behind, but I thought that you did it because you didn't want it. It's very much dirtier than when you had it last, having seen active service, but you can get it cleaned in New York, and I can't unless I send it away. I hope you get it all right and that they don't hold it up for duty...

France
10 July 1916

I've just returned from way up the firing line. My flight commander had to go there to see a big gun battery. You see we work in conjunction with the gunners, and fly over the lines and signal to them by wireless just where their shots went, and keep connecting them until they get an O. K. or bull's-eye. I had never been near the big guns before and so it was awfully interesting. Gee, they make such a noise. They let me fire one and the noise is ringing in my ears yet it was a lot of fun, and quite a change for me.

Darling, have you got an old bit of fur you don't want? I want a piece to sew on the collar of my leather coat. Any old bit will do – just to keep the draught from blowing down my neck when I'm up in the air. I shall get it all right if sent to No. 1 Squadron, RFC, France...

France
10 July 1916

Just another little bit of letter for you, although I haven't much to say. I haven't received your pictures yet, but I guess they will come here in a day or two. The post is fairly good here. Things very seldom get lost, and there is no duty on anything coming into France for any soldier in the field.

The Huns were dropping bombs on us last night, but they didn't get anywhere near us... but it gives you one or two anxious moments as they are coming down. They make a very peculiar whistling noise as they are arriving. However, it is hard to figure out where they are going to hit!

11 July 1916

I received three very sweet letters from you this morning and one from Miss Marbury; you had just received my first French letter – poor mite – I'm afraid the first few are rather miserable ones. I was so very depressed at not hearing from you. But I am not depressed any more. I am happy and I would stay here another year willingly if I could be sure that in the end I could get back to you safely, darling. Oh! I want to get back to you so badly. I shouldn't care if we didn't have a penny. I don't want any extravagant things any more.

I often think of how wonderful it will be when it is all over. We can perhaps have a little farm with lots of animals. We could buy a cheaper one and keep it for always. I was so foolish about Manhasset. If I had listened to you, dear, we wouldn't have had to sell it and get into all that trouble. But we'll know better next time. Oh! If only this war could end this winter; but I don't see how it can, and I'm here to see it through and take my chances with the rest...

Father was tickled to death getting your letter. He sent it to me with strict instructions to return it. He has your pictures and I am writing him after this to forward them on to me and I shall return those I can spare.

How is Rastus? You haven't mentioned him in your letters for a long while and I'm getting worried about him. I must close now, dear, because I have two more letters to write – one to father regarding your photos, and one to Versailles to Miss Marbury. I'd like to see her but I don't think it can be done because we are expecting a big scrap here soon, and every pilot will be needed; but I shall want to hear from her about you and your plans...

France
13 July 1916

Just a little line before I go to bed. There is an awful row going on. The continual thunder of guns outside, and the more frightful singing of the officers inside. They suffer anything from Pagliacci to Michigan. The favourite song seems to be 'The Simple Melody' from *Watch Your Step*. They didn't know how the rag part went; I showed them, and now I realise I've made one of the biggest mistakes of the war! Every night they take sides and sing on one side 'Play a Simple Melody', etc., and on the other 'O, You Musical Demon', etc., and the pianist playing an entirely different tune makes an Indian uprising sound like real music.

France
23 July 1916

... I'm sorry to write such short letters, but I don't get as much time now as last week. We are doing more work in the air, as you no doubt have read in the papers.

Last night, as I told you, we had a squadron dinner, which means that the whole squadron (consisting of 40 officers) dines at one large table and has a big champagne dinner. This was in honour of three pilots who had won military crosses. I have the job of providing all the drinks for the squadron, and I also arranged the dinner, which was a big success.

I managed to get a block of ice from a hospital in a town near here. We'd never had ice here before, and I made cocktails and champagne cup. Most of the boys got fearfully tight, but they are all very young and felt all right this morning. I suppose it does one good to have a party once in a while, but nothing will make me happy but you, darling...

France
24 July 1916

Darling, you said that one of my letters about the air raid near Bailleul was very interesting, and I'm so glad. Nearly every day I could tell you some interesting news, but I don't want to frighten or worry you more than necessary, so I try as much as I can to keep off the war in my letters, and then again I'm not allowed to put anything in a letter that might be of use to the enemy, who are in every branch of our service, and never lose a chance to get hold of a letter in the hope of finding something of interest.

Oh darling, while I think of it – you might tell Dodd that my name is 'Lieut. Vernon Castle' not BLYTH.

Civilisation must be a peach of a film, but as you say, a little gruesome. If it's anything like this war it must be terrible. I think I told you we are near the receiving hospital where they get all the worst cases to treat before they send them to the base, and some of the poor chaps are in a terrible state, and the worst cases seem to get better while others, apparently not badly hurt, die.

There is one poor chap, who has the whole of his jaws, top and bottom, blown away. Nothing from his nose down, and he's going to live, while another man, who hasn't a scratch on his body, but is suffering from 'shell shock', will die. Things here seem all out of proportion. One good thing is, nobody seems to worry about anybody else, and so things go on just as though nothing had happened.

Oh dear! I shall be glad when it's all over and I can come back to you, darling, but no one here seems to think it will be over this year even.

We have started an offensive [one of the offensives in the Battle of the Somme, which began on 1 July 1916], but it's been prepared against by the Huns ever since we started to prepare for it, and so to make any headway will cost us more than it's worth. But there is one thing the Germans must realise sooner or later, and that is: *we are capable of going on with this for ever, and we improve each year.*

France

3 August 1916

This is another busy day for us and the weather is perfect. If it doesn't come over cloudy soon, we will be dead with fatigue. We did a big bomb raid yesterday on some zep sheds 90 miles over the German lines; it was terribly exciting. We were eleven machines altogether, and all but one got back safely. That one had to come down on account of engine trouble, and I suppose was taken prisoner. We don't know yet. No German machine came to attack us, and the Archie guns were very poor; it seems that it's only just near the lines that they are any good, because they get a lot of practice, and I'm sorry to say they are becoming pretty accurate, but inland they are awfully bad shots as they very rarely get a chance to shoot, then all of a sudden eleven machines came over, and they didn't seem to know which to choose. I don't think we did much harm to the zep sheds as only about three bombs hit the right place, but it must have scared them.

The zep raids have started again on England, but they seem to be worse than us on bomb dropping. I'd like to get a chance to 'straff' a zep, but I guess I shan't until I'm sent for duty in England. I really think in the air we've got them frightened to death. I saw one today on patrol duty, and as soon as he spotted me coming towards him, he dived down and away like a stone.

Oh dear, I'll be glad when it's all over and I can fly in peace. Do you know, darling, that I'm in the RFC for five years! It doesn't mean that I shall necessarily have to stay in the Army after the war, but I shall have to do about ten weeks flying every year, and can be called upon in case of another war, which is not very likely. I presume I shall have to go to Canada to do it unless we happen to be in England.

Well, sweetie, this is all for the present. There isn't a minute goes by that I don't think of you, little mate...

France
4 August 1916

I haven't had a letter for four days and I'm getting awfully hard up for something to write you about, and I'm not feeling very well today. I guess it's the heat or something. Anyway, they are giving me a day's rest from flying, so I'll be all right tomorrow. Flying at great height gives you a headache, sometimes, and your ears crack. You know how your ears feel when you are going under the Hudson in the Tube? Well, it's like that, only much, much worse.

I hope darling you will continue to send me the New York Sunday **** (title redacted). It amuses me tremendously. It's really awfully pro-German. Gee, how I hate the Germans! The terrible things they do! I really didn't believe them when I was in America, but they are most all perfectly true.

The dragging away of all the young French girls [aged] from fifteen to twenty and making them work and be servants to the German officers is simply frightful. We are quite near Lille and the towns they are taking them from, and it makes you feel that you want to take over bombs and blow up the whole town, but of course that would do more harm than good.

France
5 August 1916

... No letter again today. Only a doughy old cake from [name redacted]. Of course it's darn nice of her, really, and I appreciate it and all that, but I suffer enough out here without having to fight home-made cake, but it will do for bomb practice.

Today is a hot air day. The General is paying us a 'surprise' visit! The equipment officers are dashing about as though they really had some work to do. The only person who doesn't seem to realize the General's importance is Lizzie. She's barking at him.

We were raided by five Hun machines yesterday evening, but they didn't do any damage as they were driven away almost as soon as they appeared. We couldn't see them as it was getting dark, but we heard the machine guns of our patrol machines, firing at them, and then one of their machines fired off three white lights which means in German 'going home'. The leading machine always fires off the lights and then the others follow. They have a whole set of signals with different coloured lights, which we are able to read. So the raid was really, what we call here, a 'washout'. 'Washout' is a word used an awful lot out here. It's the equivalent to 'nothing doing'.

I'm most awfully anxious to hear about your picture, darling. You must have started long before this. I hope you'll like doing it, dearest. I do wish I was there to help you, although I don't help, do I? I only make you nervous. Still, I'd like to be there, anyway.

This is all I can write today, sweetie. God bless you and send me a letter in the morning.

France
12 p.m., 7 August 1916

... It's simply awfully late, but I haven't had a minute to write you before! This morning at six I was called and told there was a motor lorry going to [redacted], a town quite large, but four hours' ride from here, and as I had a lot of drinks, etc., to buy for the squadron mess, I had to get up and go there, and I've been in town all day, waiting for the lorry that was to take me back.

I had quite a nice time although I was all alone. They marched in a bunch of Hun prisoners, 8,000 of them. They had horrible unshaven and criminal faces, but they looked on the whole very happy to be prisoners, and were joking away among themselves.

I did a lot of shopping and bought many luxuries that we don't get up at the front, such as fish, five blocks of ice, an ice-cream freezer, gramophone records, etc., etc.! And, sweetheart, I have bought you your coffee glasses. I had only seen them in tin and nickel, but I managed to find four in silver. They are quite beautiful, and the woman is going to send for two more just like them, and in about eight days they will be shipped off to you. I am afraid, darling, you will have to pay duty on them, as they are quite valuable-looking.

I'm very sleepy, dear, so I will continue this tomorrow, or perhaps I'd better close and write another tomorrow – more envelopes for you to open...

France
18 August 1916

I didn't have time to finish writing to you yesterday. They wanted me to play in a game of cricket, and as there were not enough officers to make up the correct amount, I had to play. It's a rotten game; worse than baseball.

Last night we had quite a rough night. Three of our pilots are joining another squadron, and we gave them a sort of farewell party, which ended with their breaking up most of the furniture and drinking all the drinks in the place. One of our guests got his face walked on by a hob-nailed boot, and it was altogether a jolly evening.

I had a postcard from Elsie Janis this morning. They are sailing for New York again, on the 28th of this month. I don't expect to get to England until Christmas time, darling, so I guess your picture will be over by then, and if we are lucky, you will be able to meet me...

I am enclosing some sweet peas which are growing in a box outside my hut. It looks quite pretty really.

Goodbye for now, my precious...

Chapter Thirteen
The Perils of War

'Of those who watched, there was not one that had not seen
him at the "Halls" in the immensely remote days of
"Gilbert the Filbert, the Colonel of the Knuts".'
Rudyard Kipling, *The Irish Guards in the Great War*, Vol. 2,
1916 – Salient and the Somme, 1923

As Vernon was sending flowers from France to Irene, their friend Basil Hallam, who loved sunshine and laughter and Elsie Janis, became another multiple in the casualties of the Battle of the Somme. Elsie and 'Ma' had not sailed for New York when Captain Basil Radford, as he properly was, died. Instead, she and her supposedly stone-faced 'Ma' both went to support the troops on the Western Front in tribute to his memory. Elsie became the first female entertainer ever allowed on a military base: she often performed nine 45-minute shows a day within shelling distance of the German Army. That was her penance for loving Basil Hallam so much. Basil hadn't liked the army, but the troops adored him as much as Elsie, who was hailed as one of the supreme morale boosters of the Great War.

Before the tragedy, she and Basil had made plans, for after the war, to live in Liverpool and start 'a family of little entertainers'. On the Western Front, Basil was constantly asked to 'perform' and all but forced to do 'Gilbert the Filbert'; if the soldiers hadn't seen him on stage, they'd heard of him. He died in freak circumstances on 20 August 1916: he was assigned to a reconnaissance RFC team, which operated from observation balloons, fabric envelopes puffed up with flammable hydrogen gas. Watchers often had to parachute out when the balloons were attacked or drifted towards or behind enemy lines. Basil, at the age of twenty-eight, wasn't so lucky. Rudyard Kipling recorded his demise in a volume of his work, *The Irish Guards in the Great War*:

On a windy Sunday evening at Couin, in the valley north of Bus-les-Artois, the men saw an observation balloon, tethered near their bivouacs, break loose while being hauled down. It drifted towards the enemy line. First they watched maps and books being heaved overboard, then a man in a parachute jumping for his life, who landed safely. Soon after, something black, which had been hanging below the basket, detached itself and fell some 3,000 feet. We heard later that it was Captain Radford [Basil Hallam]. His parachute apparently caught in the rigging and in some way he slipped out of the belt which attached him to it. He fell near brigade headquarters. Of those who watched, there was not one that had not seen him at the 'Halls' in the immensely remote days of 'Gilbert the Filbert, the Colonel of the Knuts'.

The next day's letter from Vernon to Irene reported, with cushioned preamble, the news to her. He tried to make it casual:

21 August 1916

I've just heard that we are not allowed to send any pictures – magazines – news cuttings or postcards, etc., etc., to neutral countries, so, darling, I'm afraid you won't get your pictures after all. Isn't it too bad? They have even stopped the embroidered postcards that the soldiers were so fond of sending. As it's war I guess I can give those up, but I'm sorry about the pictures, dear.

I heard last night that poor Basil Hallam was killed yesterday. He was in a kite-balloon section in the RFC, and I always thought of him as having a safe job. They were winding his balloon down when the rope broke, and as the wind was blowing towards the Hun lines, he and another officer in the balloon had to jump out with parachutes, and Basil's parachute didn't open. I hadn't seen him since I have been in France as he was stationed quite a distance from here, but I saw him in London, and he said he was awfully 'fed up' with the war. I feel awfully sorry as he was such a nice boy.

This isn't a very cheery letter, is it, darling? I will try and do better tomorrow.

Irene kept in close touch with Elsie Janis and 'Ma' but Elsie, despite her valiant war efforts, was difficult to comfort. Basil's death also brought home to Irene how close Vernon was to danger. Even if it was a veneer, they maintained positive exchanges. Irene treated Vernon to tales of her filming. *Patria* was to be the most sensational and longest, fifteen-part, serial film of all time. Echoing patriotic triumphalism, Irene was on the movie posters as Mrs Vernon Castle – 'America's Best Known and Best Dressed Woman'. Her character was Patria Channing of the 'Fighting Channings', heir to $100 million, and dedicated to freedom. She is targeted by Japanese spies and Baron Huroki, as played by Warner Oland (later, an estimable Hollywood Charlie Chan), grimaced and threatened Patria as fiercely as leading man, Milton Sills as secret-service superman Captain Donald Parr, battled to protect her.

The Baron was after the money to fund his Mexican allies. Hearst surpassed himself: the $90,000 serial was such rabid anti-Mexican/Japanese propaganda it was investigated by a US Senate committee and President Woodrow Wilson demanded changes. They didn't involve scenes involving one of the walk-ons, a young actor called Rudolph Valentino. The plot implied that the United States might soon be at war with Japan, despite Japan being an American ally. Following the Presidential request, that element was softened. Kimonos were replaced by suits and Mexico took up the slack for the evil element in the five episodes filmed in California; it's disputed whether the real Pancho Villa appears in the serial (he's not in the one hour of film which remains). Irene only commented on her own performance: 'Fortunately, I was not called on for any acting except to look terrified occasionally, and in those occasions I didn't need to act, I was.' She filmed the first ten episodes around the New York State towns of Ithaca, Buffalo, Newport and Fort Lee: her deal was that the Hollywood filming would be completed in time for her to sail to England in time to be with Vernon for Christmas, 1916. He deserved it. She told her co-stars what a hero her husband was. Vernon had written and spoken of his first flight across enemy lines and Irene often employed it as an exemplary example of Vernon's courage and dedication.

His commanding officer was determined to test his new flier's nerve. He instructed Vernon to take twenty-four pictures of the enemy trenches. That involved low flying and being within range of the anti-aircraft guns as he took his photographs, tricky enough to do without being constantly blasted at. The camera must be calmly focused on a specific area on the map framed by indicated points of the landscape. It was often wham, bang, wallop, what a picture for Vernon as he tried to focus amid the German barrage, the bursting shells going off like firecrackers around his tiny aeroplane. When the fireworks got too close he would fly off and zig-zag back and forward to prevent being too easy a target. A flash of 'Archie' banged at his tail but he snapped his photographs one by one staying just away from the German guns long enough to photograph his objective. Finally, he believed he's completed his mission and thankful for that – and being alive – he turned back to base. The trouble arrived the next morning when his Commanding Officer asked 'Castle, did you take these pictures?' A happy Vernon saluted and beamed that he had. The CO tore the photographs up in front of him. They were worthless. What had gone wrong? Vernon explained the heavy fire he'd been under – and that he'd kept taking photographs despite the bombardment but sometimes had to fly off course. The CO didn't like that answer and saw it as fear getting in the way of the job. Vernon was angry at the CO and at himself. He immediately took to the air again, flew through the acrid clouds of Archie and took the twenty-four photographs all over again. His aeroplane was peppered with shrapnel, a piece pierced the collar of his flying jacket, a more direct hit ripped his rudder and that made for a heavy return landing. The only thing that survived altogether intact were the photographs. They were on target and in focus.

Irene also revealed the letter Vernon wrote to her – it is apparently in July, 1916, but the precise day is not clear in the existing papers – about his first aerial combat:

It was a terribly cold day, and I was detailed to go up on a patrol. I had just got into my machine and started up the engine when I suddenly realised I hadn't my little prayer around my neck. Of course I am far too superstitious to go up without it, so I stopped my engine, got out of the machine, and went to my hut where I found it. I was too bundled and had no time to undress, so I tied it round my wrist. Well, I got up in the air about 10,000 feet when I suddenly spotted four Huns. Then I was glad I had gone back for my prayer, because I thought to myself: 'Here's where I get it.' I beetled off after the Huns, who were well over our side of the lines and only a few miles from the aerodrome. I gradually caught them up, and when they saw me the two behind turned on me, and as they were higher, they started to dive at me, one from the front and the other from the back, like this,

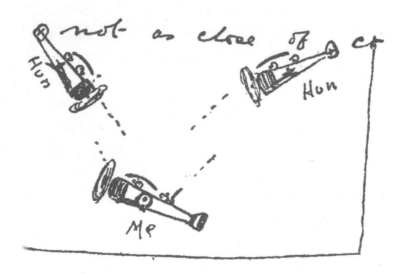

not as close of course as in this drawing of mine. My observer opened fire at the one diving at the back and apparently frightened him away or wounded him, because he beat it. The Hun in front of me had me cold really, because I couldn't tilt my machine up enough to get range on him, but I fired my gun anyway, and he like a fool turned off, which gave me the opportunity I wanted, which was to get under his tail. Now we were like this:

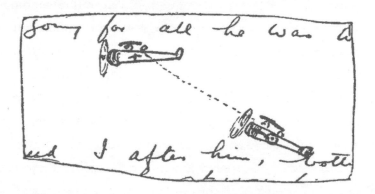

He was going for all he was worth for Hunland, I after him, both blazing away. Presently he stopped firing, and I guess I must have either hit the observer, or his gun just jammed. Then the Hun pilot tried to turn and shake me off his tail, but he couldn't, and every time I could get the light on him I blazed away. By this time we were across the lines on his side, and the Hun Archies were firing at me, but I was so darned excited I didn't notice anything. Well, we kept on for some time when suddenly his machine tipped over sideways and downward, and then started spinning like a top.

I knew I had hit him. He fell right through some clouds, and I lost sight of him for ever. When I came home I reported it, but of course as I didn't actually see him hit the ground, I couldn't very well claim him as a certainty; but while I was at lunch, one of our pilots who was working with the artillery in that vicinity said he saw the machine come through the clouds and crash into the ground. So after it was verified, I got full credit for it. It was very exciting because all the chaps on the aerodrome could see the fight. I don't like killing things, as you know, but I certainly saw red that time. Gee, I was excited.

Irene was always keen that her fellow Americans knew of the bravery of Vernon's comrades. She made available one of her husband's (undated) letters to her: 'I've really had quite an exciting morning. I was flying very low, about 4,000 feet, when I saw a Hun machine about 10,000 feet up, and just over our lines. I don't think he saw me, or if he did he didn't give me a thought because I was so low. However, I thought I had better start climbing, and if I could get above him, I might have a chance to bring him down. I climbed. My machine was not the fastest we have, so it was very slow work, and all the while the German was going round in big circles just over our trenches. When I was about 7,000 feet and the Hun still about 10,000, I looked up. Another machine diving down from about 17,000 feet came into view. At that distance I couldn't see whether it was one of ours or theirs. When it got closer, I discovered it was one of our fastest scouts and that he was coming at terrific speed. He dived right under the unsuspecting Hun and pointed his machine up and opened fire.

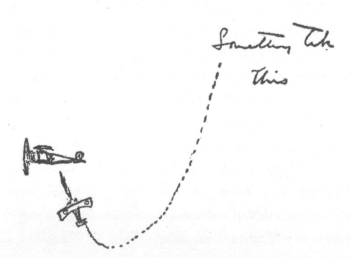

Well, the bullets must have gone into the gasoline tank, because with a big explosion, the German machine burst into flames and went crashing to the ground. The poor pilot (I really felt sorry for him) jumped out long before the machine touched the ground, but of course there was nothing left of him when he hit. Our pilot who did the job was so excited, and really it was a splendid piece of work.'

Irene, a.k.a. Mrs Vernon Castle, the title star of *Patria*, was receiving praise for *her* work but the director, his platinum-blonde girlfriend, and the late summer weather of California, which can turn anxious, slowed production: certainly, some mix of this, according to Irene. She was anxious about Vernon, wanting to see him but stuck in California. They kept constantly in touch by letter. Vernon kept them as chatty as possible but he could not rewrite the news of the day, which was also all over the American newspapers. He tried his best with pet as well as war news:

23 August 1916

... I received three sweet letters from you this morning, and I was so happy to get them. Poor dear, you seem to be suffering from the heat, so it must be awful.

The letter from [name redacted] was quite interesting. Did he promise you to get me a job in England? Because he has no influence, however good his intentions may be. He was only in England himself because he was too bad a pilot to be sent to France. As a matter of fact, I would much rather be here than in England. One feels that one is doing something here, to help. It's usually untrue, but you feel that way, and also there isn't the 'hot air' out here in France. COs and generals and things are quite human. Of course if you were in England, darling, it would be different, but until you come, I guess I'm happier here in France. The only thing I miss is music and theatres and suppers, and well-dressed women and horses and cars and dogs, etc., etc. We have everything here in the way of dust, guns and aeroplanes.

I suppose you will 'pounce' on the 'well-dressed women' and think I want them, won't you? I don't though, darling. You could only understand what I mean if you saw the revolting sights that crawl around these war areas... I get so frightfully fed up at times.

I'm so glad Elroy and the babies are still with you. It must be a lot of fun having them around. Thank you, dear, for sending Ham's letter. There is not much war in Mexico, but it must be darned uncomfortable out there. The insects and things are so annoying. We have lost Barber, our pianist. Not killed – he's gone to England, and I don't know what we will do for music. Some suggest buying a pianola, but they are hard to get around here, and very expensive.

This is all for tonight, dear. I hope you don't get bored with my letters. Yours are food and drink to me...

26 August 1916

The fur came today! Also the second episode of your movie. The fur is perfectly wonderful, dear, but much too good for my flying coat. I am going to have it fixed on my British Warm: you know, that khaki blanket coat I have. It will look splendid on that, and I can buy a piece of cheap fur for my flying coat, because it will only get splashed with oil and rain, and it would be a pity to waste good fur.

I didn't get the *Vanity Fair* with our pictures. They have censored them coming to England for some reason or other...

I'm awfully sorry, dear, you have had 'Baby' on your hands all this while. If you can find a nice home for her, I should give her away. She is really only good for breeding for a polo pony, and she makes a pretty good saddle pony, but she is too much a thoroughbred to be comfortable... You are so good to look after 'Baby', darling. I just love you all the more for your sweetness to that little nag. If only we had our farm we could keep her, but we shall one day, sweetheart, and it will be worth all this separation and we will appreciate each other much more than we could have ever done otherwise.

I shall be so glad to get the invoice for the Victor records. If there are any more good dance ones that you think we would like, you might send them direct here to France, and there won't be any duty. If it's too much trouble, darling, don't bother about it; it seems I'm always asking you for something.

I must close now, dear. Thank you again for the fur, precious...

30 August 1916

I received another sweet letter from you today, darling, and you are still suffering and in bed. Oh my dear, I hope you will take care of yourself. I just hate to think of your being ill. I don't feel any too well myself today. It's been a simply terrible day, frightful wind and rain. The job I had to do is of course postponed until the weather clears up. I was hoping that it would have been all over by this time. I just hate having something unpleasant hanging over my head. I prefer to get an order and go up straight away before I get a chance to worry over it. Now we are on an unpleasant subject, dear. If you should hear of anything happening to me, don't believe it right away, as frequently mistakes are made. A missing man might be a perfectly safe prisoner, and a wounded man only just scratched.

My precious little wife, you are so sweet to think of saving enough money to buy me a Rolls-Royce – but, darling, I don't want one, I only want you and a home. If I had one, I'd give a Rolls-Royce just to look at you for five seconds. It seems years since that last night in the little inn at 'Pewsy' [*sic*], and those six days were so short that they seem like a dream, and I haven't lived since.

I haven't received the Sunday papers for some time, dear; perhaps the censors have stopped them, as the last N.Y. [press] seemed to me to be very anti-British! Perhaps they will be sent on later.

3 September 1916

... I couldn't write at all to you yesterday as I had to be at a strange aerodrome the whole day. It's too bad, dear, I can't tell you what I was doing to be too busy to write you. We have to be so careful now in our letters, especially when they are sent to a neutral country, but I feel sure you will understand, darling, and will forgive me if my letters are a little dull.

I got two sweet letters from you today, dear. One of them enclosing two photos of 'The Movie'. It's some crock of a machine that 'Juarez' was going to take you up in. I'm glad he was shot before he had a chance to leave the ground with you... Poor child, you are certainly working hard in this picture. I hope you don't wear yourself out doing it. I'm crazy to get your 'stills', darling. I'm so interested...

I didn't get myself a soft job like [name redacted], my love, because I should feel a little ashamed if I had come all the way from the USA. just to do an office job in England, and never get to the front at all. I should like a job in England in winter, because I can't stand the cold, and if you come over, I can be with you. I shall anyway be due for leave about Xmas time.

I have never heard of a woman in the Flying Corps. I guess it's just a newspaper story. I don't want you to fly, darling, until I can teach you myself... If I could have a day in New York with you I'd be willing to walk all the way. Never mind, we will be together again soon, and then we will have lots of parties and suppers, and have the time of our lives. Gee, I wish the darned war would end...

You bet I'll go to the dressmakers with you when I get back home, darling, and you'll come with me when I play polo, won't you, sweetheart? I want to be with you all the time to make up for being separated from you for so long. Tell and I will follow you about everywhere... God bless and take care of you, sweet little mate, until I can be back in the nest again. Mates sometimes pine away and die when they are separated.

5 September 1916

It is now after 12 at night, and I'm only just back from a concert given by a hospital near here. It was quite a success, and not half bad, considering. I played my drum and did a lot of solo dancing, which made a big hit. They get a lot of singing and recitations at these things, but rarely anyone who can dance.

7 September 1916

... I have only just come down from a long patrol and although it's quite warm here, I nearly froze to death.

I received three wonderful letters from you this morning, darling. It certainly makes my day happy when I hear from you. I was very sorry to hear of your accident in the Marmon. Do be careful, darling, won't you? I don't think you can come to much harm as long as you don't drive too fast. I'll bet old Filby was scared stiff...

I'm simply crazy to get a picture of you in your soldier suit. I'll send one to the *Tatler* as you seem to be their pet for the moment.

The lunatic women that were let loose were, I think, all collected again. I feel awfully sorry for them. They have a panic every time a Hun machine comes over and drops bombs. It isn't a very pleasant sensation, as you can hear the bomb whistling through the air for about twenty seconds, and you have no idea when it's going to drop. In fact, I feel sorry when I drop them myself. I don't often do it now as I have been given a better job and better machine, and I now escort the bombing machines, to fight off the Huns should they attack, but as a rule they don't! They keep a long distance behind and follow you all over the place in case something should go wrong with your engine, and then of course they would be on you like a pack of wolves. But unless they are very superior in numbers you can usually get them running.

Oh, darling, I wish you were coming with Coralie – but you will come at Xmas, won't you, darling, and then I suppose I shall get a job in England, but if not then, a little later. They rarely keep a pilot out here more than eight months, as their nerves won't stand it, and I've been out here three months today...

8 September 1916

This morning I received the cable you sent Father.

I don't know who starts these rumours about me, but you mustn't pay any attention to them, dear. My name is down in a 'next of kin' book in the office, and should anything happen to me at all, you will be the first to hear of it, and Father next. You mustn't worry, darling, I don't stand half the chance of being killed out here as most of the yaps do at home crossing the streets.

I don't think there is a chance of my seeing Coralie for some time, dear... I received the Sunday papers from Dodd yesterday too, darling. They are awfully interesting. One of our pilots used to be an artist before the war. He is a very clever artist and I have commissioned him to paint you two oil paintings of aeroplanes in flight. One of them is finished already, but of course I'm not allowed to send it to you, but I know you will be pleased with it, darling, as it's really quite brilliant …

10 September 1916

I went out to dinner last night to one of our gun batteries, and in the middle of dinner they suddenly had a 'straf'. It was perfectly wonderful; I wish you could have been there. I fired one of the guns, and my ears have been ringing ever since. I brought my shell case home with me. I shall have it made into a lamp or something for Mother. Of course I'll have a lot of souvenirs for our home. They will be interesting after the war. I've got several now, so we can give some away. Brad will want one, and Ham too. I guess one will be able to buy them after the war, but they won't be so interesting. Mine will have a sort of little history attached.

… I do so long for the time to come when I shall be with you again. I guess you will be in England by the time I get leave – won't it be wonderful, darling?...

12 September 1916

I had a letter from Father today saying that Coralie had arrived. They are, of course, awfully excited. I shall probably get a letter from Corrie in a day or two. I wonder how long she will stay.

I'm part owner in another dog and when I teach them how to do the fox-trot he's going to give her to me. She is the sweetest little mutt you have ever seen. Just like the mutt you see in a circus with the dunce's cap on, that runs around and does nothing. She is like a toy fox terrier, only very low on the ground and coloured brown and white. Her name is Quinnelle – named after her former master, a pilot who had the misfortune to have his bombs go off under his machine. Quinnelle is going to have puppies in a day or two. The father is a Sealyiam [sic], or thinks he is. I'm dying to see the pups.

When we are not flying now we are busy building ourselves a tennis court – a hard one – so that we can play in the winter. There is an awful lot of work to a tennis court, but we expect to have it finished in a week.

The rye whisky hasn't come yet, but I expect it any day now. We are all most excited about it. I have been transferred from my flight to headquarters, which means that I take my meals with the CO (commanding officer). The mess is, of course, much better, and quite a good thing for me, as I get to know all kinds of colonels and things.

I hope all this small talk doesn't bore you, darling, but you know how I am handicapped as regards real news. I must say good night now, my dear. May God bless you and keep you safe and bring us together again very soon.

13 September 1916

Two very welcome letters came from you this morning. Also the music. Thank you a thousand times, sweetie. You do so much to make me happy... There is very little civilian population here in these parts, and absolutely no *nice* people. Only peasants. You see they are in the war area and everybody with the fare left long ago for more desirable spots.

Do you ever remember looking over the rail of a ship and seeing steerage passengers? Well, they would be first-class passengers compared to the people around here.

The French Army are quite different, I'm told. They are allowed to go to Paris very often, and also if they wish they can have their wives live in the towns they are billeted in. They also give away all kinds of medals on the slightest provocation. If I were in the French Army I should have already had the '*Médaille Militaire*' as I have done over one hundred hours' action service in the air, and anyone in the French Flying Corps who has done that gets a medal. The Germans get more medals still, judging from the prisoners we take. The French are a very wonderful people. They have all adapted themselves to this war in a most admirable way.

The rotten weather is beginning to set in now, I'm afraid. It has rained all day today, and it's so cold and miserable I don't know what I shall do in the winter. I just hate the cold weather!...

I've got a little oil stove in my hut trying to keep the puppies warm, but I'm afraid it gives off more smell than heat.

I hope you don't mind my writing in pencil, dear. It's so much easier for me and you are apt to get a longer letter this way. Sweet little Rastus – I just love to hear about his little tricks. I'm so crazy about that little ape... My candle is going out. I must close

in a hurry now. I don't think this is a very nice letter, dear, even
if you are able to read it...

16 September 1916

... My last two or three letters have been dated wrong. I've
written every day, but until today I had lost track of the date.

We are terribly busy just now. I only wish I could tell you all
about it, but I can't, darling, so you must wait until I return, and
if you keep my letters, as I do yours, we can go over them
together and I will be able to remember lots of things that
occurred. I also want to warn you, dear, that there might be a
day or two in which I shall be unable to write at all, as the
Flying Corps is not a stationary unit, especially if there is any
sort of an advance.

I had lunch with Hubert Neville today. He sends his love to
you. They are giving a concert, which they want me to go to, not
far from here. I shall go and I will let you know all about it.

What do you think? [Name redacted] has gone back to
England on 'home defence' work. He's only done a few weeks'
work out here, but he's lost his nerve and can't stand it, so he's
gone home. Gee! He's lucky, although I shouldn't like to have
people say I was frightened. I'd have to be awfully scared to
give up here, but I shall be due to come for a spell at Xmas
time, sweetheart. Oh, I do so long to see your sweet face again.
I just daren't let myself think about it or I'd get so blue and
downhearted.

France

19 September 1916

I wasn't able to write you at all yesterday we were so frightfully busy – and I'm afraid this isn't going to be a very fat letter. I will try, darling, very hard to catch up so that you won't feel neglected.

I received a letter from you today, darling, but it was rather a sad little one. You had just heard of the rumour of my being made prisoner.

I hope I never shall be, darling, but if I am you will know about it long before any rumour gets around. I don't think the war will last more than one year more any way …

France

20 September 1916

Today I received three lovely long letters from you. Gee, it's so wonderful to hear all the news, darling. I'm so excited when I get letters from you and so miserable when I don't. I'm so glad you didn't get frightened about that silly rumour about my being killed.

[Name redacted] is such a fool and an awful funk. He started to learn to fly long before I did and could have left for France long before. He speaks as if I got out here early because I was well known as a dancer, when, as a matter of fact, that has been my biggest handicap, as everyone seems to think it is impossible for one to be on the stage and be any good at anything more serious.

However, I'm pretty well installed now, and one of our senior officers told me today that he wanted to advise me to learn all I could about machines and men in the squadron, as I was one of the few pilots here who would be capable of commanding a flight, and that I would be made flight commander in a few months, in all probability.

I shall be glad to hear, darling, that we have a new woolly monkey. They must be awful cute, but I don't think there is a monkey in the world that could beat that boy Rastus.

I'm happy to say that I think there is absolutely no doubt that Germany is beaten, and will never be on the offensive again [Alas, not. The capitulation of Russia in 1917/18 released many German and Austrian divisions for the Western Front, resulting in the Ludendorff Offensives of March–May 1918, which very nearly succeeded]. Of course she can hold out, for God knows how long, but I don't think she will for more than a year. I'm due for eight days' leave in a week, darling, but I'm not going to take it, as it would be January before it came round again (that's about every three months). I'm going to put it off until you come to England and then I shall take it. I know you want me to, and I want to have you meet me, my little wife, and be the first I see when I come home. It's going to be so very wonderful, darling, I hardly dare to think of it for fear it may not come true.

It's late now, dear, and very cold, as this is only a canvas hut. This isn't a very long letter as I promised, but I will continue it tomorrow, sweetheart. I don't want to stop writing to you, but I'm shivering so I guess I'd better.

24 September 1916

First of all, let me thank you for the coffee, *Vanity Fair* and Sunday papers, which arrived today with two adorable letters which I have only had time to glance through up till now. One of your letters, darling, enclosed the one of mine with all the 'scratchings out'. It's simply too bad I can't tell you some of the news, darling, but I will have an awful lot to tell you when I see you.

Today I got an awful fright. An Archie gun almost got a direct hit on me. It shot away a big bit of my rudder, making it terribly hard for me to steer, and a piece of the shell went right through the back of my leather coat; luckily it didn't touch me, and all was all right, but of course I had no idea how bad the rudder was until I got down. As long as you keep 'zigzagging' and turning your machine, they very rarely can hit you, so I don't usually get them as close as that.

The war is going along awfully well, and there is enough excitement here to last me for the rest of my life. Darling, after the war, I have to put in my ten weeks' flying a year; of course you can be with me. You can put on your monkey-suit, and come up with me if you like!

Would you like to, sweetie? It would be such fun if we could go up together, and fly around to various places…

France
27 September 1916

I'm so sorry I can't write you the long letters you write me. It seems such a shame, but I really, sweetheart, have so very much to do all the time, and when I do get some spare time I have to do all sorts of jobs that come to me as Mess President.

I don't think I told you all the things I have to do now, but they include the collecting of all the money from the officers, for their mess bills, and paying for all the food, seeing that the men keep the place clean and the baths hot, and in fact, it's sort of a stage manager for the squadron.

I've done an awful lot of things since I've been Mess President.

I've had built a great big bathroom with three baths and a shower and a regular hot-water system, with an American furnace so that we can get hot water at all hours. Before we could only get sponge baths and unless you got there early you had to have cold water. Now everybody has a hot bath every morning, and the bathroom is one of our pet exhibits when we have guests or visitors. I've also built a big bar with running water and an ice chest, etc, etc. It's quite a lot of fun because I can get all the men I want to build and do things.

I'm going to have a tennis court built soon. A hard one, for the winter. During the cold weather we have much more spare time. I received the movie photographs this morning, darling. I think they are perfectly wonderful.

29 September 1916

Yesterday again I was too busy to write to you. Please forgive me, darling. I know you work so hard in this picture, and you need my letters badly, so I will try and not let it occur again. I used to be able to send you a picture postcard or something when I couldn't write, but now all that is stopped.

Your account of [name redacted] coming to dinner and setting his cigars off amused me immensely, dear. I can just see you.

This won't be a long letter, sweetheart, because I have quite an important job to do over Hunland. The weather is bad now but as soon as it clears up I've got to push off.

We have just heard that Romania is coming in on the Allies' side, which is good news. Our flying corps is doing awfully well. We've got it all over the Germans in that direction.

I received the invoice for the gramophone records and I guess I'll get them all right now.

I do hope you get your coffee glasses, darling. I had to send them by parcel post. How is the Marmon going? Will you send me a picture of it with its new wire wheels? Gee, I wish I could have a ride in it. It seems years since I drove a car. My poor little mate, how you have suffered with your head!

I am sending my letters to 120 [Lexington Avenue] again as by your letter, it seems you will in all probability be in New York or Newport by the time this arrives. I wonder where you are now, sweetie. And what you are doing. Oh, if I could only see you for just a minute it would make me so happy. Last night I dreamed I was leaving America and you to come to this now, and when I started to wake I thought to myself, 'It's only a dream – I'm in bed and haven't gone to the war at all,' and just then a gun woke me up thoroughly, and here I was in my hut. I told my hut-mate and he says that after the war he's going to sleep in one of these huts and have fireworks set off in the morning and an engine whizzing outside the door so he can feel thoroughly at home.

My dear, wonderful little wife, I long for you so. The suffering I endure by being away from you makes this war very insignificant to me. One day we shall be together again, my precious.

9 October 1916

… Yesterday one of our observers did a wonderful thing, while up on patrol: they were 'archied' pretty badly, and the pilot was hit on the head with a piece of shell and killed. Of course the machine began to fall, and the observer, while it was coming down, climbed out of his seat into the pilot's, and succeeded in landing the machine in the aerodrome. He made a bad crash landing, but he wasn't hurt at all. The pilot had died almost instantly. As observers don't know anything about flying except what they see, this was a splendid effort of this chap, and he will probably get the Military Cross.

The war news has been pretty good lately, but I'm afraid it will be a long time yet before it's over. It's really too bad because both sides are so heartily sick of it.

Well, little wife, I must close now. I'm so very, very sorry I can't write you a nice letter. God bless you, darling.

13 October 1916

I have just been told that I am to proceed to England tomorrow morning, and shall probably be there three days. There isn't a boat I can catch until Sunday, so I shall take that I think. After reporting to the War Office, I shall go straight to Norwich and see Father. My cold is much worse today so I don't feel very much like travelling, but it will be a change for me and I have been so frightfully miserable these last few days.

Cavendish Hotel, London
15 October 1916

I've just arrived in London. Gee, it looks good to be in a real town. I've just called up Corrie. She's coming to Ciro's with me. I'm staying at this little hotel. It's awfully nice. The chap who is on leave with me has lived here before. His name is Captain Balcombe Brown. Oh, darling, I wish you were here. There's been a lump in my throat ever since I arrived because I've been so homesick for you, sweetheart. Good night, my dearest. Excuse my haste. God bless you.

Hotel Metropole, Folkestone, England
22 October 1916

We are held up here on account of there being no boat; we were to sail at 7.30 this morning, but the boat is not leaving until tonight. This is a very dull place at this time of year. I've been sleeping most of the day. We should have been at the squadron by this time if we hadn't been held up. Joe Coyne gave us a parting dinner last night at Ciro's.

I have just heard that Norman Prince, who was in the French Flying Corps, has been killed. Did you know him? I hope, darling, you like the paintings [name redacted] is bringing you, the silver machine is the new one we are flying, the other is the one we are giving up. I must go now, sweetheart, and get my things on the boat; I'm loaded up with 200 oysters, a salmon and haddock, and numerous bottles of drinks, some sweets and a large cake and many other things. My luggage looks something like yours does when you travel.

Goodbye, my darling, I am dying to get back and see if there are any letters for me from you, sweetie.

Hotel Folkestone, Boulogne-sur-Mer, France
23 October 1916

We are held up here for eighteen hours; the train service is frightful, and I'm so anxious to get back to see if there is any mail for me, and also the oysters are sure to be bad by the time I get there, and it's been so much trouble to bring them all this way, with the scarcity of porters, etc. The salmon I had cooked here in the hotel, so I guess that will be all right, but it's rotten hanging around in these dead towns. We are just going for a long walk by the seaside to pass the time away, and then we shall go to the station and get on a train as early as possible, because there are thousands of people wanting to get back.

24 October 1916

I am happy again for the very first time in weeks. When I got back very early this morning I found seven sweet letters here, waiting for me. I've got an appalling lot of work waiting for me here in the squadron, also some rather bad news; four of my friends in the flight have been killed since I've been away, two were brought down by Archie guns, and two were shot down by a flock of German machines. It's darned hard luck, and they were four of the nicest boys in the squadron, but even this can't make me sad, darling, when I get sweet letters from you.

Now, sweetheart, I am going to take your letters, one by one, and answer any little questions that are in them. I'm so terribly sorry you have to wait so long between my letters. I am afraid the mails are getting worse instead of better. There is nothing to make them better. The more boats or men we lose in this war means the less we can spare for the mails, and so I'm afraid nothing will improve until after the war.

About my leave, darling, we are so short of experienced pilots now that we must remain in France nine months before being sent home for duty in England, unless of course one's nerves won't stand it, or something like that. My nerves seem to be quite all right so I guess I'm here for another four months, but of course nothing is sure. I might suddenly be sent back tomorrow.

Anyway, darling, I am almost sure I can get leave for Xmas, but, love, if you have to go right back to America again I don't think it would be worthwhile for you to go through those horrible journeys, and I would rather wait another month when you could come over for good, and then I would get my leave. I might have to come back here for about three weeks, and then come home to stay for some months anyway.

I do so long to have a little house, or flat or something, darling. I would give up my Merry Xmas willingly, just to have you with me for more than a week. You could have a fairly happy time in New York with Elroy's babies, so I will stay here and not come to England until you can come over to me.

I've got a dozen little jobs to do now, darling; I will stop and continue a little later. Later, I will continue this in pencil, if you don't mind, dear. I can write quicker and it's time I need just at present.

To continue with the same subject, darling: my plans, as near as one can judge, are like this. I will be here at the front ordinarily until the beginning of February, then I shall be brought home and in all probability be made a captain and given a flight in England for several months. In between that time I am entitled to a week or ten days' leave. I know you know best, sweetheart, what to do, and what you would like to do, so I must leave it entirely to you. Should anything suddenly happen, I will cable you immediately.

Darling, there is something I want you to bring me from New York, and that is a pair of binoculars with a Zeiss lens. The Zeiss is the best lens in the world, and as it's German we can't get any, but I'm sure you could buy them in America. Strong field glasses are tremendously useful to us out here. I also want a Victor record called 'Walking the Dog', a foxtrot. Will you send it to me, dear?

I'm so pleased you have got some more pretty clothes, sweetheart; won't it be wonderful when we are in London? I shall be so proud of you. Quinnelle's pups are getting quite big now, and at the age when they are a nuisance. They have to be fed because she won't nurse them any more, and they keep on getting under the floorboards of the sheds, and I have to wallow in the mud and fetch them out.

Oh! Oh! I do want a baby Rastus. If you see another one, will you bring him to me? I nearly died when I read your letter all about him. Isn't it sweet the boy not being jealous of him? I tried to get a monkey while I was in London, but I couldn't find a small one at all. I was so very sorry to hear about poor little Blackie. I wonder if he is still alive, poor little nag – it does seem a shame. I've never heard of the black-water disease before.

Your picture in your RFC suit is coming out in the *Tatler* next week. I would also like them to have one of those wonderful leaping snapshots if you can spare another one. It's nice to keep your name in the papers, all the time, and everybody I met in London asked after you, and wanted to know when you were coming back.

Gee, it's cold out here, and flying is simply terrible. I wear my leather coat, and that raccoon coat of mine over it, and we have to put ointment on our feet now to prevent frostbite, but I don't care much, darling, as long as I can get back to you eventually. I hope I continue to be as lucky as I have been since I've been out here.

France
28 October 1916

... Six wonderful letters came for me this morning. It's too good to last I'm afraid, and I shall have to go a long while before I get any more. I'm so very sorry about poor little Blackie, he was such a little peach. Poor darling, I guess you felt much worse about it than I do, because he was with you so recently. You were so sweet, dearest, to have taken so much care and trouble about him, and I'm glad he died that way rather than in strange hands. We will always remember him as one of the best little sports, and one day perhaps we will find another one like him. Every day when I think of you with your pets, darling, I thank God that I found you, who are so good to little dumb creatures. You've got the sweetest soul in the world, dear…

I don't think, darling, that you need worry very much about the German submarines that come to America… [censored)]… But I would much prefer you to come over on an American boat. I'm so anxious to know whether you think it advisable to stay and finish your picture before coming. God! When I think of your coming to me I get so excited I get a headache…

France
4 November 1916

I'm pleased to hear that Jim Europe's show was a success, and your decision was a popular one. The press cutting you sent me, sweetheart, is a lot of rot. I am not attached to the French Army, and I am no hero. I've done good work here, they say, and have made about a hundred flights over the German lines, and have led many bomb attacks, etc., but that is no more than heaps of pilots have done. Most of my work is in conjunction with artillery now, but I shall have to wait until I see you to explain it.

Darling, I hope you are not upset at my going to England, are you? I didn't want to go, but I had to as I was the only one except the Flight Commander, in our flight, who could fly this new machine. It looks exactly like the painting Coralie has for you – the one with the blue sky showing, and, by the way, darling, will you have a photo of this painting taken? Oliver, the man who did the sketch, wants one, as he keeps a record of all his work. Don't send it to me as perhaps it should not go through the mails. Just keep it and I will give it to him later.

I will do all in my power, dear, to remain here until you have arrived in England, and I think the chances are about a hundred to one against my having to be there before you. It's just as well, really, that I was there last time, because it was a change, and you can't have any idea how this place gets on one's nerves after a few months…

I've promised to go to a pierrot concert given by some Tommies tonight. I usually do a song and dance for them. When I get back, I'll finish this.

11 p.m. I've just got back, sweetie. The show was a big success, as they always are. They stand for anything out here. I'm so excited about your new clothes, sweetheart. I shall be so awfully, awfully proud of you. I'm glad you bought yourself some pearls, darling. Oh, how I wish I could have bought them for you, but I'll buy you some one day, precious, but I guess not this Xmas. I'm going to give the chaps here as merry an Xmas as I can. I shall get a tree and some coloured balls, etc. Will you send me one of those electric sets with coloured lamps? Just a small one, and a week before Xmas I shall keep back all the parcels that come for anybody, so that they can't open them until Xmas day. I shall think of you a lot that day, but I shan't be sad, because I know you will be wanting me, and will be coming to me soon.

Fancy old Minto getting first at the Fair. I'm so pleased for his sake. Well, ducky, it's past my bedtime, and I'm getting sleepy… Kiss all the babies for me, dear. Give the boy Rastus two kisses. I bet he looks a little gentleman in his moleskin coat. He must have a little uniform like ours...

7 November 1916

Today has been a terrible day. Raining all the time, and no flying, but I have had a lot of work to do on machine guns. Tonight I had to go to another concert. I am getting a reputation as a 'comic', and the result is I am sent for whenever there is a concert party around here. I don't like to refuse because it's usually for such a good cause, like buying comforts and for the poor chaps in the trenches. My God, how I pity them in this weather!

I haven't much news to tell you. There has been no mail of any description here for three days on account of the terrible storms on the Channel.

Are you going to California I wonder? If you are it will take years for our letters to get to each other. Oh, dear, I wish these two months would go by quickly. Will you send me a tin of ordinary coffee, dear? Ours is dreadful...

France
13 November 1916

Dear, I'm so sorry you didn't want me to go to England. I wish I hadn't been sent there now, although I really think I needed the change. It was so difficult anyway, to arrange anything, one way or another. If you are told to go anywhere, you go, and that's all there is to it. A chap in a squadron near here was suddenly kicked out the other day and sent to German East Africa. It happened he was very pleased, but if that had happened to me, I should have gone mad. As it is, I'm scared stiff that I shall be sent to

England [to become] a flight commander before you can get here. I'm pretty nearly the senior officer (flying) here now. I've told the CO how matters stand, and he will, of course, try and arrange it to suit me. So we mustn't worry.

Hotel Edouard, Paris
8 December 1916

I guess you will be surprised to hear that I am in Paris. I've come here for a new machine which I am to fly back, but fortunately the weather has been so bad that it's been impossible to leave. It's raining and there is a thick mist all over the ground. I arrived very early yesterday morning. I'd give anything in the world, darling, if you were only here with me. Everything here reminds me of you and the wonderful times we had together. I'd better begin at the beginning and tell you everything I've done.

When I arrived of course I had to go and report myself to headquarters, the CO of which is Innes-Ker, or Major Lord Robert Innes-Kerr [in fact, Lord Alastair Robert Innes-Ker, 1880–1936, son of the seventh Duke of Roxburghe; his brother Henry married the daughter of Mrs Ogden Goelet, the society nemesis of Mamie Stuyvesant Fish]. I think you met him in New York. He was over there with George Grossmith during the run of *Tonight's the Night*. There is also a chap there named Goldsmith, a charming man of about forty-two years, whom we know by sight very well. (He is a Frenchman.) He asked me out to lunch at the Café de Paris, which looked just the same. Louis was there and of course tickled to death to see me, and asked dozens of questions about you and Mother, etc. There is no music anywhere in Paris. I enjoyed it ever so much, especially for its sweet memories. It seems like a dream when I thought of the first time you and I went there and danced. When you come we must go there together, darling. It will be such fun.

Well, to continue my story: after lunch I left Goldsmith and went and bought my sweet a Merry Christmas present. Hooray! Hooray! Which, poor mite, I am not able to send you, but it won't be long now, and I will keep it for you. And who do you think I met on the street coming out of the shop? Maurice Soufflot! We had a drink together and a long chat which made me still more homesick for you, precious. I also met Rabajoi, and he asked me to tea at the Ritz, where they are having a sale for the Red Cross. We had tea and strolled in to the sale, and the first thing I saw was a monkey in a cage! Well, to make a long story short, he is sitting on my shoulder now trying to find a flea in my ear. He's a Japanese monkey, just a shade bigger than Rastus, and not unlike him. Of course he isn't Rastus, and never will be, but he's getting along very well.

I was three hours [with him] last night, making friends, and with the aid of a banana we have formed a relationship which I hope will turn into love, without a banana. I was obliged to give 200 francs for him, but he has been more than 200 francs' worth of fun already. The only thing is he is so darned active, and can do a flying trapeze act better than any monkey I've ever seen, and as he doesn't like to be put back in his box I am usually detained in my room about an hour longer than I intended to be. I will write you more about him, darling, later. He is going to be very happy. The only thing that worries me is flying him back. He will have to be kept so warm, and I must fly very low on account of the pressure on his little ears, but when I get him back, I'll keep him warm all the time, and he will have the monkey's long-distance flight record, and he may even become a corporal. He is tapping my wristwatch now, just like Rastus.

To go back to the Ritz sale: the most prominent figure there as a salesman was none other than Howard Sturgess. I nearly died when I saw him. He invited me to dinner at his apartment and I went. There were about ten people there, all men. Three we know – Harry Lehr, Frank Otis and Elliott Cowden. Elliott is quitting the war on account of his health, and is sailing for New York soon. Poor little Jean Renault was in the French Flying Corps, and was shot down and killed by a Boche. I stayed at Howard's until late at night, and then came home to play with little Hallad.

Today I got up late and have been lunching at the Café de Paris with some flying men who are here to fetch machines with me. I must say goodbye for now, darling. We are all going to the theatre tonight. I don't know which one.

Hotel Edouard, Paris
9 December 1916

It is very late and this is such a scratchy pen that this will only be a short note. I was at the aerodrome all morning, but it was so foggy and wet that I couldn't leave. I had lunch with some friends of Goldsmith's; they are Americans, but have lived in Paris for years. Their name is [redacted]. I met Letillier there, and he invited me to a party at his house, from where I have just come. He had music, but the latest music (American) was 'On the Mississippi', and terrible dancers, except two sisters, who were awfully good and not bad-looking. I had to go the rounds, but I danced with them as much as possible and had quite a nice evening. Letillier has a marvellous house, and of course a wonderful dinner.

Little Hallad is rather a bad ape. The chap that rooms with me here let him loose at dinner time, and then couldn't catch him again, so he thought he would be all right alone, and left him. Well, I wish you could have seen the room! It looked as though a cage of monkeys had lived in it for years. There wasn't a glass ornament that hadn't been deliberately broken. He had taken a package of safety razor blades and bitten them, one by one, into small pieces, spilled the ink, turned on the bath water, and picked the stuffings out of the quilt and a hundred other things. Tomorrow I shall put a chain on him. He has got a little cage exactly like Rastus's, but I'm afraid he will eat the basketwork. He knows me already, and when I tell him to go to bed, he scutters into his basket rather than be caught, and he prefers to eat his meals right on the top of my head.

I must go to bed now, sweetie...

11 December 1916

I am still in Paris and I am absolutely fed up with the place. There is nothing to do in the evenings except go to the rotten revues or out to dinner and tea with these society people. I was at tea at [name redacted]'s yesterday and I've never been so bored in my life. I've had all sorts of invitations from the same kind of people; they are all exactly the same as when we were here. I didn't mind them for the first few days, because they reminded me of the times when I had you here, dear, but I shall go mad if this rain and fog doesn't clear up. The funny part is, darling, I should love to live here with you, but I'm so lost without you that I would much prefer to be at the front...

I've met several of the American Legion and they can leave and take a holiday in New York any time they like. Little Hallad is so sweet, you will love him, I know, dear. He sleeps in bed with me sometimes if it is very cold, and he is a very good, clean little gentleman. His only drawback is his extraordinary activity. I can't keep him on a hot-water bottle because he bites holes in it and lets the water run out...

Café de Paris
14 December 1916

Vernon et moi, Maurice Soufflot, sommes au Café de Paris et regrettons beaucoup, beaucoup que vous ne soyez pas ici avec nous. Que de jolies souvenirs nous avons tous ici dans ce café! Espérons que ce bon temps reviendra!

This place makes us both sad, darling, because we used to be so happy here. Come back to me soon, darling.

All my love –
VERNIE

Chapter Fourteen

Continental Divide

'Hold my hand, no matter what the weather,
Just you hold my hand,
We'll walk through life together,
For you'll find in me that kind of friend,
Who will see you through till the end.'
Al Bowlly, 'Hold My Hand', 1931

'Perhaps he's been delayed,' said the reception clerk at the Savoy Hotel on the Strand. The words sent a chill through an already shivering Irene. She bustled her coat around herself to chase the goose bumps. Where was Vernon? She'd never forgive herself. With *Patria* dragging on in production she'd been persuaded – a personally promised $5,000 bonus by William Randolph Hearst had helped – to stay longer in California. Hearst had suggested she cable Vernon and ask him to postpone his leave until the New Year. After she agreed, she became sure her husband would be shot down and killed in that time. The Savoy desk clerk looked straight at her: 'There is no message.'

'Are you sure?'

'There's little private use of the cables from the Continent.'

Irene took his sympathy with her and returned to Vernon's

219

reserved and regular room. She spent forty-eight hours there, breakfast, lunch and dinner were brought to her, and she watched the white telephone on the mahogany desk across the room. It wouldn't ring, no matter how much she demanded it to. She made plans to go to Norwich but they were forgotten when there was a knock at the door and Vernon was there. She ran over and was about to crush him to her when he stopped her. A cheeky little monkey face peaked through the scarves around his leather coat. 'This is Hallad. From the Bible. Hallad be thy name.'

When the introductions were over, Vernon and Irene paid attention to themselves. She said of that time at the Savoy: 'For a few days we were able to forget the war across the Channel and lie in each other's arms, shutting the world out.'

It was as fun as in Paris when they'd lived in the attic and scooted around the boulevards for no reason but the joy of it. Again, they fuelled themselves on champagne. They walked around London, over to Covent Garden and up into theatreland and Mayfair. Vernon had cash and it added up to more than the savings from his $5-a-day military pay. He bought Irene 'wings', the brooch picked out in diamonds. That February 1917, at Selfridges on Oxford Street, he was able to buy the green-and-red striped ribbon of the Croix de Guerre ('Cross of War') that was waiting for him in France. The military decoration had only been created eighteen months earlier, to mark 'acts of heroism'. The grand French award, a bronze cross pattée on two crossed swords, was intended for distinguished bravery and Vernon had earned it. He was a war hero, mentioned in dispatches for his repeated missions over enemy lines.

As such, he and Irene were also to meet Queen Alexandra, the former Princess Alexandra of Denmark, widow of King Edward 'Bertie' VII, mother of King George V. Vernon and Irene had been invited to dance at a war-relief benefit concert at the Drury Lane Theatre in Covent Garden. The office of Alexandra, the Queen Mother with the winning and generous smile, had, with some encouragement from the British War Office, asked for them to appear. With them both in London it was an obvious fundraising opportunity and war effort morale-booster. For Irene it was a nightmare. She didn't have a thing to wear. She complained to Vernon and he smiled: 'Don't worry, I'm here. I'll hold your hand.' She 'made do' with a black chiffon evening dress she rescued from her luggage trunk. With a little sewing, it would tango and foxtrot. Rather nicely, as it turned out.

Vernon and Irene Castle, the best known dancers in the world, had not done what they were famous for in many months – danced together. They were nervous but their confidence got a boost when they were able to engaged musicians they had worked with it. There was little rehearsal time available but Irene wrote in My Husban' in 1919: 'We waited backstage for what seemed hours and hours until our coons struck up one of our old favourites. Hearing that music in a theatre again took us back several years and the encouraging and admiring faces of our coloured friends – they were seated on the stage – gave us an added confidence.' It was glorious for Vernon and Irene, the dances returned like a bicycle ride, spinning smoothly one after another, as they performed for the delighted audience.' Irene thought they were in a dream as they bowed to the Queen Mother.

They danced again at parties and enjoyed being with each other. The only mishap during those days in London was the death of Hallad the monkey, who suffocated in the Savoy hotel room. Vernon had put a coat around him to keep the always-cold monkey warm. He blamed himself for the accident. When he returned to France, Vernon eventually replaced his loss and grief with the rhesus monkey, Jeffrey.

Irene returned to New York, another nervous trip across the German-submarine-infected Atlantic, and fought her own battles, firstly to get her $5,000 'bonus' out of William Randolph Hearst (she got half) and secondly in a court case over a theatrical contract for the show *Miss 1917* with Charlie Dillingham and Flo Ziegfeld, which she won. She also signed a movie contract with Pathé Pictures, giving her early-morning starts from 120 Lexington Avenue. One of her self-described 'undying epics' was *Sylvia of the Secret Service*, in which the Viennese actor Erich von Stroheim, as a sneering German officer, began his career as the original 'man you love to hate'.

The always lovable Vernon remained in action at the front but a couple of bumps in the sky, by chance and German fighter planes, found him to be reunited momentarily with Irene and on a new mission with Walter Ash. His final letters from France begin the story:

France
3 March 1917

I've heard nothing about my leaving here yet, so I guess I can't be leaving as soon as I expected. The Huns are very active here just now, and we get fights every time we go over the lines. I shall be very relieved when I hear you are safely home, though I don't feel the least bit nervous about the boat you are on. I feel it's safer than an American boat now, but at the same time, travelling at this time is dangerous. I wonder if America is coming in? I hope they do now that you are safely home... I have a terrible time every night trying to forget little Hallad. It's very funny, but I don't seem to be able to get over his death. It does seem such a shame, and I miss him terribly.

Oh, I have something to ask you to do. There is a Canadian regiment out here, and they have about forty American chaps with them, and these chaps, the CO was telling me, are perfectly wonderful soldiers, and I wonder if you wouldn't care to send them some American magazines, books and papers? They are doing a lot of dirty work out here, and anything you send them would be appreciated so very much, and would bring a great deal of joy.

France
9 March 1917

... I am hoping to have news of you soon. I am so anxious to hear that you are safe and well. I miss getting letters from you so. Nobody writes to me but you, and so the mails have not much interest for me.

It's been another dull day today with very little doing. There really isn't a thing I can write you about, sweet. I'm not allowed to discuss the war, and God knows there is nothing else to talk about here... I am sorry, darling, to have to write you these silly letters. I guess you'd rather have them than none at all, but when you don't get any letters to answer, it's awfully hard to write.

I only did half an hour's flying today, and when I did go up I couldn't see the ground, so I had to come down again. We have got some nasty jobs to do, as soon as we get a fine day. I hope I don't get "'strafed' when I'm so near to going home...

10 March 1917

...Today has been a very busy day for us and I've got a splitting headache, so this will only be just a word or two. I brought down another Hun today. Unfortunately it was over their lines, but it was confirmed by our batteries who saw it fall down in flames. I deserve my little credit for it, really. I saw four of their machines flying in diamond formation (that's like this):

X

X   X

X

and as I was above them, I dived down on the tail of the last one and shot him down and flew away before the others had time to realise what had happened. I didn't feel like taking the risk of fighting the other three over on their side of the lines. I probably wouldn't be writing you tonight if I had. As it was, I wasn't even fired at.

There is no further news, darling. I'm terribly anxious to hear from you. I shan't be happy till I do...

11 March 1917

I wasn't able to write you yesterday. I received your cable this morning and was so very relieved to know you are safe and happy. I know, of course, I should have heard if anything should have happened to your ship, but at the same time I felt very worried.

I had a terrible experience this afternoon. It has been a very bad day and there has been no flying, but there was something very important over the lines that HQ wanted to know, and our CO was told to send up four pilots, and I was one of them. I was to go over the lines at about 1,000 feet, and the others at 2,000. Well, I had hardly got over when 'Bang!' and I got a direct hit on my machine by a Hun Archie. It hit the engine and tore about half of it away. Of course I thought I was done for, but I still managed to keep a little control over the machine, and by the grace of God, landed just behind our second-line trenches. There is hardly anything left of the machine; as it came down it hit some barbed wire, turned upside down and landed on its back. I was strapped in tight, and except for a cut on the nose and a bruise or two, am unhurt. I can't understand it, and if you could only have seen the crash you wouldn't have been able to understand how I could come out unhurt. Well, the CO says it's the last job I need to do this trip, and is going to give me easy work until I am sent home.

Tomorrow I'm going to Paris to get a new machine. If the weather is bad I shall look up old Howard and 'Papa Louis'. I'd like to be able to spend a day or two there. It seems years since you went away. Give the Crown Prince Rastus a kiss for me...

17 March 1917

... Today is such a bad day that I am unable to leave for the squadron. I am staying with the CO of the aircraft depot, who lives in a peach of a chateau. We have been playing ping pong all the morning nearly. I hadn't played it for years, but it is very amusing. I guess I shall be able to get back tomorrow. I still haven't heard when I'm to be sent home, so it's just as well you didn't stay, isn't it, darling?...

The ping-pong days were soon over for Vernon. The War Office knew how important he could be for recruitment and public support, for morale in America and he received orders to sail to New York where he would be posted on as a high profile flying instructor. Now, in early 1917, Vernon was back in America – and America was in the war. President Woodrow Wilson had held neutrality (he'd made big financial loans to Britain and France) but Germany had become seen by his voters as the evil enemy. This was exacerbated when Germany promised submarine attacks on all commercial ships crossing the Atlantic to Britain. Germany offered an alliance with Mexico, U-boats attacked US ships and America declared war on 6 April 1917. The Great War was getting greater.

The War Office in London decided the now Captain Vernon Castle was a prize gift for the Imperial Royal Flying Corps in Canada, where there was a campaign for recruits. He would provide glamour and much-needed instruction in flying in aerial combat.

To support Vernon, Walter Ash enlisted in the IRFC and was appointed his batman. Together they became a valuable presence at the Camp Mohawk training camp at Camp Deseronto in Ontario, where Vernon flew the JN-4D Canuck, as the Canadian variant of the Jenny was known. That was after he'd entered centre stage in his snazzy Stutz Bearcat with the two German shepherd police dogs, which he boarded at the Mohawk Indian Reservation, and Jeffrey – who tore around and up the officers' quarters. Vernon and all the fliers were an attraction in the rural area. Flying was a novelty and every Sunday, after church, crowds with picnics would gather around the aerodromes, to gaze at these flimsy little craft take off and fly around and land again. It was, they said, magnetic.

Vernon found he wasn't the only new instructor with a flair for fun and extravagance. He had his Stutz Bearcat; his friend Captain Jack Coats, formerly of Skelmorlie Castle, Ayrshire, Scotland, had his huge white Marmon car shipped into Deseronto. Captain Coats, who lost a lung to mustard gas in France, kept a motor launch at the harbour and it was used to rescue fliers who fell from the sky into the Bay of Quinte. The Mohawk Indian who cared for Vernon's dogs also looked after the launch.

They were a lively, if black-humoured, *Journey's End* wild bunch, commanded by Lord George Wellesley, the great-grandson of the first Duke of Wellington and a man who found himself in 'Camp Deserted' because of love. The tall, distinguished commander – a Grenadier Guard before wartime transfer to the RFC – was a black sheep in London society. When his brother died at the front, leaving his wife and two sons, Lord Wellesley had married his brother's widow – against Church of England proscription – and he and his lady, Louise, began a new life in Canada. The couple were popular in camp and in the town, promoting co-operation and recruitment.

Vernon did his bit. He was seen as a heroic flier. After hours of instruction, he would take his Canuck up to 8,000 feet to 'relax'. He'd do barrel rolls, loops and, the most tricky of all, Immelmann turns: the pilot does a half loop and then rolls half of a complete turn, the linen-covered wings struggling and digging into the air, leaving the aircraft right-way-up and flying in the opposite direction. Mechanics on the ground swore they could tell when he was at the controls as the flying was so graceful, like dancing in the sky.

The instructors bored easily. They would race trains in their planes. Lieutenant Ned Ballough was 'the wing walker'; he'd climb out of his cockpit and stroll along the wing of the aircraft, back and forward, as his Jenny flew itself. Another unorthodox manoeuvre involved Vernon, Jack Coats and Audrey and Gwen Wilmot, the sisters of their friend and fellow instructor, Eardley Wilmot. Jack Coats and Audrey Wilmot became devoted to each other, and Vernon and Gwen completed foursomes for nights out; time never did tell if that was romance or wartime flirtation. Irene knew how to rein in Vernon – she took Tell up to see him.

With her sister Elroy, who was in the Women's Ambulance Corps and with whom she'd become closer, she took his dog north from New York. Before moving to Ontario, Vernon had visited Irene and Tell briefly on the set of *Sylvia of the Secret Service*: this was the trio's reunion. Elroy stayed in town and Lord and Lady George Wellesley gave Vernon and Irene a room in their cottage and, said Irene, 'left us alone'.

In Deseronto, the only rival with Fraser's Ice Cream Parlour for entertainment, a couple of dubious bars aside, was Naylor's Theatre. It was the only theatre for miles and could show the new silent films, but no one liked them. They liked *real*. Vernon and Irene put on a show, dancing and comedy; and all profits to the air cadets. Vernon celebrated by taking Irene, against all the regulations, up in his plane for a spin, which delighted her: 'We were in his special world and he was sharing it with me.'

Vernon tried to disguise from Irene exactly what this war training truly involved: he was still risking his life every day, every time he went into the sky. He was fearless – his luck was, to him, legendary – but other instructors and would-be pilots were killed daily. At the base all were aware of the fatal potential of their endeavours yet Vernon maintained a grandeur of care about him, a parental aura. The young cadets – for Vernon was a veteran, aged twenty-nine – all adored him. He was fun but dedicated. In turn, Vernon admired their enthusiasm, their guts. There was a great deal of determination around; one instructor, Colonel Harcourt, flew with a wooden leg.

Vernon tried not to have favourites, but Alex Fraser had talent and enthusiasm and Vernon, with a minimum of forty mostly teenaged students a week, found time for extra training with Cadet Fraser. The cadet completed his preliminary training impeccably and was preparing to go solo.

On 30 May 1917, Vernon got into the back instructor's seat and Cadet Fraser took the controls up front. The official report of the flight says the young airman was making a turn at 200 feet up in the air when the nose of the Jenny dropped; he panicked and pulled the nose up too quickly, stalling the aircraft. His hands were 'frozen' on the controls and there was no way or time Vernon could correct and avert a stall. The Jenny spun out of control and smashed into the roof of a hangar. The flimsy wing fabric ripped over the front cockpit as the shaken Vernon clambered out on to the hangar roof. He called to Alex Fraser but the cadet was unconscious – or dead. Vernon ripped at the fabric surrounding the rear cockpit and through it he could see the cadet's flying jacket. It was burning. The petrol tank exploded and Vernon was thrown to the ground. The flaming plane fell through the hangar roof. Mechanics stopped Vernon running into the hangar to reach the body, which with the plane was ablaze.

Vernon was devastated by Alex's death. He brooded for weeks; he visited the boy's parents. He got shingles and was sent off to New York to recuperate from the discomfort of that and the more severe pain from the trauma. Irene said he gazed out of the window and blamed himself for sitting in the rear seat. He said it was almost certain the man in the front cockpit would be killed. Irene quizzed his thinking:

'But the instructor always takes the back seat, doesn't he?'

'That's no excuse, no excuse at all.'

There's not much sentiment in war and the front/back-seat rule was for a simple reason: the pilot-instructor was more valuable alive than the pilot being trained.

Vernon kept his thoughts close, as he did Tell, whom he took on long, reflective walks. He wrote about the incident to James Europe, who was now also in the war; he believed, correctly, that the music man crowned America's first 'King of Jazz' would understand his internal conflict.

James Europe had dealt with conflict all his life: patience and understanding, but most of all never denying your belief, were his rules for Vernon. Do what you believe is correct. In December 1916, James Europe had organised a brass band for the new 15th Infantry Regiment (Coloured) of the New York National Guard. In July 1917, with America in the war, the 15th was mobilised, and sent to France as the US 369th Infantry Regiment. The troops were integrated into the French Army: there was no place for a black infantry regiment in the American Expeditionary Force (AEF). The 369th soldiered on regardless, earning medals, distinction, huge casualties and the applauded moniker, 'The Harlem Hellfighters'. A machine gunner, Lieutenant James Europe, was also the leader of 'The Hellfighters Marching Band'.

While they fought in France, the Imperial Royal Flying Corps had more mundane but vital battles. The severe Canadian winters hampered training so finally, after long negotiations between London and Washington, a deal was done for the 84th Royal Canadian Flying Corps to move their operations to Texas, to Benbrook Field near Fort Worth. Vernon became the 'father' of the base, insisting that 'my boys' get the best of everything. Almost always by his side was Walter Ash. Some of the cadets said that they were like a vaudeville double act, always fooling about and entertaining the student fliers. Vernon would have coffee with the learners after each flight they took; the engine roar prevented sky-high education.

There were some distractions. The Texas girls offered a warm welcome to the British and Canadian flying men. Vernon and the Scots boys were told their accents were 'cute'. Not as cute as the ladies of Fort Worth, both in looks and outlook. Mrs Caroline McCluer gave the gossip of the Texas two-steppers when she was ninety-one years old. For the *Aeroplane Monthly Magazine* of December 1992, she remembered it well:

We were all excited when we heard that the British and Canadian cadets were coming to Fort Worth. We soon discovered that they would be off-duty on Friday afternoons and many of the girls I knew couldn't wait to get in their cars to drive to town and would ride up and down the streets to see if they could pick up some RFC cadets and officers. A lot of the Fort Worth boys were jealous of the British and Canadians as they looked so grand in their uniforms. A lady called Mrs Galbraith held a list of a group of girls that she could call on when the officers were going to hold a dance. We would then go to the officers' club down on West Seventh Street but were always chaperoned. Once the officers had met the girls they would telephone them to invite them to hangar parties. I used to go to the hangar parties and always had a good time.

There were also a lot of parties at the Riverside Country Club, where it was so lovely to walk from the dance floor out on to the veranda, and sit in the moonlight.

Vernon Castle would always be at these parties. He wouldn't dance but would go up and join the orchestra where he used to play the drums, and I surely do remember his pet monkey, Jeff, beating the drums.

The dances, the girls, were an escape for the increasing tensions in the Texas airspace. Benbrook Field had become a 'finishing school' for the pilots and they were taught clever aerobatics and dogfight tactics including, from Vernon, the *Dicta Boelcke*. It was clever but dangerous stuff. In the week ending Friday 15 February 1918, five pilots had died in that single week.

On that February Friday, Vernon was giving instruction on a Curtiss JN-4 (serial number: C663) and taking a young cadet called Robert Peters up from Field 3 for their first flight together. He said they'd have a debrief coffee after the flight. Vernon, as was now his rule, sat in the front cockpit. He was at the controls and had throttled down for a landing. He was only 45 feet in the air when he saw another aircraft begin to take off from the runway immediately in front of him. His wing cut his view but there was no question: he was going to smash into the other plane. He attempted the impossible: an Immelmann turn to avoid the other plane and correct the flight of his Jenny.

There is one eyewitness account from Cadet Charles Sage, who described what he saw in a letter to his father:

Another bus was about in line, just getting started prior to taking off. Apparently, the man below took no notice of the descending machine, else he would have stopped, it being one of the rules of the air that a landing machine has the right of way. Neither did the American cadet in the rear seat with Castle notice the machine taking off, else he would have given it the gas and gone on. Castle, being in the front seat, was prevented from seeing the situation due to the wings of the plane. The first thing, as I saw it, Castle caught sight of the lower plane just as his wheels touched the rudder of it. Immediately, he pulled up in the air doing an Immelmann turn. This took the plane about 75 to 100 feet off the ground and had he been another 100 feet up, the turn would have been completed. As it was, there lacked room and his plane dove straight into the ground.

The plane and Vernon were in pieces. The Jenny looked as if it had been snapped in half, wings from tail, by hand. Cadet Peters had a black eye and terrible shock. He was rescued from the rear cockpit. Vernon was horribly crushed and bleeding and jammed behind the engine; it took fifteen minutes to get him out. The officers and enlisted men trying to free him were in tears. He was taken to the on-field emergency room, but he wasn't coming back. The life had been crushed from him and he was officially declared dead twenty minutes later. They changed the roll on the airfield's list of casualties to six dead that week and there would be another dozen updates shortly.

The place was distraught. Rumours were instant. German spies were to blame. The officers and the cadets desperately wanted a better villain than bad luck. Walter Ash walked in circles around and round the wreckage of the plane. He, like most others, was in tears. Captain Castle was meant to be the lucky one, the laughing cavalier. Ash held on to Jeffrey; he'd have to look after the pet monkey now.

Irene got the news by telephone from a persistent reporter. Her secretary Lizzie Wagner said she did not become hysterical. Irene's face turned ghostly, translucent, and she went into her bedroom and hurled her body at the bed and fainted. Vernon's sister Coralie was in New York with Lawrence Grossmith, who was in a Broadway show, and she helped as much as Irene's grief would allow. Everybody wanted a comment from her as news of Vernon's death appeared on front pages in New York and London and Paris and also in Berlin. He'd earned a great deal of respect. Some acclaim was strange but well-intended: 'the butterfly who grew into an eagle', thought the *New York Sun*. No one could think straight.

It was forty-eight hours after Vernon's death became public that Irene issued a statement through Lizzie Wagner: 'It was a brave man's death, and it is not a woman's part to complain.'

Chapter Fifteen
High Flight

'Oh! I have slipped the surly bonds of earth,
And danced the skies on laughter-silvered wings;
Sunward I've climbed, and joined the tumbling mirth
Of sun-split clouds, – and done a hundred things
You have not dreamed of – wheeled and soared and swung
High in the sunlit silence. Hov'ring there
I've chased the shouting wind along, and flung
My eager craft through footless halls of air...
Up, up the long, delirious, burning blue
I've topped the wind-swept heights with easy grace
Where never lark or even eagle flew –
And, while with silent lifting mind I've trod
The high untrespassed sanctity of space,
Put out my hand, and touched the face of God.'

Pilot Officer John Gillespie Magee, No. 412 Squadron, Royal Canadian
Air Force, killed, aged nineteen, when his Spitfire was in a mid-air
collision with a training aircraft over Lincolnshire,
England, 11 December 1941

The *Sunshine Special* train took Vernon's funeral casket to New
York for a farewell that was early Valentino. The morticians
had cared for his body and, resplendent in his IRFC uniform,

Croix de Guerre pinned to his chest, he was laid out on public display at the funeral parlour's chapel on Main Street in Fort Worth. There were many thousands of people on the streets and scores of state police and Texas Rangers keeping them from turning their mourning into a hysterical and dangerous display.

Several hundred women, including Caroline McCluer and her dancing friends, gathered at St Andrew's Episcopal Church, but there was no room available for them, or Walter Ash, to hear the prayers to send Vernon off. The church was packed with uniforms and dignitaries. Women from starlets to Gloria Swanson, who knew and did not know Vernon, spoke to the newspapers of their sadness. Irene waited in New York for Vernon's return.

Late in the afternoon with the services complete but the tears not dry, Vernon's coffin was wrapped fondly with the Union Jack and escorted to the depot of the Texas and Pacific Railway. Members of the 84th Flying Corps squadron flanked the caisson drawn by six black horses and saluted by a military band and gunfire. Children ran behind it while most everybody else, soldiers and civilians, just stared, heads bowed and bared. The train, the *Sunshine Special*, waited and puffed. The *Houston Post* reported: 'Men wiped tears from their eyes, the sobs of women were audible above the slow, measured tread of the funeral procession.' At Union Station, a guard of honour of airmen opened a pathway to the train. Captain Frederick Fedgewick of the Royal Flying Corps was responsible for the transit; thousands for the overwhelming sadness of the day. As Jack Coats said, Vernon would have liked it.

The funeral in New York would have impressed him even more. He really did make an entrance.

Irene was in charge. The reaction to Vernon's death had been remarkable and the public display of grief as lavish as her arrangements. Flowers were heaped in the car with Vernon's casket as the *Sunshine Special*, the regular stopping commuter train between Forth Worth and New York, whistled and stopped en route across America and up towards New York. Around 1,000 people met the train at Grand Central Station and Vernon was moved to Campbell Funeral Church, where he lay in state like royalty. It was from there that the funeral proper would begin but first, like a river, hundreds who knew him or wished they had streamed around his coffin for two hours.

At 11 a.m. on 19 February 1918, the funeral cortège moved off at a perfect ragtime pace, slowly, to the Church of the Transfiguration, the New York entertainment world's 'The Little Church Around the Corner' on East Twenty-Ninth Street. Irene had alerted the church that 'many Negro friends' would be there and they were in three-buttoned suits and white shirts and black ties, as neat and as much in 'uniform' as the fighting men from Britain, America and Canada. The Coloured Musicians Union was responsible for a host of flower farewells. Vernon's drummer friend Buddy Gilmore was given a moment with him before the coffin was closed. There were famous faces, Ethel Barrymore, friends, Bessie Marbury, and surprises; Maurice Mouvet, the supposed great dancing rival, appeared to say goodbye. Irene, dry-eyed and pale, was led into the church by her brother-in-law Lawrence Grossmith. She performed perfectly, her strength in the moment surprising her. Her mother and Coralie helped, but also the honours being bestowed on Vernon by senior military personnel. Major Lord Alastair Innes-Ker, commanding the Royal Flying Corps detachment, led the funeral to Woodlawn Cemetery (named a National Historic Landmark in 2011) to the north of the city in the Bronx. The mourners could see each other in the polish of the procession, all that was unusually bright, shining, on a dark, damp and drizzly February day in 1918.

At 120 Lexington Avenue that evening, the one-time surgery of Irene's father, the family remembered Dr Foote's constant urging following any family mishap: 'I don't want anyone to get upset.' They smiled at that and it helped a little and they talked of Vernon and life and death and said all the things aimed at comfort. They told stories of Vernon's antics, his goodness, his wildness, his daft ways with money, his generosity and love of life. Irene was quiet a little later when the others talked of how it began, of the days in Paris – before they were the most famous couple in the world. The way it was, when Alexander was the leader of the band:

Come on along,
Come on along,
Let me take you by the hand
Up to the man …

Irene did imagine flying in the air around Vernon, never ever afraid with his arms around her at the Café de Paris. The crowd chanting 'Bravo, bravo!' as she and Vernon went on dancing, which was the way it was always meant to be. When there was a hint of a pause in the action, in the insistent rhythm of the song Berlin stole from Scott Joplin, the cry went up for more, more, more. And Vernon and Irene danced on.

At the end of March 1918, a letter, which Vernon had lodged with his family on a visit to Norwich two years earlier, to be sent on by his sister Gladys, arrived at Lexington Avenue.

My poor little widow:
When you get this letter, I shall be gone out of your sweet life. My only thought, darling, is for you. I don't want you to be unhappy. Death is nothing to me, sweetheart. I don't feel it and

perhaps the giving of my life has done some good. It is only you who suffer, my baby, so you must be brave for your own sake. You may be sure that I died with your sweet name on my lips, and my only wish for your future happiness. You are the sweetest thing God ever made, dear. You must marry again, and have babies, and I will be a happy memory, darling. Be brave and don't cry, my angel,

VERNIE

Book IV
Twilight Time

'Cocktails and laughter – but what comes after?'
Noël Coward, 'Poor Little Rich Girl', *On With the Dance*, 1925

Chapter Sixteen

Dancing in the Dark

'When purple-coloured curtains mark the end of day
I'll hear you, my dear, at twilight time.'
The Platters, 'Twilight Time', Mercury Records, 1958
(writers: Buck Ram, Morty Nevins, Al Nevins, Artie Dunn)

London, 14 June 1923.

It was just, just not good enough, complained Irene, as she danced with the man who was dancing with the girl who'd danced with the Prince of Wales.

Billy Reardon listened patiently. He was used to this nagging as the other half of their dance team. On the advice of Irene and Vernon's loyal friend Elsie Janis, the clean-cut and impeccably elegant Reardon had joined the Castle 'family'. He was good. Fred and Adele Astaire were impressed. They'd helped to choreograph the Castle–Reardon touring show. It was a little – just a little – like old times for Irene.

Except there wasn't always enough room to dance with the Prince of Wales.

Their show at the Embassy Club was presided over by Luigi, who had taken control of the fashionable nightclub three years earlier. It was not as extravagant as Rector's in New York, but was still imposing and over the top, famed as the best dance club in London, with five-star food and drink, discovered along a marble passageway at the Piccadilly end of Old Bond Street.

It was also the haunt of 'the darlings', the society girls of England seeking the company of Edward, Prince of Wales, and his enthusiastic partying friends. The Embassy was one of hundreds of London dance clubs which had taken off like a mad, swirling Irish jig since Vernon and Irene had taught the world to dance. Tea dances at the Savoy or the Piccadilly Hotel were five shillings. The Astoria Dance Hall and the Regent Palace wanted two shillings. Private clubs were much more – the Embassy entrance fee was £21 – and were the world of the Bright Young Things: compulsory evening dress; cocaine and champagne optional, but habitual. Suntans were essential and diluted iodine did the job when the Riviera proved inaccessible, or dull.

Irene most adamantly had no interest in the Bright Young Things or the drugs and all that jazz. The 'fashion' era she had helped to create was not *her* thing. Yet, she liked the Embassy Club: two glass doors took you into the restaurant-dancing room decorated in violet, jade green and white; sofas and tables lined the walls, which were covered in mirrors – if you were paying a fortune to be there, it was reassuring to see you were part of the crowd. The tables had green electric candlesticks with shocking pink shades; amber lights offered soft glows from the ceiling. In the centre of the room was the dance floor. The music was provided by Bert Ambrose, known by the cognoscenti only as 'Ambrose', and his seven-piece band. ('Ambrose' was so admired at the Embassy that when he took off to New York for more money, he was persuaded to return by a telegram from the future, briefly, King Edward VIII: 'The Embassy needs you. Come back – Edward.')

Yes, Irene liked the Embassy, but so many people wanted to see her dance that there wasn't room to do so. She and Billy Reardon had been hired for £350 a week (a working family could rent a house for £50 a year) and the demand was so great that Luigi extended their run by three more weeks. As the crowds arrived, Luigi, in a quest for a return on his investment, moved tables closer and closer to the dance floor. One Thursday evening, Irene maintained there was only the equivalent of a theatre aisle left to dance on. She complained again to Billy Reardon and then told their employer: 'We simply can't do it. There finally comes a space too small to dance in and this is it. Every time I'd lift a foot off the floor I'd kick somebody's teeth out.' As she stood in the club's kitchen, Luigi asked: 'What can I do? They descend like locusts and all of them have big parties. The Prince of Wales, he brings ten people. What should I do? Evict him?'

They invoked a Café de Paris solution and moved the front-line tables out of the way during the dance performance and, like everyone else, the heir to the throne picked up his chair. Irene recalled in her memoir: 'The Prince of Wales was there so often I felt I knew him well. He would come over to our table and sit down. He was charming to us, and many evenings we went to our places with him, taking a few members of the orchestra to provide the music. The party would last all night at Earl Portarlington's or some other noble house, and scrambled eggs and coffee were always served before the party broke up.'

Irene tried to teach the Prince of Wales to dance in style but although he was good at the Shimmy and Heebie Jeebie, he was no Vernon Castle: 'Edward pump-handled when he danced and was stiff and led badly. When you put these faults together, you have a very bad dancer. He told me: "You dance too highbrow." I never did know what he meant.'

Irene might complain *to* Billy Reardon but she had no complaints about him. They danced wonderfully together: the foxtrot, the tango, the Castle Walk. Still, the memory of Vernon hovered. That summer in London, the *Dancing Times* review of the Embassy Club show reminded those who'd forgotten: 'There has only been one Vernon Castle in the world.'

Irene knew that better than anyone.

In 1918, without Vernon, she had found herself bewildered. She had been wary of the upcoming and fast-living but not yet lost generation at her heels, and conscious of her obligation to herself and her husband's memory. She contributed to them by pushing herself into war relief benefits and doing what she did best – dancing. She appeared at concerts across America as part of the war effort, but found herself most effective by simply dancing with soldiers at events pushing sales of Liberty war bonds. She said it stopped her thinking of 'what might have been'. She made a determined effort. With the war perilously balanced, she joined Vernon's brother-in-law Lawrence Grossmith and a string of other silent-screen stars to make the 1918 morale-boosting film *The Common Cause*.

As the Great War ended, she was a movie star. *Patria* had been a great success of the serial format and Irene was offered and took role after role: for a time it seemed she was in a new film every other month. Many of them were filmed across the Hudson River in Ithaca, New York State, where movie pioneers Ted and Frank Wharton established film studios pumping out blood and thunder serials, cliffhanging three- and five-reelers of exploits and perils, all aimed at screams and thrills for audiences who returned week after week. Irene was often in peril. Or in the Tap Room of the Ithaca Hotel, having dinner with Lionel Barrymore or envying Pearl White's new outfit or escaping the attention of Oliver Hardy, who hadn't yet found Stan Laurel to agitate.

The work moved west and so did she, on a three-picture engagement. Billed as Mrs Vernon Castle, she was with the kings of Hollywood: Charlie Chaplin, Douglas Fairbanks Senior and William S. Hart, friend of Wyatt Earp and Bat Masterson and the template for the movie cowboy. She adored Chaplin, who screened his films for her and Douglas Fairbanks: 'The little man would sit hunched up in his chair while Doug and I died laughing over a scene. Charlie would call the technicians and tell them what changes he wanted. He was the absolute boss, a complete perfectionist…being hailed as the comic genius of the world.'

Fairbanks wasn't so funny. The grinning hero of *Robin Hood* and *Zorro* was married to heiress Anna Scully, mother of Douglas Junior, and having an affair with his also-married (to Irish actor Owen Moore) mistress and future wife, Mary Pickford. The lothario invited Irene out for an evening drive to see Hollywood at night. He wanted a little more than the view and Irene was 'vastly disappointed' – as much by the great screen lover's seduction technique as the attempt, which she harshly thwarted. She found it safer with William Randolph Hearst and Marion Davies, who themselves were a confusing arrangement.

It was a complex time for her, as it was for Fairbanks and Hearst and their carnival of partners. While she wondered 'what might have been?' with Vernon, so too did the gossipmongers fixated on their marriage. Irene could be very grand in a turn-of-the-century New Rochelle manner, but deference to that society had all but gone; enlisted men and officers had fought the Great War together and class barriers were casualties too, such sensibilities squashed into the middle. Irene swanned above all that and her airs and graces invited opprobrium; she was a tantalising target.

Some said Vernon had fallen in love with Gwen Wilmot while

training in Canada and was going to marry her; his friend Johnny Coats did marry Gwen's sister Audrey in September 1918. The rumours fed on each other, the purveyors of them unable to resist, especially with the scaffolding around the so, so wonderful image of Vernon and Irene Castle increasingly shaky. It made for conversation and newspaper column space to rumble that monument about. Vernon's letters – which, yes, were archived by Irene – did not reflect anything but devotion to his wife. There is no hint of (other than army) censorship in them. Gwen Wilmot genuinely believed she was important to Vernon – but his family saw it as nothing more involved than a wartime flirtation with an impressive girl. Irene believed the 'beautiful side of his nature' was shown in Vernon's will, which was made on 28 September 1915. It was sent for probate on 6 May 1918: 'I, Vernon Castle, being of sound mind and mindful of the uncertainty of life, especially that I am about to enlist in the English Army, do declare this to be my last Will and Testament. I direct the payment out of my estate of all my just debts and funeral expenses. The rest of and residue of property I give unto my beloved wife Irene Castle, to be her property absolutely and in fee for ever. I make this disposition of all my estate, not only as a token of my deep love and sincere affection for my dearly beloved wife, but in grateful recognition of the happiness which I have enjoyed in her society during all our wedded life, and the great assistance which she has during all that time rendered to me in my professional work and career.' Irene said the will was 'phrased in human tenderness unusual, I am told, in such documents. I glory in the affection that it expresses for me.'

Irene, publicly and to those around her, was strong and adamant about 'getting on'. She was also afraid – and alone. All her life she had been 'managed', by her mother and by the influential men in her life: her father and Vernon. Both of them were gone and, for the first time, she saw herself in jeopardy. Her mother had suffered a stroke and her recovery was slow. Neither Vernon nor the endearing Dr Foote — 'Now, don't excite yourself' — was available to open their arms and comfort Irene. It was alien to her: there had always been a man about her house; it was the New Rochelle way.

Robert Treman filled the vacancy. He was personable and, with a confidence arrived at from being the son of the banker, the man who controlled the money in Ithaca, New York. Irene met him when she was filming in the suburban town where his parents were leading figures: his mother played the harp, his father was the citizens' stoical patriarch. They rather owned the place and were not much taken by an 'actress'; being one of the land's most prominent war widows brought more vulgar attraction. Irene, lost and distraught, quietly married Robert Treman on 21 May 1918. It was three months since Vernon's death.

The marriage was a life raft. She remained Mrs Vernon Castle professionally and to her new in-laws and, maybe, to herself. The new marriage was built on comfort, not love; a safety net of fondness at an emotional time but accidents, despite precautions, can happen. Irene was aware she was a social outsider in Ithaca — but she was also a star. She left her business affairs, $63,000 in stocks and bonds, and their expansive home on the outskirts of Ithaca to Robert Treman: she carried on with her wartime fundraising and agreed to appear at benefits, visit wounded soldiers and make a film for the Red Cross in London.

She'd stay at the Savoy, which she knew so well. With bizarre happenstance, it involved her in the dark, decadent side of British society — and accusations of involvement in the drug death of a glamorous showgirl-actress. It should have been a cameo, for the death of Billie Carleton involved a cast of astonishing scene-stealing characters with more perils than Irene or Pauline, and all the rest, had ever faced on film. Irene was made a leading lady; for newspapers, the *Daily Sketch* especially, and Noël Coward it provided *succès de scandale*. Headlines and circulations heightened and Coward, who knew those involved, captured events in his 1924 play *The Vortex*.

Irene was presented in newspapers as the best friend of the victim — and indeed, as she told Scotland Yard detectives, she had been laughing with Billie Carleton only hours before the actress was found dead at the Savoy. Yet she had only met her that Armistice Night of 27 November 1918. London that evening was a carnival. Irene was invited to a Victory Ball at the Albert Hall by the American portrait artist Ben Ali Haggin. The ball, sponsored by the *Sketch* in aid of the Nation's Fund for Nurses, was a fancy-dress affair: Irene wore a Persian boy costume complete with elaborate turban, which Ben Ali Haggin had created for her. She felt like a princess in it.

The Great Victory Ball, aimed at raising £500,000 for a nursing college, attracted an eclectic mix of costumes, from Elizabethan to Mardi Gras mermaid, Britannia, women wrapped in silk and pearls and men dressed to theme with the Great War itself. Irene with her huge turban stood out even from that crowd.

Billie Carleton didn't see her but many guests told her about 'the Persian boy look'. Billie, who planned a career in Hollywood, was most aware of Vernon and Irene Castle. In 1915, she had taken Irene's role in Irving Berlin's *Watch Your Step* in the West End. Her career had flourished — she was working and friendly with theatrical stars Gertrude Lawrence and Beatrice Lillie — but so had her drug habit. She'd begun smoking opium after being given it at Murray's Club on Beak Street. Cocaine had arrived with Reginald de Veulle, a transvestite fashion designer, and heroin with the heavily dependent actor Lionel Belcher. Billie liked all of it – Ada Ping Yu, the Glasgow-born wife of her Limehouse connection Lau Ping Yu, believed her consumption to be 'beyond human' – and had a daily opium supply from the Chinese dens in London's Docklands. Her drug use had hurt her career, but she'd had a run of good roles in 1918 and by that November had become, briefly, the youngest leading lady in London's West End in *The Freedom of the Seas* at the Haymarket Theatre. She was twenty-two years old. After her performance, sixteen days after the First World War had ended, she went on to the Victory Ball wearing a diaphanous creation made for her by Reggie de Veulle at his Bond Street shop. The *Daily Sketch* described her evening:

'It seemed that every man there wished to dance with her. Her costume was extraordinary and daring to the utmost, but so attractive and refined was her face that it never occurred to anyone to be shocked. The costume consisted almost entirely of transparent black georgette.'

All Billie Carleton wanted to see was Irene costumed as 'the Persian boy'. Dancing on excitement and supplies from Billie's silver box of cocaine, she and her friends partied on till 4 a.m. When they returned to Billie's rooms at the Savoy – on the same floor as Irene – a floor waiter was sent to ask if an overexcited Billie could see Irene's costume. In the early hours she tried on Irene's turban. It was too big for her and they laughed and talked about Billie's plans for Hollywood, Irene telling her: 'You'll be wonderful there. They like blondes.'

Billie Carleton, the illegitimate, Bloomsbury-born Florence Leonora Stewart, who'd jumped from the wrong side of the tracks and back again, via chorus line and centre stage, didn't make California. Her maid found the girl with too much charm dead in her room several hours after she'd said goodnight and left Irene's room. Her cocaine case was by the bed. It wasn't empty. Still, her death was ruled an overdose.

In America, Irene got the treatment: newspapers picked up the 'best friend of Billie Carleton' angle and the story was presented with huge photographs of Irene and 'doctored' prints of the two fudged together. Irene screamed lawyers when she was implicated as a drug fiend. They advised her to hold back even when a nine-part newspaper series with imaginatively forged letters about her and the death of Billie Carleton began running in the *Syracuse Herald*. Irene believed no one was looking out for her.

Scotland Yard had told her she would not have to give evidence at the inquest. It was a relief. The inquest, as reported by *The* (London) *Times* on December 1918, was told that the dead girl and Reggie de Veulle, the son of a British vice-consul at Le Mans, hosted opium parties at de Veulle's Mayfair flat at 16 Dover Street. These evenings were 'disgusting orgies' at which Ada Ping Yu, 'the high priestess of unholy rites', cooked the opium through the night and into the following afternoon: 'After dinner the party provided themselves with cushions and pillows, placed these on the floor, and sat themselves in a circle. The men divested themselves of their clothing and got into pyjamas, and the women into chiffon nightdresses. In that manner they seemed to prepare themselves for the orgy.' Billie Carleton would arrive at 16 Dover Street after her shows and, 'after disrobing, took her place in this circle of degenerates'. The inquest was given full details of the night Billie Carleton died:

For the Victory Ball, Carleton commissioned an outfit representing France from de Veulle; as it was to be a 'dry' event, she also ordered some cocaine for the occasion. Having dined with Fay Compton [the actress sister of author Compton Mackenzie], Carleton arrived at the ball and met Lionel Belcher, who had a silver box of cocaine for Carleton, given to him in the gentlemen's lavatory by de Veulle, who was wearing a tight-fitting harlequin costume.

Carleton, Belcher, and a friend returned to Carleton's flat at the Savoy Court in the early hours of Sunday morning, where Carleton changed into a kimono; breakfasted, the friends left. At 10 a.m. she rang a friend. At 11.30 a.m. Carleton's maid arrived for work, and found her mistress snoring. At 3.30 the snoring stopped. The maid tried to wake Carleton, and called for a doctor. He administered artificial respiration and an injection of brandy and strychnine, to no avail.

Billie Carleton was believed by her friends to have died from the prescription drugs she frequently used to alleviate her regular cocaine 'hangovers', but this was not considered at the inquest. It was all evil drugs and 'The Yellow Peril' from Limehouse, imagined in 1912 as the home of Dr Fu Manchu by the English author and Harry Houdini's friend, Sax Rohmer. The coroner gave transparent direction to the jury – Reggie de Veulle was guilty in supplying the cocaine that caused Billie Carleton's death. This was despite evidence of her addiction. He was later acquitted of manslaughter and jailed for eight months, without hard labour, after pleading guilty, with Ada Ping Yu, to a charge of conspiracy to procure cocaine. Ada Ping Yu got five months *with* hard labour. Her Chinese husband Lau Ping Yu got a £10 fine. He had many connected clients.

In America, Irene got most of the attention. It's not hard to see why: the most famous dancer in the world linked to London dope fiends and the death at the Savoy of a star, a leading lady of the West End stage. You'd read it.

Which is, of course, what the good people of Ithaca did.

Irene was upset but not anguished; that came a few weeks later with the murder of James Reese Europe. He had played on battlefields, for Generals Pershing and Gouraud, and for the troops as they went 'over the top' in the trenches. With his 369th US Infantry 'Hellfighters' he had provided a ragtime fanfare for the war effort. After one huge concert in Paris, one of the band bowed towards him and announced he had launched '*ragtimitis*' in France. Indeed, on his safe return to America in February 1919, he carried on the crusade for *his* music: 'I have come from France more firmly convinced than ever that Negroes should write Negro music. We have our own racial feeling and if we try to copy whites we will make bad copies. We won France by playing music which was ours and not a pale imitation of others, and if we are to develop in America we must develop along our own lines.'

The 'Hellfighters' band had paraded up New York's Fifth Avenue before crowds of more than a million people on their return home in February. They'd been saluted as they marched and played from Madison Square Garden to Harlem. Europe and Noble Sissle had written 'On Patrol in No Man's Land' in the final days of the war and it was an instant hit, one of eleven recordings the 'Hellfighters' band made in March 1919. On the back of huge sales, especially to returning servicemen, a nationwide tour was arranged; the billboards proclaimed: '65 Battling Musicians Direct from the Fighting Fronts in France – The Band That Set All France Jazz Mad!'

The tour was a sensation, which was why he was performing on 9 May 1919 at what was to be the first of three concerts at the old and barn-like Mechanics Hall in Boston. It was wet, chilly in the city, and the band leader had developed a bad flu. But he wanted to be on stage for the packed house, which included Al Jolson, who was there with the cast from *Sinbad*, which was in rehearsal over from Huntington Avenue at the Boston Opera House. He felt much better by showtime, most certainly in spirit. Governor Calvin Coolidge (the future thirtieth US President) had personally asked him to play the next day at the State House; he was also invited to lay a wreath at the Robert Gould Shaw Monument, a great honour, as Shaw had commanded the courageous black soldiers of the 54th Massachusetts Voluntary Regiment during the Civil War.

None of that took place. After surviving the deadliest war ever, during the concert's intermission he was killed by one of his own band in a sad, ridiculous scuffle.

He'd admonished drummer Herbert Wright, aged twenty-four, for walking off- and onstage during performances. Wright had a tantrum: he threw his drumsticks down and began a tirade of abuse: Europe did not treat him well, and he was tired of getting blamed for others' mistakes. He flew at Europe and, suddenly, there was a penknife in his hand. It looked innocuous, harmless, but Wright jabbed the blade into Europe's neck. It severed his jugular vein.

The band leader died at 11.45 p.m. in Boston City Hospital's emergency ward. He was thirty-nine. His friend, the 'father of the blues', W. C. Handy, composed his thoughts, as he did his music, intelligently: 'The man who had just come through the baptism of war's fire and steel without a mark had been stabbed by one of his own musicians. The sun was in the sky. The new day promised peace. But all the suns had gone down for Jim Europe, and Harlem didn't seem the same.'

James Europe's death was written in 'King of Jazz Dies' head-lines around America and the world. He was granted the first ever public funeral for an African-American in the city of New York. On the morning of 13 May 1919, his body lay in state at the Paris Undertakers on 131st Street, near his home in Harlem. Thousands visited and walked solemnly by the open casket. The funeral procession involved hundreds and was watched by thousands; there were six cars just for the flowers, which included two bouquets from Irene: one from her, one from Vernon. At the end of the procession, Ford Dabney, who was so often a visitor at the Castles' home with James Europe when they had created the sounds for those special dances, led the members of that original Castle House band. They wore black armbands and carried their musical instruments by their side. The integration of the mourners, the absence of any 'colour line', was so rare it was itself a story. All around St Mark's Episcopal Church on West Fifty-Third Street it was jammed, as was the church, with the American, French and British governments and forces heavily represented. It was a heroic event before his burial, with full military honours, at the Arlington National Cemetery.

Irene cried even more on 25 May 1919 at a memorial service for James Europe at the Olympia Theatre in Philadelphia when, along with Theodore Roosevelt Jr., and many, many other historic names, she was moved by the emotion of the baritone of a young singer, aged twenty-one, called Paul Robeson. Fred 'Deacon' Johnson, leader of the Black Musicians Union, spoke to all mourners in what was a civil-rights beginning: 'Before Jim Europe came to New York, the coloured man knew nothing but Negro dances and porter's work. All that has been changed. Jim Europe was the living "open sesame" to the coloured porters of this city. He took them from their porter's places and raised them to positions of importance as real musicians. I think the suffering public ought to know that in Jim Europe, the race has lost a leader, a benefactor, and a true friend.'

Irene certainly had.

Chapter Seventeen

Shall We Dance?

'I'm puttin' on my top hat
Tyin' up my white tie…
Dancin' in my tails.'
Irving Berlin, 'Top Hat', 1935

'With no clothes on at all? Nothing? Dreadful!' It wasn't just Mrs Harrison, who gossiped with Mrs Hurst and her spinster sister Dorothy, who was shocked at the news. Irene Castle Treman had posed in the altogether: naked, nude, without a stitch, revealing all – and more – and was shameless about it. Most of sensitive Ithaca trembled to ask for detail, apprehensive the answer might result in a swoon. Irene, as Mrs Treman, lived in a stone-built house in Cayuga Heights, north of Cornell University, with a swimming pool, the only one in town, and servants and animals, monkeys and dogs and birds galore, which the locals, and her in-laws, found beyond eccentric. So, too, was her ongoing career. What got the lips pursing and the net curtains twitching was the story that she'd paraded herself starkers.

Life had been so much easier before the war. Irene, disenchanted with Ithaca and Robert Treman, found solace in the past and in planning her dance tours with Billy Reardon. The Astaire brother and sister were happy to work with her during breaks from their own shows.

All that was abruptly halted by the death of her mother. Mrs Foote had been confined to home following a series of strokes, but in May 1922 there came one too many. Irene was distraught and felt her mother's death 'was the end of the beauty and graciousness of an era she carried with her'. Good or bad, depending on circumstances, that time had gone. It was a period typified by her mother's final placement: in the family plot at the cemetery at Jamaica, Long Island. Irene's grandfather had bought the ground decades earlier and positioned a single but big headstone emblazoned 'FOOTE'. A gregarious man, he'd invited his friends to join him there and as Irene looked around on the day of her mother's funeral, the Foote name was in the minority; there were many other names on smaller headstones around the plot. Growing up in New Rochelle, she'd known most of them: 'The tenderly, crazy world of my youth was reflected even in the plot where I left her.'

That difficult day, Irene pledged to show her love and devotion and memory of Vernon in an ongoing tribute. She decided on a marble statue of a nude woman for Vernon's grave at Woodlawn Cemetery. She would pose for it and, on enquiry, found the most eminent female sculptor was Sally James Farnham. She was one of the few women artists successfully receiving large-scale commissions and what snared Irene was her creation, for the Venezuelan government in 1921, of the tribute to Simón Bolívar, which stands at the head of the Avenue of the Americas in New York City. Farnham, who had Frederic Remington as a mentor, made *End of the Day*: an impressive sculpture of a female figure with head bowed and in a crouched pose atop Vernon's tombstone.

It sits before a marble semi-circle, held above it by four pillars. It's a sad sight: sorrow trapped in marble.

The ashes of Zowie, the English bulldog the Castles were gifted by Dr Foote, and Rastus and a few others from their menagerie, including Jeffrey, are buried around the Castle monument. The pets have their own 'Castle' headstone. Other pets and strays are remembered at the world's first pet cemetery at Hartsdale, New York: the 'Peaceable Kingdom' is itself a monument to animal lovers. It includes a 50-ton above-ground mausoleum for two spaniels, and the War Dog Memorial, which was dedicated after the First World War; the first public tribute to military canines. Irene visited often. She was also a constant presence at Woodlawn Cemetry where in 1953 she had her grief for Vernon permanently preserved and her memories mummified when *End of the Day* was recast in bronze.

Her second marriage didn't have much of a chance. Her in-laws regarded her as an 'actress', which to them was the wrong side of Grand Central Station. Her husband 'lost' her $63,000 in stocks in an investment and as she was touring she only felt 'half married'. She jettisoned the other half in 1923 and that year became entangled with and married Major Frederic McLaughlin, who was interested in money, coffee, ice hockey, and her. A tycoon in wealth, through McLaughlin's Manor House coffee, and sports (as the first owner of the Chicago Blackhawks), he chased Irene to the altar. She designed the original sweater for the Blackhawks Hockey Club – and comfortable family life. She carried out Vernon's wish for her to have children: Barbara, born on 25 January 1925 (died in 2003), and William (born 17 July 1929; died 2012).

McLaughlin, sixteen years older than Irene, liked his own way and he was extremely settled in it. From their Tokyo honeymoon onwards, he and Irene were at war – as she was an animal-rights activist. She had a platform: she remained 'the best-dressed woman in America', was featured in fashion articles every month and presented *The Life of Irene Castle*, a weekly 15-minute radio version of her Paris days with Vernon, Zowie and Walter Ash, who had died after a long illness in 1924. She organised a dog sanctuary in Chicago and soon 'Orphans of the Storm' was established, placing stray dogs in homes. It was a 'foster' arrangement, for Irene kept track of how the animals were treated. She became a champion of animal rights, fighting cases of animal cruelty and against vivisection. Ernest Hemingway got a blast. He was present with Irene and some 'pals' of William Randolph Hearst – J. Edgar Hoover, Winston Churchill and Vernon's polo opponent Will Rogers – at Hearst Castle, San Simeon, California, when Hemingway's tales of his passion for bullfighting set her off: 'If you call that a sport, you'd better stop drinking Spanish brandy.' Hemingway, it's said, had another bottle of Hearst's best after the fiery encounter.

Her marriage floundered and so did she. The children held her focus and her animal-rights campaign work filled the time, but she couldn't replace the excitement of the dancing days with Vernon. Through the Great Depression she was lucky holding on to her own lucrative fashion and cosmetic advertising contracts; and McLaughlin's Manor House kept the family financially insulated. Despite legal moves, they did not divorce but lived 'together but separately'. Irene, when schooling allowed, travelled Europe with the children. She also began a clandestine arrangement with an advertising executive, George Enzinger.

She was chased by distress. Bessy Marbury died on 22 January 1933, and her widowed sister Elroy succumbed to cancer on 16 July 1934. Every event brought back thoughts of 'what might have been' with Vernon. Most dramatic in doing so was the offer in 1937 for the rights to film the story of Vernon and Irene Castle.

It was a serious big deal, a project for RKO (Radio-Keith-Orpheum) Pictures, one of Hollywood's big five studios and home to behemoth talent like Katharine Hepburn, Cary Grant and 1933's *King Kong*. Irene was paid $20,000 for the rights and she became 'technical adviser'. Her contract gave her powers over the story; she worked in tandem with the screenwriter Oscar Hammerstein II but was sharp with her opinions over costumes and hairstyles. Her blessing of Fred Astaire as Vernon was instant. She was less generous about and to Ginger Rogers. Irene wanted the fashions to be exactly as she had designed and worn them. Ginger Rogers, a screen sensation, had her own image to protect: there was no way she was cutting her hair. Irene nit-picked. The director Hank Potter says in the RKO files about her: 'She wanted one sequence shot over again only because Ginger, who was supposed to have come back from riding, had no hat on, and Irene said: "I wouldn't be caught dead riding without a hat." And, oh, the arguments and pleadings that went on about that.' The same RKO files show that Irene had alerted the film-makers about the hat before the scene was shot.

The RKO documents are extensive and show the under-standable conflict between Irene, who wanted it the way it was, and the Hollywood giant, which wanted the entertainment. Yet it was Hollywood's Censorship Office that stopped Astaire and Rogers as Vernon and Irene being seen touring with black musicians when *The Story of Vernon and Irene Castle* was seen in cinemas in 1939. The original plan of producer Pandro Berman was that James Europe's orchestra would be as they had been: all black musicians. The Censor's Office sent a memo to RKO: 'This would give serious offence to audiences throughout the southern part of the United States and your studio is likely to be deluged with protests.' This prompted the RKO purse-string executives in New York to memo the Coast in telegraphese: 'Southerners are certain to dislike use coloured orchestra Castles' picture and since it cannot make any difference entertainment wise strongly advise use of white men. No one remembers what they used and we should not take chance with coloured.'

The RKO exercutives' indifference to the reality, to the Castles' openness to all around them, their trail-blazing emancipation in the entertainment world, was insistent and Irene found her objections were not negotiable. There would be white musicians in the film, or no film. Even the then immediately relevant Oscar triumph for Hattie McDaniel, as Best Supporting Actress for her cinematic landmark role as Mammy in *Gone With the Wind* (1939), made no difference. But... but... Hattie McDaniel was the first African-American to win an Academy Award. For RKO, tomorrow, as Vivien Leigh's Scarlett O'Hara was most adamant about, was another day. There would be white musicians in the film, or no film. RKO didn't give a damn. Which is also why Walter Brennan, the wonderful and white character actor, stretched himself to remarkable thespian heights and became the black Walter Ash. RKO said casting a white actor gave the screenwriters more freedom to project the character into the story which, in 1939, was 'a period piece'.

Sadly, the real Walter Ash did not get to review the film, which featured Lew Fields playing himself, if thirty years younger. The renowned critic Frank S. Nugent of the *New York Times* did, on 31 March 1939:

Broadway, which does not believe in miracles, has been referring to the casting of Fred Astaire and Ginger Rogers in the Music Hall's *The Story of Vernon and Irene Castle* as a 'natural' and in a sense it is. Certainly there are no two persons in the world today more perfectly qualified to celebrate the history of the famous dancing team, the Castles, than the famous dancing team of Fred and Ginger.

At first glance they seem to be a benign gesture from drama's divinity... but the story of the Castles happens to be a story of a tragedy and that is where doubt rears its ugly head. Rogers and Astaire have been so closely identified with light comedy in the past that finding them otherwise employed is practically as disconcerting as it would be if Walt Disney were to throw Mickey to the lions and let Minnie Mouse be devoured by a non-regurgitative giant. Frankly, we prefer not to think of Mr Astaire's Vernon Castle being killed in a training plane and Miss Rogers' Irene staring, tearfully, at phantoms dancing in an empty garden. We've been conditioned to seeing only their lighter and brighter side. Of course, that's the truth of the Castles – more's the pity – and Mr Astaire and Miss Rogers have presented the story so sweetly and so well that we must criticise ourselves, not them, for our doubts about it.

There is nothing presumptuous in their impersonation of the most famous dancers of their generation, nothing like the second-rater's 'impressions' of the first-rater. They are dancing at the top of their form all the way, and that's high enough to do the Castles no discredit. They have had the charity, too, to modernise the steps just enough to shake the mothballs from the old ballroom routines. The Castle Walk, the first tango, foxtrot and maxixe might have seemed comically unsensational had they been rigidly reproduced. Astaire and Rogers modified them about as much as the Castles themselves might, were they repeating them today.

Frank Nugent wrote that we prefer happy endings. That can't always be. Yet there can be hopeful conclusions. Towards the close of the film, Vernon and Irene/Fred and Ginger are seen dancing a waltz. In the movie Vernon, in uniform, has returned from his daredevil photographic mission over enemy lines. Irene/Ginger is relieved he's safe and they dance; the only fully developed waltz Fred Astaire ever performed throughout his film career. The sequence is two minutes and ten seconds of film history: it's the imaginary last dance of Vernon and Irene Castle, and truly the last dance of Fred Astaire and Ginger Rogers in their landmark series of 1930s RKO musicals.

The film-dance expert Professor John Mueller offered in a critical analysis of the film: 'The most moving aspect of the duet is the way the dancers gradually take mental leave of their nightclub audience to focus on each other.' He describes the form of the waltz and concludes: 'They rock gently in that position, then all movement subsides – the ultimate hesitation – and they gaze at each other: secure, content, together, and alone in a crowded public arena.'

Vernon and Irene were always at their best on the dance floor, she safe and swirled around him like his favourite tie, he strong and confident in holding her, wearing and caring for all her hopes and fears. Irene buried a great deal of herself with Vernon.

The passing of Frederic McLaughlin in 1944 left her formally free to be with and marry George Enzinger; Irene outlived him too. He died from cancer in 1959 and, despite her record, she never stopped talking about getting married again. She was always vainly alert for another Vernon until she died on 25 January 1969, two days after suffering a stroke. She was seventy-five. By then, Echo Bay, that sheltered inlet on Long Island Sound, with the swimming and the Rowing Club and the English string bean sitting in the sun, was memory.

Irene had made plans for her reunion with Vernon. She is buried alongside him at Woodlawn Cemetery: together again, gracefully prized in marble, bronze and time gone, commemorated as the couple Vernon so celebrated in a letter:

'We did have such wonderful times, didn't we, darling?'

Postscript

Love Story

*'It is the custom to look back on ourselves of the boom days with a
disapproval that approaches horror... But it had its virtues, that old boom:
life was a great deal larger and gayer for most people, and the stampede
to the Spartan virtues in times of war and famine shouldn't make us too
dizzy to remember its hilarious glory.'*
F. Scott Fitzgerald, 'Echoes of the Jazz Age', 1931

Irene Castle, with her determination to achieve perfection, did
not give Ginger Rogers an easy time during the filming of
The Story of Vernon and Irene Castle. In turn, Ginger Rogers took
no hurt from that. She said she and Fred Astaire were determined
to capture the essence of the period and 'celebrate the creative
energy of two authentic originals'. In 1980, she wrote of gathering
in an RKO screening room with Fred Astaire and their director
and producer and recalled her memory of seeing Vernon and
Irene on film, the still-existing, ever-so-short reel-and-a-half silent
sequence of them dancing:

> We saw the two famous dancers, minus music, dancing with
> their characteristic style and class. Yes, they were the epitome

of class. That quality came blazing forth from the silent screen. Grace, style, dignity, class! It was thrilling to be transported back to their generation, to recognise the joy these two elegant individuals brought to their appreciative public. Such a flow of at-oneness. I felt I could read their mutual affection as they journeyed across my vision.

Our motion-picture script on their lives was infused with the love they had for one another; and now I felt sure it was true as I watched their arms entwine, around and around again, while they looked at each with such respectful admiration.

Oh, our script must be telling the truth.

They had to be in love with one another.

I wouldn't have it any other way.

Time, fashion and the Great War intruded on the partnership of Vernon and Irene and, in turn, on their legacy. For a moment, they were the most famous couple in the world; how they danced and looked remains, more than a century later. Names may fade, but they say love lasts for ever. As Ginger Rogers insisted, we wouldn't want it any other way.

Author's Note and Acknowledgements

(Bertie Wooster:) 'As a dancer, I out-Fred the nimblest Astaire.'
P. G. Wodehouse, *Joy in the Morning*, 1946

I saved Fred Astaire's life.

Well, rescued him from possible injury, at least. It was 1978 and he was about to be assaulted by my mother-in-law. We – that is, my wife, her parents, and I – were making our way to our seats at the Santa Anita Park racetrack in Arcadia, CA. For his part, the dancer was strolling most appropriately to the winners' window. A lifetime devotee of the ponies, Astaire was a vision of insouciance. His horse had won the first of the afternoon's races. It was going to be a wonderful day.

The sun played across his smile as Doreen, my mother-in-law, saw him. She had visited us in Hollywood several times and met movie stars like Cary Grant, but this was oh, so very, very different: this was Fred Astaire! She and her husband, Victor, had spent a lifetime as enthusiastic ballroom dancers. They went to classes, they were involved in competitions and weekly dance events in

331

London. They'd seen all the Fred and Ginger movies, been raised on tales of the Great War and Vernon and Irene Castle. They'd waltzed through the television years with Victor Sylvester and the *BBC Dancing Club*, and with Peter West (and the many others) introducing couples on the same channel's *Come Dancing*, the ballroom-dancing competition that began in 1949 and which, decades on, is now *Strictly Come Dancing*.

All this love of dancing boiled over in Doreen when she spotted Fred Astaire no more than a quickstep away from her. At her side, I sensed her about to charge at the elegantly dressed, but slightly built, seventy-nine-year-old star. She leaped, and with great difficulty, I pulled her back from her target and her enthusiasm. Fred Astaire turned at the confusion and smiled. He was nonchalant, unaware that he'd been about to be bowled over and hugged breathless in a torrent of fan adulation. He wandered on: simply watching him walk was worth the price of admission, all my bad bets. He had an inimitable style, remarkably resilient in his twilight days, so adroit it was difficult to imagine he could ever put a foot wrong. Yet even heroes carry some clay on their feet.

After 'living' with Vernon and Irene Castle for some time it was easy to spot their errors in life, but just as easy to allow their eagerness for fun, for dancing and making others happy, to compensate. They entertained before Gertrude Stein's 'Lost Generation', which was an altogether more self-interested bunch with pleasure the sole point of existence. Publicly, the Castles existed in the lightest of dream worlds which, given their era, was an escape route from fear, hopelessness, poverty, prejudice – albeit briefly, for many. Anything can happen in dreams, and Vernon and Irene Castle all but demanded that theirs should become more fact than fantasy. You can see thirty seconds of their magic in a sequence from their silent film *Whirl of Life* (1915), which duplicates their breakthrough performance at the Café de Paris, using the link: http://www.danceheritage.org/castle.html.

Of course, in their world, where electricity supplied light and not much else, their fame communicated itself by astonished word of mouth, and by newspapers. Which is why I am indebted to the New York Public Library at Lincoln Center, the Billy Rose Theatre Collection, and access to the scrapbooks of Vernon and Irene Castle. Luckily, the couple created a great deal of newsprint, and it is a tribute to the archivists of the printed word that so much remains. Public libraries and those of newspapers and magazines worldwide were invaluable, as were the Internet forums celebrating the heritage of dance and the theatre. The Theatre and Performance Archive of the Victoria and Albert Museum in London was an inspirational source. Members of Irene Castle's animal charity, Orphans of the Storm, were most kind; anyone interested further in their work can find them at: http://www.orphansofthestorm.org. As they can more information about the times of Vernon and Irene Castle from the bibliography which follows.

There is a memorial in Benbrook, Texas, at the crash site where Vernon was killed, on the southwest edge of Fort Worth. Directions: going west, take exit 429 off Interstate 20 on to US 337/Benbrook Blvd; south for one mile, then left on to Sproles Drive; then third left on to Vernon Castle Avenue. The impressive monument is topped with the metal sculpture of a biplane, and beneath it a plaque gives the specifications of the aircraft used for training. Written below is: 'He Danced With Death'. In Norwich, England, there has been a long campaign to have a memorial established for Vernon Castle. Norfolk historians point out that Edith Cavell and Lord Nelson are the only people from the county who, along with Vernon, have been honoured by major Hollywood films. It does seem about time.

The lives of Vernon and Irene Castle were of a much different time. We live with anxious sensibilities, hoping Thursday recyling will save the planet. Vernon and Irene rather believed that making people happy would do it. It certainly involved less stress. Of course, in their lives there were pliable personalities and the egomaniacs to work them over. Irene, and especially Vernon, seemed, justly enough, to dance around them. Maybe somewhere they still are. It's a nice thought. I have tried not to censor the language or attitudes of the Castles or those who were part of their lives, or the writings of the time. It is how they behaved not how they talked that defined their purpose. I can sense the banshees of probity arranging a meeting about that. There is really no need. It was of its place just as it is out of place a century and more later. Then, unpleasant words in reference to race and all their derivatives were as the shorthand slang of language today, and much in common use. (Strange, given our twenty-first-century casual use of bad language, that swearing rarely appears in reported events and public appearances.) I have tried not to allow Vernon and Irene, and all others in this narrative, to show any knowledge of what is going to happen. They didn't have the benefit of hindsight, and I hope I have censored mine. For instance, Vernon as a fighter pilot was as romantic and extraordinary a figure as the astronauts who followed, but he had no sense that man would walk in space in the second half of what to him was a fledgeling century. Yet, all those years before Sinatra, he and Irene flew audiences to the moon in their unique way. Katharine Hepburn said of Astaire and Rogers: 'She gave him sex. He gave her class.' Vernon and Irene gave each other the love you can see in their dance.

Author's Note and Acknowledgements

I feel privileged that Craig Revel Horwood, an expert in dancing and its history, took the time to read the manuscript in advance and contribute his foreword. The 'ten' was most welcome, especially as it's a score remote from my efforts at the Castle Walk.

I thank my wife, Lesley, for the dancing and the idea. Further, on class acts, I am indebted to Toby Buchan, the Executive Editor of John Blake Publishing, for help and guidance, energy and that most precious of things, enthusiasm.

DOUGLAS THOMPSON, Lavenham, Suffolk

Dramatis Personæ

'The Grand Duke was dancing a foxtrot with me
When suddenly Cyril screamed 'Fiddledidee'
And ripped off his trousers and jumped in the sea,
I couldn't have liked it more.'
Noël Coward, 'I Went To A Marvellous Party', 1938

P. T. (Phineas Taylor) **Barnum** (1810–91): an outrageous entertainment entrepreneur, a somewhat wicked genius known as the 'Shakespeare of Advertising', who marketed tricks and 'human curiosities' and his 'Grand Traveling Museum, Menagerie, Caravan & Hippodrome' into millions of dollars. The Broadway show *Barnum* (1980) was based on his life.

Irving **Berlin** (1888–1989): the greatest songwriter in American (and quite a lot other) history. From 'Easter Parade' to 'White Christmas' he was a hit from the start with 'Alexander's Ragtime Band' (1911) and 'What'll I Do' (1924) and 'Always' (1925) and continued to be from 'Top Hat (1935) to what could have been his anthem: 'There's No Business Like Show Business' (1954).

Oswald **Boelcke** (1891–1916): one of the 'fathers' of German aerial tactics in the Great War; on 28 October 1916, he took to the air with Manfred von Richthofen ('the Red Baron') and Erwin Böhme, another ace, and three others for his sixth patrol of the day. In a rush, he did not lock his safety belt. The German pilots became involved in a dogfight with several DH2s of the RFC. As Boelcke closed in on Captain Arthur Knight, in the chaos of the air he and Böhme collided with each other. Remarkably, Boelcke, twenty-five years old, who suffered the most damage – his top wing was gone – recovered some control and as his Albatros DII fell out of a cloud he crash-landed apparently safely; yet, without his seat belt, and he never wore a helmet when flying, the impact killed him.

James 'Diamond Jim' **Brady** (1856–1917): American financier and philanthropist, he made his money from the railways and clever investments, collected diamonds (with a twenty-first century value of more than US $56 million dollars), and loved the actress Lillian Russell and eating. Charles Rector called him 'the best twenty-five customers I ever had'.

Fanny **Brice** (1891–1951): the groundbreaking/legendary singer ('Second Hand Rose') and actress immortalised by Barbra Streisand in the film *Funny Girl*, 1968.

Eddie **Cantor** (1892–1964): from the *Ziegfeld Follies* of 1917 he had hit songs, 'If You Knew Susie', 'Makin' Whoopee', rejected the lead in *The Jazz Singer* (the first 'talkie'; see Al Jolson, q.v.) but went on to become an American favourite on stage, radio and television.

James J. 'Gentleman Jim' **Corbett** (1866–1933): knocked out John L. Sullivan in the twenty-first round in New Orleans on 7 September 1892, for boxing's World Heavyweight Championship. After he lost the title to British boxer Bob Fitzsimmons on 17 March 1897, he never returned to championship form and went into acting, remaining a celebrity name. Errol Flynn played him in the Hollywood tribute, *Gentleman Jim*, 1942.

Glenn **Curtiss** (1878–1930): a founder of the American aircraft industry. In 1908 he joined a pioneering research group, the Aerial Experiment Association, founded by Alexander Graham Bell at Beinn Bhreagh in Nova Scotia, to build flying machines. He flew the first officially witnessed flight, founded the first military flying school and designed and built aircraft including the JN-4 'Jenny' that Vernon Castle worked with. New York's LaGuardia Airport was known as the Glenn H. Curtiss Airport when it opened in 1929.

Charles Bancroft **Dillingham** (1868–1934): his greatest credit was launching Irving Berlin on Broadway with *Watch Your Step* which, of course, brought such fame to Vernon and Irene Castle. He also brought Russian prima ballerina Anna Pavlova to America in 1915.

Grand Duke **Dmitry** Pavlovich (1891–1942): the man who romanced Irene Castle was believed by the British Government to be the Emperor of Russia (he was a first cousin of the murdered Tsar Nicholas II). For his part in the murder of Rasputin in December 1916 he was banished to the Persian front, but after the October Revolution the following year toppled the Tsar his safety from serving soldiers could not be guaranteed. He was given refuge by Sir Charles Marling, the British representative to Tehran. Marling convinced the Foreign Office that his man was the next Emperor and the Grand Duke was allowed into the UK, the only Romanov permitted to live in England. He moved to Paris a couple of years later. He was first cousin to the Duke of Edinburgh: his mother, Grand Duchess Alexandra Georgievna was a daughter of George I of Greece and Olga Konstantinovna of Russia.

Lucy, Lady **Duff Gordon** (1863–1935): as Lucile she was the first English designer to find worldwide acceptance. She 'invented' models and catwalk shows – the mannequin parade – and with outlets in Paris, New York and Chicago, she was the original international couture brand, designing for clients like Irene Castle. Her name and designs live on with mentions in the television series *Downtown Abbey* and *Mr Selfridge*. She and her husband, Sir Cosmo Duff Gordon, Bart, survived the sinking of the RMS *Titanic* in April 2012.

Isadora **Duncan**: (1877–1927): the American dancer who wanted to return dancing to a high art form but found herself branded more at pavement level for her sexual and drinking antics. Gloriously bisexual and a Communist, she had become a citizen of Soviet Russia when she was killed in a car accident in Nice, the result of the flowing silk scarf she always wore becoming entangled in one of the car's spoked wheels. It provoked the comment from Gertrude Stein: 'Affectations can be dangerous.'

Douglas **Fairbanks** Senior (1883–1939): Hollywood director, actor, screenwriter and swashbuckler: *Robin Hood*, *The Thief of Bagdad*, *The Mark of Zorro*. He was a wily businessman, co-founder, with D. W. Griffith, Charlie Chaplin and Mary Pickford of United

Artists, and a founding member of the Academy of Motion Pictures and Sciences; he hosted the Academy's first Oscars ceremony in 1929. His marriage to America's sweetheart Mary Pickford made him 'the King of Hollywood'. That title vanished with the introduction of talking pictures. Irene Castle would have smiled at the title of his last film: *The Private Life of Don Juan* (1934).

Lew **Fields** (born Moses Schoenfeld; 1867–1941): Vernon Castle's mentor, he appeared as himself in *The Story of Vernon and Irene Castle*. A legendary Broadway name, the sometimes nasty banter in Neil Simon's *The Sunshine Boys* is based on his relationship with his early partner Joe Weber. Fields always regarded Vernon as a son.

W. C. **Fields** (1880–1946): American actor, comedian and writer, fired from *Watch Your Step* by Vernon. He died from the booze that made him famous through his act on stage and in silent and talking pictures, films like *The Bank Dick*, 1940 which included the scene:

Fields to bartender: 'Was I in here last night, and did I spend a $20 bill?'

Bartender: 'Yes.'

Fields: 'Oh boy, what a load that is off my mind… I thought I'd lost it.'

Elinor (Sutherland) **Glyn** (1864–1943), the younger sister (by one year) of the equally remarkable Lucy, Lady Duff Gordon (q.v.), aka Lucile, was a somewhat self-elevated sensation, the *Fifty Shades of Grey* novelist of the early twentieth century. Her racy and 'romantic' fiction earned her a reputation. As did her equally 'romantic' affairs during her marriage to Essex landowner Clayton

Louis Glyn with several aristocrats including Lord Curzon and the sixteen years younger Lord Alastair Innes-Ker, brother of the Duke of Roxburghe. That dangerous liaison with the young Innes-Ker was the catalyst for her 'scandalous' novel *Three Weeks*, about an exotic queen who seduces a young British aristocrat; it landed Elinor Glyn on the tiger skin of the doggerel and with tremendous book sales. Her notoriety took her to Hollywood where she worked with Valentino and 'styled' Gloria Swanson on *Beyond the Rocks* (1922). She created the 'It' concept, an appeal which some women and some men simply just had. 'It' was not a euphemism for sex or personality appeal. It was just 'It'. When Elinor Glyn pronounced that Clara Blow had 'It' the actress became a star, and an everlasting symbol of the Roaring Twenties, from her role as shopgirl Betty Lou Spence in *It* (1927). Elinor Glyn wrote for Hollywood and became one of the early female directors. She had 'It'. When told that occult-themed British author Denis Wheatley's novels had been translated into forty languages, she asked whether they were in English yet…

William Randolph **Hearst** (1863–1951): a great man and a monster, a publishing tycoon and vicious enemy but a sorry romantic; Hearst, the model for Orson Welles's *Citizen Kane* (1941), started in 1887 with the *San Francisco Examiner*, which he crowned 'The Monarch of the Dailies', and launched his international news empire and propaganda from then on. He was a tabloid-style genius, a populist, and his newspapers dictated not just policy but sometimes events having been credited for bringing on the ten-day Spanish-American War of 1898. The supporters of Hearst's much maligned 'yellow journalism' said his papers 'wore their feelings on their pages'. Hearst was innovative and introduced, among so much more, Vernon Castle's favourite cartoon strip, Krazy Kat. Irene Castle balanced her friendship with Hearst's wife Millicent (they never divorced) when he began openly living with his mistress, the actress Marion Davies, in California. His monument – other than *Citizen Kane*, by which his legend is much informed and is regularly voted the best film ever made – is Hearst Castle on 240,000 acres of California at San Simeon out on the Coast. It is magnificent, was employed as the estate of Marcus Licinius Crassus in the film *Spartacus* (1960), and remains one of the great attractions and examples of personal indulgence, created to keep Marion Davies at home and happy. Overlooking the Pacific about four hours' drive either way between San Francisco and Los Angeles, Hearst Castle was donated to California half a dozen years after its creator's death. The marvel which Hearst named La Cuesta Encantada, the Enchanted Slope, is a State and National Historical landmark and open for tours: 750 Hearst Castle Road, San Simeon, CA 93452, United States.www.hearstcastle.org.

Harry **Houdini** (Erik Weisz; 1874–1926): born in Budapest, magician, debunker of fake spiritualists, showman, a kindred spirit of P. T. Barnum (q.v.), but his exploits as an escape artist have never been fully explained – other than that he escaped.

Elsie **Janis** (1889–1956): her efforts with her mother in supporting the troops during the Great War following the death of her lover, Basil Hallam Radford, the creator of 'Gilbert the Filbert', during the Battle of the Somme saw her become 'the sweetheart of the AEF'. Her work with and for the American Expeditionary Force was coupled with that for British soldiers on the front lines: she toured the Western Front with her show and performed – hits like 'Give Me the Moonlight, Give Me the Girl'– close to where the action was taking place, one of the first Americans to do so in this 'foreign war'. She helped sales of Liberty Bonds. She recorded her experiences in *The Big Show: My Six Months with the American Expeditionary Forces* in 1919 and it is available in 2014 free of charge on line, and for a fee in printed format, from the Library of Congress in Washington, DC. She married again in 1932 to Gilbert Wilson, who was sixteen years younger. By 1938 she was living alone – and quite lonely – in Beverly Hills, California. Her last film co-starred Peter Cushing and the British actress and lover of the gangster Bugsy Siegel, Wendy Barrie. It was titled *Women in War* (1940).

Al **Jolson** (born Asa Yoelson in Lithuania; 1886–1950): known throughout the 1930s as the 'world's greatest entertainer' he appeared (in black-face) in the title role of the first talking picture *The Jazz Singer* (1927). His energetic style, racing into the audience and up and down the aisles, helped define modern musical theatre. After the attack on Pearl Harbor, he was the first American star to entertain troops in the Second World War. He did the same during the Korean War.

Jerome **Kern** (1885–1945): prolific composer of songs for the theatre and Hollywood and one of the greats of the twentieth century: more than seven hundred songs, eight Oscar nominations and two wins, 'The Way You Look Tonight' (1936) and 'The Last Time I Saw Paris' (1941). Often collaborated with Oscar Hammerstein II, who worked with Irene on *The Story of Vernon and Irene Castle*.

Maurice **Mouvet** (1888–1927) and Florence **Walton** (1890–1981): the great dance team rivals of Vernon and Irene Castle, they married in 1911 and were among the most successful couples in modern ballroom dancing until their divorce in 1920. Walton, from Wilmington, Delaware, made her stage début in the chorus of Lew Fields's *The Girl Behind the Counter* in 1907. dancing and singing in the chorus. Although born in New York, Maurice Mouvet grew up in Paris where he began dancing; a great innovator, the tango and the Apache became their signature dances.

Arthur **Murray** (Moses Teichmann; 1895–1991): born in Galicia, a region of Austria-Hungary, he landed at Ellis Island in 1897 and aged seventeen was working for Vernon and Irene Castle as a dance instructor, having been one of Vernon's pupils. He began teaching ballroom dancing, moved into mail-order dance instruction – steps were shown by foot diagrams – and launched the 'Arthur Murray Dance Studios'. From 1950 to 1960 *The Arthur Murray Party* ran on televisions and in time there were nearly four thousand studios with his name around the world: in 2014 there were still nearly two hundred.

Cole **Porter** (1891–1964): composer and songwriter and one of America's greats, from 'Let's Do It, Let's Fall in Love' (1928) and 'Anything Goes' (1934) to 'True Love' (1956), as well as scores of shows and other songs. His work is employed again and again and he appeared as a character for Woody Allen in *Midnight in Paris* (2011).

Paul **Robeson** (1898–1976): from his early appearance at the memorial for James Europe, the singer–actor–activist was close to controversy. In the 1928 London premiere of *Show Boat* (Jerome Kern [q.v.] and Oscar Hammerstein II) at the Theatre Royal, Drury Lane, he captured for ever 'Ol' Man River', taking it to ultimate spiritual heights. Some black critics attacked the play for using the word 'nigger' but the show was hugely popular, as was Robeson, who was invited to take part in a Royal Command Performance. He became a film star with *Sanders of the River* (1935), although that project was criticised for its portrayal of colonial Africa. Robeson's politics found him blacklisted during the McCarthy era. Times changed: in 2004 the United States Postal Service put him on a 37-cent stamp.

Blossom **Seeley** (1891–1974): born Minnie Guyer in San Francisco, the barnstorming Blossom Seeley became the 'Queen of Syncopation' and a champion of ragtime and, later, jazz. She was an inspiration with successful songs, including 'Some Of These Days' (made famous by Sophie Tucker, q.v.), but had her own major hits: 'Way Down Yonder In New Orleans' 'Yes Sir, That's My Baby', and her signature song – and Vernon and Irene's Paris salvation – 'Toddling the Todalo'.

Sophie **Tucker** (1887–1966): the 'Last of the Red Hot Mamas' was born Sonya Kalish on the way from what is now Ukraine for a new home in America. Aged sixteen, she ran off with a beer-truck driver called Louis Tuck. That ended with a son, Albert, divorce and her stage name of Sophie Tucker. 'Some Of These Days' became her theme song and she wowed America and then Europe, a tour that inculded a Royal Command Performance at the London Palladium in 1926. She worked on for the next four decades until just months before her death from kidney failure.

Rudolph **Valentino** (1895–1926): Rodolfo Guglielmi did his apprentice dancing in New York and was enraptured by Vernon and Irene Castle before he, in turn, conquered the world. His silent movies included film landmarks *The Sheik* and *The Four*

Horsemen of the Apocalypse (both 1921), and *Blood and Sand* (1922). As the great Latin lover he was one of the first screen idols, setting the standard for celebrity adoration and mania. When he died, aged thirty-one, the outpouring of grief was quite overwhelming; mass hysteria doesn't cover it. His fans, some of whom even wanted to kill themselves to join him in the hereafter, had never even heard him speak. But they'd seen him dance, moving elegantly across the screen.

Florence **Walton**, *see* Maurice **Mouvet** and Florence **Walton**

Ned (Edward Claudius) **Wayburn** (1874–1942): born in Pennsylvania in 1906, he founded the Headline Vaudeville Production Company working with Lew Fields (q.v.), Flo Ziegfeld (q.v.) and the Shubert brothers. He was the chief choreographer of the *Ziegfeld Follies*. His choreography, with which he helped Vernon Castle, involved acrobatics and tapping and a symmetry from the minstrel shows that he adored. He was a populist, using the tango, the Turkey Trot, the Grizzly Bear and, later, the Charleston, in exaggerated form for stage shows. He created the 'Ziegfeld Walk' and began the careers of Mae West, Barbara Stanwyck, Groucho Marx and Clifton Webb.

(Thomas) Woodrow Wilson (1856–1924), the twenty-eighth President of the United States; elected for a second term in 1916 on the platform 'he kept us out of the war', Wilson was a committed Presbyterian and defender of right against wrong, and a year later took his country into the Great War to 'make the world safe for democracy'. A moralist, he achieved much social reform and won the Nobel Peace Prize in 1919 for his work towards creating the League of Nations.

Herbert **Wright** (1895–year unknown): the killer of James Europe was charged with first-degree murder but, after reports by court-appointed 'alienists' (the psychiatrists of the day) he pleaded guilty to manslaughter in Boston Superior Court and Judge George Sanderson immediately sentenced him to between ten and fifteen years in Massachusetts State Penitentiary. Wright, whom James Europe's orchestra had 'adopted' from Jenkins Orphanage in Charleston, South Carolina, and given a chance with several other musicians, was paroled eight years later, on 1 April 1927.

Florenz 'Flo' **Ziegfeld** Jr (1867–1932): the *Ziegfeld Follies*, a series of revues which launched glamour and glamour girls were his invention, via Paris and the Folies Bergère, and he helped the careers of Fanny Brice (q.v.), Will Rogers, Eddie Cantor (q.v.), Marilyn Miller, Ruth Etting, and himself to the showgirls he found most attractive: he married Billie Burke, who played the Good Witch in *The Wizard of Oz* (1939). He produced *Show Boat* in the theatre he built on Broadway with backing from William Randolph Hearst (q.v.). The Ziegfeld Theater was demolished in 1966; a movie theatre of the same name opened a short distance from the original site in 1969.

Bibliography

'When you leave me,
Ya know it's gonna grieve me.'
Shelton Brooks, 'Some of These Days', 1910 –
the anthem of Sophie Tucker

Badger, Reid, *A Life in Ragtime: A Biography of James Reese Europe*, Oxford University Press, New York, 1995

Bankhead, Tallulah, *Tallulah: My Autobiography*, Harper & Brothers, New York, 1952

Batterberry, Ariane and Michael, *On the Town in New York: The Landmark History of Eating, Drinking, and Entertainments from the American Revolution to the Food Revolution*, Scribner, New York, 1973

Baxter, John, *Paris at the End of the World: The City of Light During the Great War, 1914–1918*, Harper Perennial, London, 2014

Bergreen, Laurence, *As Thousands Cheer: The Life of Irving Berlin*, Da Capo Press, New York, 1996

Boelcke, Oswald, *An Aviator's Field Book – Being the field reports of Oswald Boelcke, from August 1, 1914, to October 28, 1916*, FQ Books, London, 2010

Bradley, Patricia, *Making American Culture: A Social History, 1900–1920*, Palgrave Macmillan, London, 2009

Brooke, Rupert, *The Complete Poems*, Sidgwick & Jackson, London, 1942

Caffin, Caroline and Charles H., *Dancing and Dancers of Today: The Modern Revival of Dancing as an Art*, Dodd, Mead and Company, New York, 1912

Carruthers, Bob and McConnell, James R., *Recollections of the Great War in the Air,* Pen and Sword Aviation, London, 2013

Castle, Irene, *Castles in the Air*, Doubleday, New York, 1958

Castle, Mrs Vernon, *My Husband*, Charles Scribner's Sons, New York, 1919

Castle, Mr and Mrs Vernon, *Modern Dancing*, Harper & Brothers, New York, 1914

Cooper, Diana, *Autobiography*: *The Rainbow Comes and Goes, The Lights of Common Day, Trumpets from the Steep*, single-volume edition, Penguin Biography, London, 1961

Curnutt, Kirk, *A Historical Guide to F. Scott Fitzgerald*, Oxford University Press, Oxford, 2004

Curtis, Susan, *Dancing to a Black Man's Tune: A Life of Scott Joplin*, University of Missouri Press, Columbia, 1994

Davies, Marion, *The Times We Had: Life with William Randolph Hearst*, Ballantine, New York, 1989

Doctorow, E.L., *Ragtime: A Novel*, Random House, New York, 1975

Douglas Home, Jessica, *Violet: The Life and Loves of Violet Gordon Woodhouse*, Harvill Press, London, 1997

Duff Gordon, Lucile, *A Woman of Temperament*, Attica Books, London, 2012

Eliot, Valerie and Haughton, Hugh (eds), *The Letters of T.S. Eliot*, Volume 1, *1898–1922*, Faber and Faber, London, 2009

Erenberg, Lewis A., *Steppin' Out: New York Nightlife and the*

Transformation of American Culture, University of Chicago Press, Chicago, 1984

Etherington-Smith, Meredith and Pilcher, Jeremy, *The 'It' Girls: Lucy, Lady Duff Gordon, the Couturière Lucile, and Elinor Glyn, Romantic Novelist*, Hamish Hamilton, London, 1986

Fields, Armond and L. Marc, *From the Bowery to Broadway: Lew Fields and the Roots of American Popular Theatre*, Oxford University Press, New York, 1993

Fitzgerald, F. Scott, *Basil and Josephine*, Alma Classics, London, 2014

—, *The Diamond as Big as the Ritz and Other Stories*, Penguin, Harmondsworth, 1962

—, *The Great Gatsby*, Penguin, London, 2010

—, *This Side of Paradise*, Penguin, London, 1974

Franks, Arthur H., *Social Dance: A Short History*, Routledge, London, 1963

Fussell, Paul, *The Great War and Modern Memory*, Sterling, New York, 2009

Gallafent, Edward, *Astaire and Rogers*, Cameron & Hollis, Scotland, 2000

Glendinning, Victoria, *Edith Sitwell: A Unicorn Among Lions*, Orion Phoenix, London, 1993

Golden, Eve, *Vernon and Irene Castle's Ragtime Revolution*, University Press of Kentucky, Kentucky, 2007

Hastings, Max, *Catastrophe: Europe Goes To War 1914*, William Collins, London, 2013

Hayes, Helen and Dody, Sandford, *On Reflection: An Autobiography*, Lippincott, Philadelphia, 1968

Hoare, Philip, *Wilde's Last Stand*, Duckworth Overlook, London, 1997

Hunt, C.W., *Dancing in the Sky: The Royal Flying Corps in Canada*, Dundurn Press, Toronto, 2009

Janis, Elsie, *So Far, So Good: An Autobiography*, E. P. Dutton & Company, New York, 1932

Langtry, Lillie, *The Days I Knew*, Panoply Publications, London, 2000

Leider, Emily W., *Dark Lover: The Life and Death of Rudolph Valentino*, Faber and Faber, New York, 2004

Lewis, Alfred Allan, *Ladies and Not-So-Gentle Women*, Viking, New York, 2000

Kellner, Bruce, *Carl Van Vechten and the Irreverent Decades*, University of Oklahoma Press, Oklahoma, 1968

Marwick, Arthur, *The Deluge: British Society and the First World War*, Bodley Head, London, 1966

Mendes, Valerie and De La Haye, Amy, *Lucile Ltd: London, Paris, New York and Chicago: 1890s–1930s*, V&A Publishing, London, 2009

Mackenzie, Compton, *Extraordinary Women*, Martin Secker, London, 1928

Mackrell, Judith, *Flappers: Six Women of a Dangerous Generation*, Pan Macmillan, London, 2013

McBrien, William, *Cole Porter: The Definitive Biography*, Harper Collins, London, 1998

Martin, Christopher, 'The Castles and Europe: Race Relations in Ragtime', MA thesis, Florida State University, 2005

Mueller, John, *Astaire Dancing: The Musical Films*, Knopf, New York, 1985

Pakenham, Thomas, *The Boer War*, Weidenfeld & Nicholson, London, 1979

Pearl, Adam H., *Paris Sees it Through: A Diary 1914–1919*, Hodder & Stoughton, London, 1919

Pickford, Mary, *Sunshine and Shadow*, Heinemann, London, 1956

Procter, Ben, *William Randolph Hearst, The Early Years, 1863–1910*, Oxford University Press, New York, 1998

—, *William Randolph Hearst: The Later Years 1911–1951,* Oxford University Press, New York, 2007

Richthofen, Manfred, Freiherr von and Boelcke, Oswald, *Richthofen & Boelcke in Their Own Words*, Leonaur, London, 2011

Riley, Kathleen, *The Astaires: Fred & Adele*, Oxford University Press, New York, 2014

Seldes, Gilbert, *The Seven Lively Arts*, New York, 1924

Sennett, Ted, *Hollywood Musicals*, Harry N. Abrams, New York, 1981

Shulman, Irving, *Valentino*, Leslie Frewin Publishers, London 1968

Smith, Jane S., *Elsie de Wolfe: A Life in the High Style*, Atheneum, New York, 1982

Sparke, Penny, *Elsie de Wolfe: The Birth of Modern Interior Decoration*, Acanthus Press, New York, 2005

Swanson, Gloria, *Swanson on Swanson*, Michael Joseph, London, 1981

Yarsinske, Amy Waters, *Flyboys over Hampton Roads: Glenn Curtiss's Southern Experiment*, The History Press, South Carolina, 2010

Ziegler, Philip, *Osbert Sitwell: A Biography*, Pimlico, London, 1999

—, *Soldiers: Fighting Men's Lives, 1901–2001*, Chatto & Windus, London, 2001

—, *King Edward VIII*, HarperPress, London, 2012

Index

Index

Index